Vow *of* Silence

SUZANNE WALSH

MARDLE

First published in 2021 by Mardle Books
15 Church Road
London, SW13 9HE
www.mardlebooks.com

Text © 2021 Suzanne Walsh

Paperback ISBN 9781914451034
eBook ISBN 9781914451089

A CIP catalogue record for this book is available from the British Library.

Every reasonable effort has been made to trace copyright-holders of material
reproduced in this book, but if any have been inadvertently overlooked
the publishers would be glad to hear from them.

Typeset by Danny Lyle
Printed in the UK

10 9 8 7 6 5 4 3 2 1

Cover image: L-R: Callie (holding handbag),
Joseph (in pram), Anthony (standing) and Suzanne kneeling down.

Vow *of* Silence

For my daughter Melissa, my parents Ann and William Walsh, and for my siblings Carol, Peter, Nicholas, Marguerite and Damhnait.

About the author

Suzanne Walsh was born in Dublin on 10th March 1948.

She had one daughter, Melissa. She lived most of her life in London, but later on spent a lot of time in Los Angeles, where Melissa had relocated as a celebrity make-up artist. Suzanne passed away from cancer in October 2018.

It was one of her final wishes that her memoir be published.

Edited by Nicola Pittam

An award-winning journalist, author and screenwriter, Nicola has lived in the US for the past 24 years, first in Los Angeles, where she met Melissa on a celebrity photoshoot over 15 years ago. She now lives in South Carolina – the Deep South – and works as a journalist while also writing books, movies and TV shows… and has learned to say: "Bless your heart," a lot!

Introduction

I couldn't believe what I had just done. My sister Callie was laughing her head off but in the back of my mind I knew what I'd just done really wasn't that funny. I'd just spit on a grave. But it wasn't just any old grave. It was a mass grave – of nuns.

I was disgusted. Not with myself but with the grave, right there in front of me. It brought back so many horrific memories.

I'd decided to visit the cemetery near Dunleary, Dublin, to pay respects to my parents: William, who was affectionately known as Billy to everyone, and Ann, as well as my eldest brother Anthony, a member of the Royal Engineers, a regiment of the British Army. After laying flowers on their graves, my sister Callie and I took a slow walk through the cemetery when we came across the mass grave.

I was shocked and horrified that these nuns had been buried next to decent people. I felt it completely defiled the cemetery. Spitting on the grave had been an automatic reaction. My body just reacted to seeing a list of names that I thought were buried in my past. I had tried not to think of them – Sister Concepta, Sister Josephine among others – and the horror they had inflicted on me and my sisters.

For my three sisters and I had been abused by these same nuns more than 50 years ago when, by a sad series of events, we were left in their care while our mother had to travel to London looking for work. We lived for four years in the orphanages of Dublin. No one knew of the horrors that happened behind the orphanage doors. I guess back then no one would've believed us anyway. Nuns being abusive? How could they? They were servants of God. They were revered and feared in equal measure by the community. But behind the doors of the church they were simply just feared by the children they ruled over. Beatings were a daily occurrence; even the babies didn't escape the cane or a lashing from the rosary beads for doing something as simple as crying or wetting their nappies. We were starved and given scraps while they feasted on hot meals, and then made to work from early morning until midnight.

The nuns might've preached to us about going to hell if we didn't behave but we were in our own hell every single day with no one to tell or turn to. We only had each other, and I think without my sisters I would never have survived.

We never told anyone what happened – certainly not our mother – after we were constantly threatened by the nuns. It was a secret we kept as children and had kept with us for more than 50 years – until the Ryan Commission was introduced by the Irish Government in 1999.

It took them 10 years to investigate what happened and many former victims came forward to give testimony about the abuse and neglect they suffered in 60 different residential 'Reformatory and Industrial Schools' operated by the Catholic Church in Ireland. I had put my name down to testify but was never called in the end. They had so many thousands of people willing to come forward and speak about what happened that they didn't need my testimony.

At the end of the 10 years, in May 2009, the Commission published its report in five volumes, with an executive summary containing 43 conclusions and 20 recommendations. They said:

Overall: Physical and emotional abuse and neglect were features of the institutions. Sexual abuse occurred in many of them, particularly boys' institutions. Schools were run in a severe, regimented manner that imposed unreasonable and oppressive discipline on children and even on staff.

Physical abuse. The Reformatory and Industrial Schools depended on rigid control by means of severe corporal punishment and the fear of such punishment. A climate of fear, created by pervasive, excessive and arbitrary punishment, permeated most of the institutions and all those run for boys. Children lived with the daily terror of not knowing where the next beating was coming from.

Neglect. Poor standards of physical care were reported by most male and female complainants. Children were frequently hungry and food was inadequate, inedible and badly prepared in many schools. Accommodation was cold, sparse and bleak. Sanitary provision was primitive in most boys' schools and general hygiene facilities were poor.

Emotional abuse. Witnesses spoke of being belittled and ridiculed on a daily basis. Private matters such as bodily functions and personal hygiene were used as opportunities for degradation and humiliation. Personal and family denigration was widespread. There was constant criticism and verbal abuse and children were told they were worthless.

Reading the report at the time was like reliving it all over again. All the memories came rushing back. But even then I was still reluctant to tell anyone what had happened. I was still ashamed of what I'd been through, what my sisters had been through. It's not something you can just chat to someone about over a dinner party.

But finally, after seeing the nuns' grave, something in me snapped. I wanted the world to know what had happened. I wanted to shout from the rooftops what these awful women had done. They had been given these children to look after and care for but they had abused that right and privilege. But more than that, they had abused their position with God. And I so badly wanted them to pay for it the way I've paid over the years. And I've paid for it dearly with my health and throughout my life. I have Crohn's Disease and have suffered five heart attacks over the years. Once when I was in the hospital I had the Last Rites read to me twice. The doctors believe a major contributing factor is the neglect and malnutrition I suffered as a child. I believe it's all down to eating scraps every day and not being allowed to eat fresh fruit or vegetables or even meat, even though one of the orphanages had an orchard and another had a chicken farm.

Introduction

All of those nuns are long dead now but the memory of what they did still lingers. It will never go away. But I hope that by telling my story it will help other victims come to terms with what happened and, hopefully, for me, finally lay some ghosts to rest.

Some names have been changed to protect not only the innocent but also the evil.

Chapter One

I will never forget the feeling of absolute terror, then the sick feeling of apprehension as I stood in the parlour of the orphanage facing the big wooden door.

Just moments earlier my mammy had said goodbye and walked away, out of the door and out of our lives. None of us can remember anything about the actual journey from home or our arrival at the orphanage in 1958, not even the parting from our mother. I don't know if she kissed us goodbye or what her parting words were. We must have been in shock since it was surely one of the most momentous events ever to have happened in our young lives.

Everything before and after that point is clear in my mind though, even after 50-odd years, so it's not the passage of time that has made us forget but most probably the stress of the preceding few months. The ordeal of leaving our family and home was more than I and my two young sisters could cope with. Imelda can't even remember being in that institution at all. She has completely suppressed the traumatic memories.

But right at that moment as I stood in front of that door, I was trying not to cry. I wanted to be strong for my younger sisters Sinead and Imelda, who were each clutching one of my hands tightly.

We had no idea when we would see Mammy again. She was going to London to try to find work so we could all be together again. My daddy had recently passed away from cancer and Mammy couldn't afford to keep the house together and feed me, my three sisters and two brothers without a job. And she couldn't get a job in Ireland, a single mother with six mouths to feed in the 1950s. The only place she could work as a secretary to earn money was across the water in London.

So here we were. In the Catholic Church-run orphanage St Vincent's in Dublin, staring at a big wooden door, not knowing what or who was behind it. We were rooted to the spot, fixated on the highly polished brass doorknob as we waited for it to turn, fearful of what lay on the other side.

Our bodies tensed at the sound of approaching footsteps click-clicking importantly along the bare floorboards. My terrified little sisters, who were just five and seven years old, grasped my hands even tighter and desperately tried to hide behind me as the person paused momentarily outside.

I was only ten years old myself but in that moment, I became the adult. The one comforting object in the room for my terrified sisters. So I couldn't show fear. I didn't want them to see that I was just as frightened as they were. They were looking up to me now to be the big brave sister. So, I bent down to Sinead and Imelda and whispered, "It's going to be alright, you'll see."

Chapter One

Usually the job of brave sister was taken by our older sister Callie, but she hadn't come with us to St Vincent's right then; she was staying at home with Mammy for a little while longer to help with the task of packing up the house, and also as a comfort for her until she left for London within a few short weeks. She would join us later.

So we three felt so alone, totally bewildered and lost. We stood transfixed for a moment, almost without breathing. Even though we had been expecting it, we were startled when the door was thrust open and an intimidating-looking nun appeared. Completely filling the doorway, the enormous white starched headdress and long black robes accentuating her height, she looked like a giant, monstrous penguin and seemed just as terrifying. Sinead blurted out, "Who is that? I'm scared," while Imelda simply made a whimpering noise. I was so transfixed by the sight in front of me, I couldn't get any words out. I don't know what kind of welcome we had been expecting but we weren't too surprised when she just gave us a cursory glance and then, without even a smile or any welcoming words, raised her hand and imperiously beckoned us: "Come with me." Turning with a swish of her robes and clank of the rosary beads hanging from her waist, she strode through the doorway.

I had to pull on Sinead and Imelda's hands as they were rooted to the spot. Again I bent down to whisper as I didn't want the nun to hear me. "It's going to be okay, don't be afraid, she's just a big silly penguin," I told the little ones. They both giggled before clapping their hands over their mouths, afraid they'd made too much noise.

Of course their giggles were an immediate threat. The nun spun round, glaring at us. There were no kind words, no sympathetic caresses or even affectionate looks. We'd just been separated from our mammy for the first time in our lives but it was all 'business as usual' for the nuns. If she had any emotions, they were being well hidden under her veil. But even though those first few moments alone were scary and desolate, we had no idea of what lay in store for us over the next four years. Entering an alien world expecting to be cared for, instead we were to be abused and exploited by the representatives of the Catholic Church. Their doctrine of love for their fellow men didn't extend to the pitiful little souls in their care, as we were very soon to discover. Our crime, and that of most of the other children in the institution, was that we were fatherless and vulnerable – in other words: perfect victims.

The orphanage and Catholic Church dominated and dictated the lives of the mainly poor, working-class people of the district. It wasn't long after the end of the Second World War when jobs were very scarce everywhere in Europe, especially so because of the millions of soldiers that had returned from the war seeking work. Competition for jobs was extremely fierce. The majority of families in the locality were Catholic and extremely large, as women were expected to continue giving birth as long as they were able, no matter whether they were capable of doing so either physically or financially.

Because of this the orphanages in the 1950s and 1960s were filled with local children, just like us. It wasn't unusual for the children to still have a parent alive, trying to earn some

Chapter One

money and savings so they could unite the family back together again. It was a sad but not uncommon state of affairs. Of course, we didn't know this at our age. All we knew was that Mammy was going away and we had been separated from her and our brothers Anthony and Joseph, who had been taken to an orphanage especially for boys.

There was only one thing we could do. Still holding hands, we reluctantly followed the nun's black robes across the threshold to begin our new life as 'orphans'.

Chapter Two

We weren't complete novices in the art of institutional living, however. Just four years earlier, in 1954, when I was six years old, we had gone through the distress and upheaval of our mother's nervous breakdown, which had led to us spending time in various children's group homes in Dublin.

During the months that Mammy was hospitalised in the sanatorium, Daddy must have had his work cut out trying to juggle everything. As well as working full time at the Guinness Brewery in St James' Gate, alongside the River Liffey in the centre of Dublin, he made frequent trips to the hospital to visit Mammy and to both children's homes in different parts of Dublin to see all six of us children. My eldest sister Callie and I, along with our two brothers Anthony and Joseph, spent a few months in a group home called Linden, which catered for both boys and girls.

The two youngest girls, Sinead and Imelda, who were just babies then, had been placed in another home for toddlers and young babies located in a different part of Dublin. This home was called *Tír na nÓg* (*Gaelic* for 'Land of the Ever-Young') after the mythical land of the Irish fairies. In Irish mythology, time stood still in *Tír na nÓg*; one never grew old, the climate was always temperate and there was no sorrow or pain. It was an enchanted place, full of love, where the inhabitants sang, danced and feasted all day.

Linden, on the other hand, was anything but an enchanted place. The building was entirely functional and included a refectory for the children's meals, dormitories, classrooms, offices and a hospital ward. Wintry grey skies and the stark leafless trees in the grounds didn't help to improve its appearance. Bone-chilling winds whistled through our clothing as we played in the gardens under rain-laden skies, penned in by high red brick walls and huge wrought-iron gates. Although the bitter cold made our ears sting, teeth chatter and fingertips numb, we were glad to be able to escape from the staff and the strict routine for even a short while.

Being only six years old at the time, I don't remember much about my time at Linden. I don't recall the names of the staff or the other children, but I can recall many of the incidents that happened during our short stay there. There is one person I remember but only because of what happened afterwards: Mrs O'Riley was her name. She later became a victim of Nurse Mamie Cadden, an infamous back-street abortionist operating in Dublin at that time. Mrs O'Riley was left dying at the side of the road when her abortion went wrong. She had been living in Linden with her children while her husband was working abroad and became pregnant by another man. The trial of Nurse Cadden made headline news. She was sentenced to death, which was commuted to life imprisonment, and she later died in an insane asylum.

The horrible institutional food was utterly unforgettable. Once, I was made to sit alone at the dining table all afternoon in front of a dish of cold, slimy, lumpy tapioca that we had christened 'frog's eyes'.

I'd made fun of the 'frog's eyes' in front of all the other girls. The dishes had been put down in front of us and straight away I used my spoon to scoop out a big serving of this lumpy, slimy slop and turned to Callie, thrust the spoon at her and imitated a frog. "Ribbit, ribbit," I mimicked from the back of my throat as Callie burst out laughing along with the rest of the girls at the table. Of course, no one in charge found it funny, especially when they ordered me to eat my 'frog's eyes' and I refused. There was no way that sludge was going in my stomach!

The staff didn't know just how stubborn I could be when they forbade me to leave the table until I had finished every single bite. I sat there with my lips clamped firmly shut despite threats of dire punishment. They would have had to break my teeth to force any of that glutinous mess past my lips. After a couple of hours I won the battle of wills: they gave up the unequal struggle and sent me back to class, with the dish of cold tapioca pudding still lying congealed and uneaten on the table.

It might've been a small insignificant defeat for the staff but for a six year old it was a momentous occasion – a victory! It's something that I even remember to this day with great satisfaction.

On one of his visits, Daddy brought us some sweet juicy oranges. Callie and I were in awe, turning them over and over in our hands, but the minute Daddy left, someone appeared, snatched them from us and said, "Give them here, no snacks allowed but I'll make sure you get them with your lunch. We'll share them out."

We didn't mind sharing with the other girls but once the oranges were out of our sight, of course we never saw them again. Strange as it may seem now, oranges were an exotic fruit in Europe in 1954 as they, along with bananas, had been in very short supply during the grey, austere years of the Second World War.

During those six years of war in Europe, German U-boat submarines sank hundreds of ships carrying essential supplies, which led to severe shortages in the war-torn countries of Europe and the rationing of almost everything. It wasn't until the mid-1950s that rationing came to an end and even basic goods were freely available again in the stores, so even though oranges and other fruit were on shelves, they were still seen as a treat in our house and we were heartbroken when those oranges disappeared.

I've had a myriad of health issues over the years, all tied in with the malnutrition and the time I spent in the orphanages. And even during the short time we were in the children's homes, I regularly fell ill. Developing big red styes on my swollen eyelids was a particularly painful memory for me. These styes were treated with eye drops by members of the staff, some of whom were rougher than the others in their application; one held my head in such a vice-like grip that I'm surprised she didn't pull my head off. I can still feel it now. Then, as if things weren't bad enough, I also developed a fungus called 'ringworm' on the top of my head. They had to cut away the hair around it, leaving a bald patch so the air could get to my scalp. Then to top it all, I got extremely painful, pus-filled boils called 'whitlows' around my fingernails. What a pitiful sight I must have looked with my half-closed eyes, scabby head and throbbing fingers.

This was the main reason why I was sent to the hospital ward to attend lessons with the sick and disabled children who lived in the home. It was a strange sight to see the other pupils laid out in rows of beds with the teacher standing in front of a blackboard at the top of the ward. As I was the only able-bodied child there (although I was not actually disabled, in another sense, with all my ailments, maybe I wasn't what you would call completely able-bodied) I sat on a chair in the middle aisle between the beds facing the teacher. Perhaps I was in quarantine, who knows? The only question being: where did I acquire all the infections from in the first place? Nobody in authority could – or would – answer that question!

It's hard to describe the mixed emotions we felt when Mammy came to visit us in Linden shortly before her formal release from the sanatorium. Although it had only been about six months or so since we had seen her, I felt a bit shy in her company. She seemed remote somehow, a bit like a stranger really. This was possibly because she was wearing sunglasses and smoking a cigarette in a long holder. I had always thought she was beautiful but now she looked extremely glamorous too, with her white trench coat and jet-black hair, just like a movie star, or even a spy, and so stunning.

Mammy didn't inhale the smoke, though; she just puffed at the cigarette and blew out clouds of smoke, a bit like Marlene Dietrich in the movies. In the early 1950s, part of her medical therapy had been an introduction to cigarette smoking, along with electric shock treatment, something that is now considered outrageous and barbaric in these more enlightened and health-conscious times. Once she took off her sunglasses and hugged and kissed us, the strangeness disappeared and she became our Mammy again.

All this had happened a couple of years previously and our lives had since returned to comparative normality. 'Normal' was something we had taken for granted once and probably would again in the future when the insecurity of our experience, if not exactly forgotten, had become more of a distant memory. I sometimes think our time in that place might also have implanted a small seed of cynicism in my soul. Up until then it had never occurred to me that there might be some adults who didn't like children and could be vicious and nasty for no apparent reason. It was also the first time we had been so dominated by figures of authority in such a closed community.

Now, though, we were home again, and all was right in our little world... but sadly not for long.

Chapter Three

Our home was in the leafy Dublin suburb of Clontarf, just a few minutes' walk from the seafront at the Bull Wall, an island at Dollymount. The beach was nearly two miles long with beautiful white sands and hilly grass-spiked dunes.

In the summer it was a haven for the poor people from the city slums. Families spent long summer days on the beach relaxing from the stresses and strains of their lives; the mothers boiled billycans over open fires to make tea and cook the crabs the men caught in the rock pools alongside the sea wall, while the children played in the sea and built sandcastles on the beach.

I look back with fondness at our picnics on the beach, eating sandy jelly sandwiches and sipping from a shared bottle of soda. Callie pretended to swim by moving through the foamy waves with her hands on the sea bottom. Back then, I didn't realise it was sleight of hand and was very impressed by her swimming ability.

Surrounded by fields and woods, Clontarf was a perfect place for families with children; you wouldn't have guessed that we were only about 15 minutes' journey by car from

Dublin city centre. Our house bordered the massive St Anne's Estate just across the dusty lane at the back of our house. All this land, consisting of approximately 250 acres, was our playground. It had once belonged to members of the Guinness brewing dynasty who had lived in the white mansion at the top of the long tree-lined drive. This was later demolished because of fire damage, after which the Guinness family sold the land to the City of Dublin in 1939. The grounds of the estate later became a public park that stretched all the way down to the seafront at Bull Island Nature Reserve overlooking the horseshoe-shaped Dublin Bay.

We knew everybody for miles around and were on first-name terms with lots of people, both children and adults. It was a very sociable, carefree life. Along with our vast army of friends, we organised sports days in the fields of St Anne's Estate and played tennis at Eason's tennis club on Mount Prospect Avenue even though we didn't know the rules of the game but made up our own as we went along.

Some summers, families of tinkers – Irish gypsies or travellers – made their camp in the fields. They had hordes of unkempt children and their horses and dogs roamed unfettered around the fields. The tinkers' shelters were made from bits of tarpaulin thrown over the bushes and they lit fires at the entrances to cook their food and to keep warm at night. Blackened pots of water swung from wooden branches arranged over the fires.

To supplement their food, the men made traps and caught some of the numerous hares that ran freely among the grassy mounds before disappearing down the numerous burrows that dotted the fields. The men called at all the houses to ask the housewives if they wanted their kitchen knives sharpened, and the gypsy women, with babies in their arms and small children clinging to their skirts, tried to sell us 'lucky heather'.

After a while, just when we had got used to their presence in the fields, they disappeared like phantoms in the night. The only visible reminders of their existence were the piles of garbage they left behind.

On summer evenings Callie and I eagerly waited outside the tennis clubhouse to see the big girls arrive for the weekly dances so we could admire their beautiful dresses. Big flouncy skirts and stiletto heels were fashionable then. We stood, agog, outside the clubhouse watching as the girls danced the jive and bopped around as their ponytails swung and their skirts bounced. Though we longed to be like them it wasn't our time as we were destined to be 1960s teenagers.

But oh how we longed! I would memorise the steps as the girls whirled round and round the room. We watched the dancing, standing on tiptoes so we could peer through the windows, until someone came out and shooed us off home. They would tell us: "You youngsters shouldn't be out at this time of the night. Be off home with you now." We did as we were told but were back again the next week with our noses pressed against the window. Callie practised the jive with her friends and sometimes co-opted a protesting Anthony into being her partner to dance the boy's part, while I would lie in bed at night and imagine it was me jiving and bopping around the dance floor. I didn't need a partner, it was just me, flying light as a feather with nothing to hold me down!

Chapter Three

When I was about eight, some new houses were built at the top of our road. We were fascinated by all the activity and spent hours sitting on a pile of bricks watching the builders work and asking endless questions. One bricklayer was nicknamed Curly because he was completely bald. He was so friendly and patient and always welcomed our company. We marvelled at his ability to carry big loads of bricks over his shoulder in his wooden brick hod and greatly admired his skill at bricklaying. The boys envied his muscles and tried to flex their own non-existent ones. Curly loved having such an appreciative audience and played to the gallery. At the end of the day, if we were still there, he would give us a lift home in the wheelbarrow. He'd tell us, "Hop in!" and we took turns hopping in and out along the way.

An old white-haired night watchman called Ned, who could have been any age but must have been somewhere between 60 and 80, set up home in the builders' tent when the building site closed for the day. I wouldn't image that he would have made much of a watchman, as he couldn't run very fast if he had to chase burglars because he was so old and rickety. Every evening he lit a great big blazing fire and boiled his billycan to make tea. Later he stoked up the fire with lots of wood for extra warmth in the chilly small hours of the night.

When we finished our dinner, we older children told our mothers that we were going to say hello to old Ned, who was just like a grandfather to us. We joined him around his fire for a singsong of Irish rebel songs and sang our little hearts out. Two of my favourites were "The Wild Colonial Boy" and "Danny Boy".

At eight o'clock on the dot, our mothers would call us home and we obeyed, protesting that we were not tired enough for sleep during the light summer evenings.

"But, Mammy, we're not at all tired," we would protest.

"Don't 'But Mammy me'. You're almost asleep on your feet. You're so tired you'd sleep on a harrow," Mammy would tell us. Of course, she was right: we were usually asleep as soon as our heads touched the pillows.

Charlie the Ice-Cream Man was one of the summer attractions we most looked forward to and was one of the highlights of our day. Charlie was a well-known local character who pedalled around the district selling ice cream and candy from a big container on the front of his bike. His pedalling powered some kind of generator that kept the ice cream frozen. On hot days we would see him coming up the road furiously pinging the bell on his bicycle, while his face turned bright red from the effort and he sweated profusely from the combined effects of the heat and the cycling.

At the sound of his bell pinging in the distance as he made his way laboriously along the road, children would appear from all directions and dash into the houses.

"Quick, quick, Mammy, Charlie's here. Please can we have some money?" we'd beg. Mammy would dole out a few pennies. We grabbed the money from her outstretched hand and ran out the door. "Make sure everyone gets a share," she shouted after us.

We sprinted up the road after Charlie with our pennies clutched tightly in our hands. Sometimes we bought 'lucky bags' which he had made up himself. If we were lucky they contained more than just a few candies: some of them might contain a little toy as well and that was how they got their name. The older boys would try to distract Charlie while Paddy Fagin (whose family later won a fortune on the Irish Hospitals Sweepstake – the forerunner of today's big state lotteries) and his friend, Spud Murphy, tried to steal a few candies. Charlie was always too quick for them, though.

"I know what you're up to behind my back sonny, don't think you can get away with it," Charlie would say.

They all laughed because they knew it was just a game and they would try again the next time. On the odd occasion they were successful, but not very often because Charlie was just too sharp for them: "I've got eyes in the back of me head, so I have, sonny. I know all your tricks, so don't think you can outfox me."

Chapter Four

The area was full of young families and almost every one had, at the very least, a couple or more children, except for the Protestant families who didn't seem to produce nearly as many babies as the Catholics.

Europe's baby assembly line was in full production in an effort to replenish the populations recently decimated by the Second World War. Ireland was doing more than its fair share for the cause even though it had remained neutral during the conflict and hadn't lost even a fraction of the number of people that other European countries had.

Parts of Europe lived under the yoke of the Catholic Church. Ireland and Italy, in particular, were staunchly Catholic, so there was no problem when it came to producing lots of babies, either wanted or unwanted, to fill the churches on Sundays.

Our family of six children wasn't even considered large in that context. There was one family just up the road who had 18 children, something that wasn't unusual or remarkable in Ireland at that time. Artificial birth control, such as today's freely available birth control pill, just didn't exist then. The Catholic

Church was one of the controlling forces in Ireland and it was the Church to which the politicians deferred. Catholic doctrine preached that it was a member's divine duty to God to procreate and contraception was a sin.

The reality of this policy was that sex became either a case of abstinence or the production of ever more unwanted children, sometimes leading to back-street abortions when people became desperate. Most people obeyed the Pope's edict without question, whether they could afford to feed, clothe and educate a large family or not, and unfortunately most of them couldn't.

Still, what did it matter to the Catholic Church – they always had a full congregation in the church on Sundays to pay their dues both in cash and kind. They also had a ready supply of pupils for their schools, which were subsidised by the government; so the more pupils the better, as each one meant extra money for the Church.

Our house had nothing much to distinguish it from the many others in our neighbourhood, but it was a great achievement for our parents to have a house in the suburbs along with a mortgage.

As was the case in most suburban houses, the sitting room at the front of the house was reserved for more formal occasions. The room most used was the comfortable combined family room and dining room with polished wooden floors and flowery wallpaper. A big dining table stood in the middle of the room and the window looked on to the garden framed by the trees in the wood just over the unmade lane. An old wooden clock ticked away on the mantle shelf over the open coal fire and a framed print of Frans Hals' painting of the 'Laughing Cavalier' looked down at us from the wall.

There was a big sideboard along one wall that the boys used as a stagecoach when they played their games of Cowboys and Indians, with Anthony sitting on top as the driver and Joseph the Cowboy sitting in the bottom section firing his guns at the chasing Indians. We girls were the Indians, of course.

I wasn't interested in playing their game and Mammy would try to persuade me: "Go on, please do it for me, Suzy, so I can get on with things." I'd finally relent and agree to play: "Okay Mammy, but just this once, I don't like playing stupid Cowboys and Indians and I want to read my book."

In the evenings Daddy helped us with our homework while we all sat around the big table. Anthony and Daddy both loved maths and spent long hours together doing equations. Curly-haired Anthony was very clever and studious but with a quiet, laid-back sense of humour. His great ambition was to go to university. He was very witty and loved to tease us and play pranks, especially on Imelda and Sinead, who fell for his tricks every time.

Although there was an eighteen-month age difference between them, Sinead and Imelda looked almost like twins, both dark-haired and blue-eyed and nearly the same size. Sinead was the younger of the two but the more dominant one. They played together all the time and were constantly bickering over their toys. In fact, they quarrelled over everything and anything.

Sinead had been born feisty. When she was a baby she would stand up in her crib, scream, defiantly grab the side rails and rock it across the floorboards to bang her head against the wall in a fierce temper because she didn't want to go to sleep. The Irish saying for her was, "That one suffers from a double dose of original sin," meaning she was double trouble. That certainly proved to be the case; she was always defiant and usually in some sort of trouble – a real hothead!

Anthony loved to make fun of Sinead and Imelda. When Sinead's legs got sunburned, he called her "old beetroot legs". Outraged, she went to find Mammy to complain: "Mammy, that Anthony's a very bad boy. He called me 'leetloot legs'." Mammy was bemused: "Leetloot legs? What?" Exasperated Sinead repeated it: "You know, leetloot legs."

Mammy had to ask him, "Anthony, what's she talking about? What did you call her?" And she was left laughing when Anthony told her he'd actually said: "Beetroot legs". Then we all fell about laughing together and Sinead stomped out of the room in a temper. Meanwhile Leetloot Legs became her nickname for a while, a moniker that she hated.

Imelda, by contrast, was the 'good girl'. She always did as she was told and tried to please everybody. Her only vice was that she loved anything sweet, especially chocolate. Imelda was always the first suspect if any of our candy went missing or the cookie jar was empty. We usually didn't have far to look for the culprit, although sometimes it could be said that she was unfairly blamed, being the immediate suspect even when it wasn't her fault; some people were known to take advantage of that fact!

When we were all in bed, and hopefully asleep for the rest of the night, Mammy and Daddy relaxed and listened to the wireless on a small table beside Daddy's armchair. On the other side of the fireplace Mammy had her own armchair and a bookcase filled with her much-loved and well-read collection of books and poetry.

This was in the pre-television years as the technology had only recently been invented and financially was out of reach of most people anyway, our family certainly. Only the rich could afford them, and it would be quite a few years yet till it became generally available and affordable for the general population.

This meant we made our own entertainment and spent hours outside making up stories and playing in the woods. We had our own special tree that we nicknamed the Crow's Nest. It was our favourite tree because it was small enough to manoeuvre our way up through the branches which spread out in such a way that it was easy for us to climb. Sitting on top of it, we could see the ships sailing into Dublin Bay, heading up the River Liffey to tie up beside the quays to unload their cargos.

We were also extremely proud of the fact that our family home stood on the site of the historic Battle of Clontarf, which took place on Good Friday in the year 1014, when Brian Boru, the legendary warrior and last High King of Ireland, was victorious over the invading Danish Vikings. Shortly after winning the battle against the invaders, some stray Norsemen who were fleeing the battlefield stumbled upon his tent and killed Brian and his guards.

It wasn't difficult to imagine that in the distant past other people might have sat on top of our Crow's Nest to spy on the Viking ships sailing into Dublin Bay and beaching their longships on the strand at Clontarf.

Chapter Four

Like most children, we had wild imaginations and would spend hours concocting and then acting out our made-up stories while then having the freedom to play outside and in the woods. Little did we know that soon that freedom we took for granted would be cruelly taken away through forces beyond our imagination or control.

Chapter Five

It was just another lazy Sunday afternoon. Without warning, a great commotion erupted from the kitchen. Imelda ran into the hall, quickly followed by Sinead and Joseph. They looked as guilty as hell. What had they been up to this time? Mammy appeared in the doorway, looking hot and harassed: "I can't do anything with all of you in here. Go out and play or do something, but just give me some peace and quiet."

She looked imploringly at Daddy: "Billy, will you get these children from under my feet for a while so I can cook the dinner without constant interruptions." Daddy put his paper down: "Who wants to come for a walk?" "Me," said Joseph. "Me," Sinead shouted, echoed by Imelda.

Sinead and Imelda ran out of the back door in a state of great excitement. It was what Mammy called their "mad half-hour" when they needed to let off steam as they were so full of energy that they usually got into mischief of some sort or the other. This usually happened on Sunday afternoons without fail, for some reason that nobody could fathom.

Chapter Five

"Ann, what time do you want us back?" Daddy called. Mammy put her head around the door with a look of relief on her face: "About an hour. That should be plenty, thanks."

We all began scrambling around to find shoes and coats. I hated wearing shoes; as usual, they had gone missing and I was looking for them but struggling to find where I had last discarded them. Eventually I found them, randomly thrown under the dining table.

Daddy leaned down from his six-foot height to help me tie my shoelaces. He and I looked most alike out of all the family. The other girls took after Mammy with their dark Celtic looks, whereas Daddy and I had blonde hair, probably inherited from some Viking ancestor. Both boys had brown hair, midway between the dark Celtic and blonde Scandinavian.

"You'd lose your head if it wasn't attached to your shoulders," Daddy laughed. I giggled, grabbed hold of his hand and smiled up at him: "Please take us to St Anne's, Daddy." He smiled and tenderly stroked my head, telling me, "Anywhere you want, Suzy."

It wasn't difficult for me to get my own way. Apart from my blonde curls, big blue eyes and angelic looks, I was a little shy but this only seemed to enhance my appeal. I could usually get away with blue murder as nobody thought I could ever do anything wrong. Old women, complete strangers, were always giving me candies and money. They would say, "You're such a little dote, so you are." A 'dote' is an Irish expression meaning 'a lovely little thing'.

I shouted to Mammy as I dashed past the kitchen door, "Bye Mammy, see you later." She called back, "Bye Suzy, have a good time."

The two girls and Joseph were already at the top of the garden. I quickly caught up with them. Joseph was standing on the railings of the gate swinging it back and forth. He was nearly eight now and a bit small for his age, probably on account of his asthma, the debilitating respiratory condition he had had since babyhood. The rusty hinges of the gate squeaked as he swung back and forth. Sinead wanted to climb on the gate too but he wouldn't stop to let her on. She was getting really angry. Her little face was contorted in fury as she shouted at Joseph, "You horrible boy. If you don't let me on I'll tell Daddy."

But Joseph wasn't intimidated by her threat and swung even harder while Imelda and I stood and watched the entertainment. "Daddy said we could go to St. Anne's," I told her. At that moment Callie came up the path behind us followed by Daddy. Her long black curly hair tumbled around her shoulders. She looked like a smaller version of Mammy and was just as beautiful.

"Get off that gate before you fall and hurt yourself," she told Joseph. She thought she could boss the rest of us just because she was the oldest, but we usually did what she told us anyway because she was a natural born leader. Joseph wriggled away from her grasp as she tried to grab hold of him and gave us a cheeky grin over his shoulder as he ran off across the dusty lane and along the path we had trodden through the long scratchy grass leading to the woods. "Don't go too far ahead. Wait for me at the ditch," Daddy warned us.

We stood behind Joseph in single file, waiting at the side of the shallow ditch while he jumped down onto the big tree branch at the bottom. From long practice, we were accomplished at crossing the log. Balancing carefully with outstretched arms, we ran the few feet across and grabbed the bushes at the edge of the ditch as we climbed out into the cool green of the woods.

This ancient wood was one of our favourite places to play. The tops of the trees formed a canopy and through the sides the sunlit green fields stretched off into the distance as far as the eye could see. Standing amongst the trees was like being in a tunnel and the only noise was the sound of the soft wind rustling the leaves and occasionally the movement made by a small animal in the bushes.

We picked big bunches of bluebells and wild daffodils here in the spring and proudly took them home to Mammy to display in a vase. In the fall, we collected the fallen nuts from beneath the big chestnut trees and threaded them with string to play a game of conkers. Almost every day during the summer holidays we took jelly sandwiches and a bottle of water with us and spent most of the day playing in the woods and fields, climbing trees, running up and down the grassy hills. Other times we played our own version of baseball.

In later life, I found refuge in this beautiful place again but this time only in my dreams. When times were bad I would dream that I was playing here again with my brothers and sisters, once more a little child without a care in the world. It was my calm, go-to place that I kept stored for when times got tough.

Callie had nicknamed one of the hills 'Fairy Hill' because there was a fairy ring near the base. A fairy ring is a naturally occurring ring of mushrooms sometimes found in forested areas. In folklore, fairy rings are thought to be the location of gateways into elfin kingdoms or places where elves and fairies gather and dance. We liked to imagine sometimes that we caught a glimpse of a fairy out of the corners of our eyes. All in all, it was a special place and seemed to have a magic all of its own.

Another of our favourite activities was collecting birds' eggs from their nests and sucking out the contents through pinholes at either end of the egg so as to preserve the shells without them turning bad.

We fished for tadpoles and frogspawn in the little streams that ran through the woods hoping they would hatch, but to our disappointment they never did. Sometimes we visited a farm a few miles away to watch the pigs in their sty, and would poke them with sticks when the farmer wasn't around. We also especially loved exploring St Anne's Estate, though, because there was so much to see and do.

Clutching his handfuls of pebbles, Joseph told us excitedly, "I'm going to throw stones at the dead dog in the lake to try and sink it." He ran off towards the woods bordering the long drive leading to the ruined mansion. Imelda looked at Sinead: "Race you." They sprinted after Joseph. Callie automatically shouted after them, "Don't go near the water."

I strolled along on the tufted green grass with the warm sun on my back. Although the summer was nearly over, we would still play here in the fall and winter. We especially loved it when it snowed and we made huge snowmen, rolling giant snowballs around the fields, competing to see who could make the biggest one.

Callie and Daddy strolled a little way behind me. She was 12 years old now and not so interested in our childish games anymore. As I glanced back, the two of them were deep in conversation.

When I reached the edge of the woods, the others were waiting for us to catch up while they stopped to get their breath back. Joseph was completely out of breath and wheezing away after his run up the fields. Because it wasn't unusual for us to see him like this, we weren't at all alarmed because we knew he would get his breath back in a minute. His asthma didn't deter him from doing anything he wanted, though, and he enjoyed all the rough and tumble of most little boys his age.

On one occasion Mammy had taken him to hospital for treatment and settled him into his bed in the children's ward. She kissed him goodbye and said, "I have to go now. I'll be back tomorrow. Be sure and be good for the doctors and nurses." Joseph smiled up at her and said, "Don't worry Mammy, I'll be okay."

She fretted all the way home: "Will he be okay? I hope he won't be lonely? Still, he should be okay. There are lots of other children in the ward and he's a friendly little boy so at least he'll have company." Her conscience troubled her, though, at the thought of him all by himself in that lonely hospital bed. She hated leaving him there. She did a few errands in the city and when she arrived back home she got the surprise of her life: who should be sitting in the armchair but six-year-old Joseph with a big grin on his face.

A stunned Mammy asked him, "How did you get here?" Joseph just smiled and told her, "On the bus!" So you can imagine that this little stroll in the woods on a Sunday was nothing to a great adventurer like Joseph, in spite of his medical condition. After a few minutes he recovered his breath.

"Look what I've got." He opened his fist to show us a handful of little stones he had collected for throwing in the water. "Give us some," demanded Sinead. But Joseph was stubborn and refused to hand any over: "No, get your own." Sinead demanded, "Where'd you get them from anyway?" Keeping them tightly in his fist, Joseph admitted, "In the back lane."

Sinead scrambled around under the trees looking for stones but there weren't any loose ones as the ground was compacted hard. She found some little twigs scattered around which she gathered up and put in her pocket before turning to Daddy who was standing nearby: "Daddy, tell Joseph to give us some of his stones." Daddy smiled down at Joseph: "Be a good boy and give your sisters some." Never one to refuse anything Daddy asked, he grudgingly handed each of us one little stone.

Joseph took off before Daddy could persuade him to part with any more, running around the edge of the lake and stopping every so often to peer into the murky water looking for the golden-haired dog. Sinead and Imelda followed him. I stood at the edge of the water and lobbed my stone into the muddy depths. It made a plop and disappeared without a trace. Sinead and Imelda followed Joseph around the lake. They reappeared from behind some shrubs with poor Joseph wheezing and gasping for breath again. He was bent forward with his hands on his knees, struggling for air.

As soon as he could talk, his little face crumpled with disappointment. He told Daddy, "The dog's not there anymore."

Daddy tried to console him: "Never mind Joseph, whoever owned it probably took it home to bury." Joseph was upset but tried not to show it too much: "But I wanted to throw stones at him and sink him."

We half-heartedly threw some more pebbles and bits of stick in the water but eventually lost interest after realising how hungry we were. I had a hollow feeling in the pit of my stomach: "I'm starving. Can we go home now Daddy?" I wasn't the only one who was hungry and looking forward to the Sunday dinner, so Daddy corralled us all to head home: "Okay Suzy. Come on everyone, we'll head home now. You three now be careful how you go and don't get too far ahead." Daddy and Callie kept us in sight all the way home, continuing their conversation as they walked along behind us at a slower pace, arms linked.

Extremely hungry now and ready for our dinner, we crashed through the back door and into the dining room; Anthony was already seated at the table holding his knife and fork, waiting for us to sit down so he could begin his meal: "You should have told me you were going for a walk. I'd have come with you."

We'd totally forgotten about Anthony as we'd all dashed out the door for our walk. "You were out and we didn't have time to look for you." Anthony crossly told us off: "Well, you could've tried. I was only up the road on my bike."

Anthony was disappointed to have missed an opportunity to go for a walk with his father, whom he adored and always followed everywhere. He was 11 and gradually becoming more and more self-sufficient. His friends now were the big boys and he played more with them these days than he did with Joseph.

Not that Joseph cared much anyway because he was very popular and had loads of friends himself. Anthony didn't like his brown curls anymore and had recently persuaded Daddy to let him have them cut off at the barbers. It made him look so much older. Callie and Anthony were great friends and spent a lot of time together when he wasn't out with the big boys. He admired her because she was so strong and fearless and a match for any boy.

As usual, Callie took charge of us as we all dove for the table: "Make sure you all wash your hands before you sit down, especially you Joseph, you're filthy. How do you always get so mucky?" Joseph grinned and went off to wash his hands. "And don't forget to wash that dirty face while you're up there," Callie added.

When we were ready, Mammy served our Sunday dinner. For a few minutes there was no sound except the contented scraping of knives and forks on plates as we polished off the food like a pack of starving hyenas.

But before long Joseph was chattering away: "Anthony, guess what?" "Let me tell him," Sinead shouted impatiently and before Joseph could get a word in, she said, "We saw some squirrels. They eat their food like this." She made little nibbling movements with her mouth. Annoyed, Joseph shouted over her, "I was talking to him first. Anthony, the dead dog isn't in the lake anymore." Callie screwed her face in revulsion: "Ugh, Daddy, tell him not to be disgusting when we're trying to eat." Daddy suppressed a smile: "That's not a nice thing to talk about at the dinner table, Joseph. You can tell Anthony all about it after dinner." "Okay Daddy," said a subdued Joseph, as he hunched down in his chair. He soon brightened up, though and began telling us some silly jokes.

This was a typical dinner time in our household with everyone chattering away or telling jokes. When our meal was over, Daddy swallowed some tablets and lowered himself painfully into his comfortable armchair beside the fire. He gently closed his eyes and drifted off into a doze.

He got tired very easily now and spent a lot of his time dozing in the chair. One of his favourite pastimes had been swimming at the Bull Wall in the evenings and he could no longer manage to do that or even play football with the boys in the fields. Mammy put her finger to her lips: "Shhhh, be quiet and don't wake Daddy. He's not feeling too well so go off and play for a while. Callie, please help me in the kitchen."

They tiptoed out of the dining room into the kitchen and closed the door. Lately, they seemed to have lots of secret conversations that would stop when any of us came near. It was so intriguing. I wondered what they were talking about now but I couldn't hear anything with the door so firmly closed.

We weren't aware of just how serious Daddy's illness was. Leukaemia was something we had never heard of. In those days, children were very unworldly compared to now. We didn't have very much contact with the big world outside of home and school. There was no television or technology, and we got all our information from parents and schoolteachers and the church.

Most people didn't have home phones and to keep in contact with our relatives we either had to write letters or travel to see them. Besides, with Daddy it had happened so gradually that they were able to keep it from us till almost the very end. Looking back now through adult eyes, I just don't know how we never realised what was happening.

Anyway, how could they have explained to us that he would soon be dead? We weren't really old enough to accept the concept of our father's death; very old people died but not our young father.

We didn't know then that Daddy had just a few short months left to live. Of course, we knew that he couldn't work because he was ill, but we didn't ever imagine that he was going to die. There was no inkling of the terrible tragedy that was unfolding and of the shattering events that were soon to befall us.

Within a few short months our happy little world would be torn apart. Maybe it was better we didn't know because we couldn't have done anything about it if we had. They say ignorance is bliss and we didn't know it then, but at least we had those last few months of innocence before our whole world changed forever.

Chapter Six

Joseph and Anthony had needed new school uniforms for the new term as they had outgrown their old ones. Christmas was also looming on the horizon with all its attendant expenses, at a time of the year when our family finances were already tight.

After much discussion, Mammy and Daddy took the decision that she would go to London to work for a few weeks to earn some extra money to try to ease the financial position. With the money she could earn there they would be able to buy Christmas presents for us, all the while keeping up the pretence that everything was okay. They had decided to treat us to a very special Christmas. We didn't know it then, but this Christmas would be the one that we would always remember as it would be our last as a complete family.

One Sunday when we were gathered round the dinner table, Mammy, looking very serious, said, "Your Daddy and I have something very important to tell you, so everybody please be quite and listen."

This caught our attention. We fell silent, stopped eating and turned our attention to Mammy. She told us, "You know that

Daddy hasn't been able to work for a while. Well, I'm going to go to work in England for a few weeks because we need money for Christmas."

Ah, so that must have been what they had been discussing behind closed doors. "Where's England?" asked Sinead as Mammy told us, "It's another country across the sea." "Mammy, are we going with you?" "No. I won't be away for long. You're staying here with your daddy. Callie will help Daddy to look after you till I get back."

I was upset at the thought of Mammy leaving us again. It seemed so soon after the last time when we had to go into the children's homes. The tears welled up in my eyes and I got a lump in my throat.

I choked back the tears before I asked, "Mammy, I'm going to miss you so much. How are we going to manage without you?" Mammy smiled and tried to reassure me: "Don't get upset Suzy. You're not going in a home, you'll be staying with Daddy this time." "Yes, don't worry, you'll be okay with me," said Daddy.

I was so relieved to hear that we weren't going into the home again because I had visions of them making me eat the horrible food and putting nasty things in my eyes.

Daddy put his arms around me: "It won't be for very long. Just a few weeks and before you know it Mammy'll be back home and then it'll be Christmas." The mention of the word Christmas had a magical effect on the younger ones. They started to discuss what Santa Claus would bring them this year, while I considered the implications of this startling news as it gradually sank in.

Chapter Six

I still had a million questions racing through my brain: "Mammy, will we be going to school while you're away?" I was so crestfallen when she replied, "Yes." "Oh." That was a big disappointment. Still, it wasn't too bad because the Christmas holidays would soon be here and we would have lots of time off then.

I started firing yet more questions at poor Mammy: "Who's going to do the cooking and the housework? Oh, and the shopping?" She smiled fondly at me as she made it clear our big sister Callie was now going to be in charge: "I'm sure you'll all help Callie with everything, especially with the cooking, Suzy."

Before we knew it, Mammy was on her way to London and somehow life at home carried on without her. We were really unsettled by her absence as this was the second time in just a few short years that we had been parted from her. Daddy constantly reassured us that it wouldn't be for long and that she would be home in time for Christmas. At least we had Daddy this time and he did his best to make us feel safe and secure.

He often asked me, "Are you okay Suzy? It won't be long till Mammy's back home. I know she misses you as much as we all miss her." He tried his best to be both mother and father to us. At least he was always there now because he couldn't work anymore, and had become a familiar fixture in his armchair by the fire in the dining room.

My teacher at Bellgrove School, Mrs Hughes, must have known about our family situation even if we didn't, because she started calling me up to the front of the class to sit by the fire. Every day at the mid-morning break she gave me one of the bottles of free milk that were provided for the poorest children in the school.

By this time, Daddy spent most of his day sitting in his armchair by the fire. Despite his constant pain, we weren't aware of the terrible agony he must have been suffering as he managed to keep it from us. He couldn't even help us with our homework anymore as he couldn't concentrate for long because he was in so much pain. Callie nursed him tenderly and the doctor visited him regularly. Anthony kept him company as much as possible and Joseph tried to keep him amused with his silly antics and jokes. But sometimes even that couldn't help.

Before becoming ill, Daddy had been very active. He was such a kind, easygoing man who was adored by all the family. Most weekday evenings we would wait at the bus stop in Mount Prospect Avenue to escort him home from work. Other times he cycled home, and we watched out for him coming up the road, running alongside him all the way to our house.

He was like a Pied Piper, coming up the road with a gaggle of excited children surrounding him, all trying to talk at the same time. Neighbouring children joined the procession and by the time we reached our house there was quite a crowd tagging alongside him. We saw him to the front door where Mammy had dinner waiting for him. He played with the younger children for a while before they went to bed and later helped us with our school homework.

While Mammy was working in London, Callie took on the big task of looking after all of us. She kept the household running as best she could, but it was still an enormous task for a 12 year old to shoulder, even though she was extremely capable and good at everything. Most of the work fell on the two of us, with me doing the cooking, even though I could barely see over the top of the stove. How I managed not to get burned or scalded, I'll never know, especially as I had to stand on a chair to reach the back burners.

Poor Daddy was too ill to do anything now and he seemed to doze most of the time. He tried to play with us sometimes but even the smallest effort exhausted him. His face was drawn and haggard and he was always deathly pale. Anthony rushed home from school every day to be with him and spent long devoted hours by his side, only moving when absolutely necessary. He pulled over a chair beside Daddy's armchair and read his comics while Daddy slept fitfully beside him.

Daddy didn't have much of an appetite and struggled to eat the meals I cooked for him. I was so proud of the food I'd made and wanted him to enjoy it. I'd present him with his dinner while he sat in the armchair: "Look what I made for you Daddy." He tried to show some enthusiasm, even though he hardly had the strength to take a bite: "You're such a good cook, Suzy. Your Mammy will be very proud of you when I tell her how well you've done."

"Thanks, Daddy. Try and eat a little bit more," I coaxed him. But no matter how hard I tried, he was too sick to eat. But of course he didn't want me, or any of us, to know that. He completely downplayed how sick he really was and promised he'd eat something later on: "I'm feeling a little bit sick at the moment, but I'll have some more later."

He was such a kind person and instead of letting me know that he had no appetite for the food I had cooked for him, he pretended he was hungry so as not to hurt my feelings. Even when he was that sick, he was thinking about us and not himself.

Surprisingly, the younger ones were well behaved most of the time and didn't really cause Callie or me any problems. That winter the weather was bitterly cold and there was a light covering of snow on the ground when I took Joseph, Sinead and Imelda up the road to the green post box to post their little scrawled letters to Mammy, which they had laboriously written with Daddy and Callie's help.

I made sure they were well wrapped-up with gloves, scarves and woolly hats. Because they couldn't reach the opening, I had to lift Sinead and Imelda up to post their letters, but Joseph was just tall enough to reach if he stretched on tiptoes. On the way back I kept a tight hold of Sinead and Imelda's hands to stop them running into the road.

"Make sure we all keep together and don't you run too far ahead Joseph. Wait at the corner for us in case there are any cars coming," I automatically cautioned him as he ran ahead of us. "I really miss Mammy. I wish she was here," sighed Imelda, her lips trembling and eyes glistening. "So do I," echoed Sinead. "When's she coming home, Suzy? How long is it now?"

I knew I had to distract them. "Soon, just a few more weeks," I said. "And then it'll be Christmas and Santa will be coming to see you. He'll give you lots of presents if you're very good and don't argue with Imelda. Why don't you count the Christmas trees in the houses? Oh, look, I can see one there."

Chapter Six

Christmas – the magic word. The three of them began discussing what they wanted from Santa and that occupied them all the way home. It took their minds off their longing for their mother. They knew that Christmas wasn't far away now, and she would be back home before long. Our Christmas decorations had already been hung and our stockings were ready for Santa's visit. We were also looking forward to our annual trip to see the pretend Santa in one of the big department stores in the city centre.

Of course us older ones no longer believed in Santa but we still kept up the pretence for the younger children. Anyway, Christmas was still a pretty exciting time and, best of all, we didn't have to go to school for ages and could play with our friends whenever we wanted.

Most households didn't have home phones then unless they were wealthy; we were no exception, so Mammy had arranged to call the local public phone box on Friday evenings when Callie would be there to answer it.

At about six o'clock every Friday evening Callie would say, "Daddy, I'm off to the phone box now. Is there anything you want me to tell Mammy?" And Daddy would give her a list of things he wanted her to pass on.

One Friday evening Callie rushed back from her visit to the phone box, ran up the front path and erupted through the front door in a state of great excitement. "Mammy's coming home tomorrow," she shouted as she ran into the dining room.

Chapter Seven

We were thrilled. There was no school tomorrow as it was a Saturday so we would all be at home to welcome Mammy when she arrived home after travelling all night from London. She was catching the Friday evening train to Holyhead from Euston train station in London and then the overnight ferry to Dún Laoghaire. We couldn't contain our excitement and ran around the house in a wild frenzy.

We were all rapid-firing questions at Callie, as she'd been the one to tell us the exciting news. I demanded, "What time's Mammy coming tomorrow, Callie?" Poor Callie didn't really know all the answers and tried her best to keep us happy: "I'm not sure. She'll be getting a taxi from the ship." "How long is it till she comes now?" asked Sinead. Callie told her, "It's hours and hours yet. You'll have to sleep first." It took a long time to get to sleep that night because of all the excitement!

Next morning, we eagerly sprang out of bed at first light without any urging and excitedly ran down the stairs expecting Mammy to be there. "Is Mammy here?" we all cried out and were all left downhearted when the response was, "No, not for a long time yet."

Callie checked us over to make sure we looked presentable when we had finished washing and had dressed in our best Sunday clothes. She was exasperated by the state of us. Callie wanted us all looking our best for when Mammy arrived, although it was a full-time job trying to keep the younger ones clean and tidy for longer than ten minutes.

Callie reprimanded Sinead: "Look at the state of you. For God's sake, go and get dressed properly and don't let Mammy see you looking like a tinker."

"Don't worry, I'll clean her up," I volunteered. I took her upstairs to the bathroom, washed her face and hands and put a clean sweater on her. Then I attempted to brush her hair quickly as she struggled to get away. In the end she wriggled out of my grip and I told her, "You'll do."

Anthony, as was his usual task, got Daddy a bowl of hot water and his razor to wash and shave. He pretended to have a shave too, imitating Daddy as he scraped the stubble from his chin while Joseph stood and watched and made jokes.

Anthony worshipped his daddy and was always eager to be in his company. Before Daddy got sick they went to the Bull Wall on summer evenings where they swam in the sea, with Daddy diving off the rocks. Daddy had taught Callie, Anthony and Joseph to swim there. When it was especially windy and the sea was choppy, Anthony and Joseph didn't swim with Daddy but instead sat in the men's bathing shelter or on the wall above the huge rocks, where they could keep an eye on his clothes as they watched Daddy swim.

We didn't know until later, but our Daddy was a real hero, and not only to his family. He had saved a man from drowning in the River Liffey in the centre of Dublin. On his way to work in the Guinness brewery one morning he saw the man fall in the water. Daddy dived in and saved him and then calmly continued on his way to work. I can only imagine what the reaction of his workmates was when he arrived at work late and in his soaking-wet clothes.

After a hurried breakfast, Callie cleared up and then made a last-minute check to make sure the house was clean and tidy for Mammy's arrival. "Suzy, keep an eye on those two for me and make sure they keep themselves clean," she said, indicating Sinead and Imelda, who were standing on tiptoe eagerly looking out the sitting room window.

I couldn't sit still and was still inquisitive: "I wonder where Mammy is now Callie." "She'll probably still be on the ship. It's a long way across the sea from England, you know," she replied with great authority. I finally joined Imelda and Sinead and we crowded into the space at the front window. There was an air of intense excitement coming from them. They were so happy that they even forgot to bicker for a little while.

We monitored every passing car. Every time we heard one approaching we shouted, "Car, car!" There was a collective sigh of disappointment when none of them stopped outside our house. To amuse ourselves during our long wait we breathed on the glass and drew pictures on the fogged-up panes. After a while we got fed up with standing and dragged some chairs from the kitchen to kneel on. Callie came to see what all the noise was about, scolding us, "Make sure you take those chairs back to the kitchen when you're finished with them."

When the taxi drew up outside with Mammy in it we stampeded out of the front door to greet her. She laughed at our excitement and very enthusiastic welcome. The boys proudly carried her heavy suitcases into the house as she paid the cab driver. Someone shouted to Daddy, "Daddy, quick, Mammy's home." He couldn't but be aware of that fact with all the commotion going on outside the front door.

Once inside in the hallway, Mammy gave each of us a hug and a kiss, although the boys tore themselves away from her embrace as quickly as they could as they were at an age when they found it embarrassing to be kissed, especially Anthony, whose face turned bright red as we giggled at him.

Mammy laughed and hugged us all again and told us, "I've missed you all so much." A chorus of excited voices chimed back, "We missed you, too, Mammy." It was such a feeling of relief and security to know that she was home again.

We followed her into the dining room. Daddy eased himself slowly and painfully out of the chair to embrace her. Although she didn't say anything or show any adverse reaction at the sight of him, she must have been shocked at his condition. He had deteriorated such a lot since she had been away and it showed in his gaunt, pain-wracked face, the black circles under his eyes and the enormous weight loss, which was very apparent as he held on to the arm of the chair. They embraced and he sank slowly back into his seat.

We all crowded around Mammy, excitedly chattering and trying to grab her attention. She was very happy to get such an excited reception and laughingly pleaded with us, "You'll have to talk one at a time, I can't hear myself think." "Mammy, you sit in your chair and I'll make you a nice cup of tea," I said, before running off to the kitchen to put the kettle on the stove to boil and get the cups and saucers ready on a tray.

I lovingly arranged slices of the apple pie that I had made especially for her (and hidden overnight so that Imelda couldn't eat it) on a plate. Mammy was so pleased when I carried in the tray. It was such a great thrill for me when she said, "I dreamt of your lovely apple pies when I was in London."

Imelda, meanwhile, sneaked out to the kitchen to help herself to a big slice. When I went back to the kitchen there was hardly any left. There was no mistaking the identity of the culprit from the guilty look on her face and the smattering of crumbs around her mouth and on her sweater.

We were so glad to have Mammy home again and she was so happy to be back too and smiled a lot. Daddy was pleased and seemed to have perked up a lot. He had missed her, too, although he had tried to be strong for us. When we had cried for her he comforted us by saying, "I miss Mammy too, but she'll soon be home. Won't it be nice to have her back for Christmas?"

It was so exciting. Mammy had brought lots of luggage and packages with her, some of which contained Christmas presents for us. Callie helped her hide them all over the house in inaccessible places, away from little prying eyes, so that we wouldn't discover them before the big day.

Later, Mammy tried to answer all our eager questions about London. She told us what a big place it was and about the trains that ran under the ground. We were puzzled because we couldn't understand how trains could get under the ground. It was difficult but she tried to explain the underground railway system. Joseph was fascinated and asked, "But how do they get trains under the ground Mammy? Do they go in a tunnel and then come out of the other side or what?" She told him, "No, they stay under the ground all the time and go round and round in circles." Joseph still couldn't get his head around the idea of the trains being underground: "But how do they get them in there?" And Mammy was just as perplexed as he was! "I don't know. I never thought about it before but I'm sure your Daddy would be able to tell you," she said, neatly passing the buck.

It was soon pretty obvious Daddy didn't know the answer either but he tried not to let Joseph know that: "Not now, Joseph, I'll tell you later."

Mammy promised Joseph that when he was bigger she would take him to visit London and he could see the trains for himself. Then, looking over at Daddy, she said, "Go and play for a little while now, I need to talk to Daddy. Callie, share out these candies between you."

We eagerly followed Callie into the sitting room. When we all sat in a circle on the floor, Callie shared out the English candies and bars of chocolate Mammy had brought us. She went round and round the circle: "One for you, one for you, and one for you." Because she was so quick we couldn't keep track of what she was doing; I suspect we didn't quite get our fair share and there might have been a bit of sleight of hand going on, but there were so many different types of candy anyway that we had more than enough to keep us happy.

Life was back on course now that Mammy was home, although the two younger girls were still feeling a bit insecure and followed her around the house, right on her heels, for the next few days, just to make sure she didn't disappear again. We resumed our daily routine and after a while it seemed like she had never been gone.

Chapter Eight

Our big obsession was Christmas, only a couple of weeks away now. Every afternoon after school, I went up to the newsagent's shop at St. Gabriel's to buy the newspaper for Mammy and Daddy. It had little red Santa Clauses and sprigs of holly printed on some pages. The younger children looked through the pages to see who could spot the little Santa Clauses first, and when Mammy had finished reading the paper we would cut them out to keep.

With mounting anticipation, Callie and I endlessly discussed our forthcoming trip to see Father Christmas in the big department store in the city centre. I'd ask Callie, "Will there be lots of sparkly lights? Will the big tree be there?" Callie would laugh and tell me, "Yes! They have them every year!" I'd carry on, "Will Santa give us presents?" Laughing again, Callie would reply, "You know Santa doesn't exist!" But I was insistent: "I know but we'll still get a present though won't we?"

We also occupied ourselves writing lists of what we planned to buy after the little ones had seen Santa, then changing our minds and crossing off items, reinstating them and adding others. Although we didn't believe in Santa anymore, we didn't mind keeping up the pretence if it meant we received presents on Christmas morning. When the others weren't around we whispered together about the packages that Callie had helped Mammy transfer from her suitcases and hidden around the house.

I mused, "I wonder what I'm getting." Callie knew what all the presents were but refused to betray Mammy's confidence and tell me. "I know but I'm not telling you. You'll just have to wait and see," she smirked. Infuriated, I left the room in a temper, slamming the door behind me.

Sinead and Imelda ran around the house, up and down the stairs, singing and chanting, "We're going to see Santy, we're going to see Santy." Their excitement was catching and the atmosphere in the house was brighter than it had been for quite a while now.

The boys pretended not to care about our trip to the city but they couldn't suppress an occasional glimmer of excitement. Even Anthony, the stoical elder brother, allowed a little smile to cross his face at the mention of our forthcoming trip. Of course, Joseph was his usual nonchalant self and took it all in his stride.

The big day soon arrived and we were all up at the crack of dawn. We rushed around getting washed and dressed and were all ready by the time Mammy called us to breakfast: "If you're ready, sit down at the table. Your food will be done in just a few minutes."

"Can we go and see Santy now, Daddy?" begged Sinead and Imelda. He laughed: "The shops won't be open for a long time yet." Mammy was busy and became irritated at the incessant refrain from Imelda and Sinead: "When are we going to see Santy? Is it time yet Mammy?" At one point she crossly told them, "If you don't stop annoying me, you won't be going anywhere at all."

They knew she didn't mean it, but we were all so excited that we had to work off energy while we were waiting for our food and went outside to run around the frosty garden. We didn't even notice the freezing cold. When breakfast was ready, Mammy called us in. The others were eager to get going and gobbled their food down as quickly as they could, but I was way too excited to eat. Mammy tried to coax me: "Try to eat something Suzy. A cup of tea isn't enough. You'll need some nourishment inside you. It's going to be a long day. If you don't want porridge, what about some toast and marmalade?" I pulled a face as I insisted, "I'm not really hungry. Okay, but just a small one."

I managed a few small mouthfuls. The others had already left the table and were playing outside in the back garden. It had started snowing lightly and I could see them through the window, running around the garden trying to catch the snowflakes in their outstretched hands and on their tongues. At long last it was time to leave for the bus. We didn't have to be told to put on our coats and were ready and waiting by the front door, eager to be on our way, like racehorses waiting for the off.

Before we left the house Mammy asked, "Now, does anyone need the bathroom before we go?" Nobody did, as we had already been a thousand times. So she made sure we were all dressed warmly ready for the trip: "Have we got everything? Joseph, fasten the buttons on your coat. It's cold outside. Keep yourself warm and make sure the cold doesn't get to your chest."

Daddy joined Mammy; they looked at our eager faces and exchanged smiles: "Let's go." We didn't need telling and, despite his asthma, Joseph was already halfway down the road to the bus stop. His footprints in the newly fallen snow pointed the way ahead of us as we ran to catch him up.

Poor Daddy was so thin and gaunt, his face as white as the snow falling gently around us. He walked slowly, linking arms with Mammy and Callie. Anthony walked in front of them and frequently glanced back, anxiously checking that Daddy was okay. Although he was very worried about him, he tried not to show it. Sinead and Imelda lagged a short way behind Joseph. They were too young to be aware that anything was seriously wrong with Daddy. As they passed each house, they admired the beautifully decorated Christmas trees covered with twinkling coloured lights that stood in the front windows. The trees and bushes were adorned with a heavy dusting of snow. It looked just like a scene from a snowy Christmas card.

Even though it was Christmas, that didn't stop Imelda and Sinead from competing like they always did. Only this time it was over what Santa was going to bring them. "I'm going to ask Santy for a bike," said Sinead. "I'm going to ask him for a doll that walks and talks," replied Imelda. "Me, too," insisted Sinead. "No, you can't. I'm having it," said a pouty Imelda. But Sinead was not giving up her new dream of a doll that walked and talked: "I can if I want to." This, of course, sent Imelda into melt-down mode: "I'm going to tell Mammy on you."

They argued all the way to the bus stop, until they became distracted by the sudden appearance of the bus approaching in the distance. They started running to catch up with Joseph: "Wait for us Joseph." He got to the bus stop first and was waiting there, red-faced and breathless, when we arrived.

"Daddy, can we go upstairs?" he implored with shining eyes as we all clambered on board. "Oh, goody, let's go upstairs," shouted Sinead. Daddy couldn't make it up the stairs in his condition and gently told Joseph, "It's best if you stay down here so we can all be together. There's enough room for all of us down here but not upstairs."

Behind us, other excited children were running for the bus. The conductor waited until everyone was safely aboard and sitting down before he rang the bell for the driver to move off. Daddy gave Joseph the long string of tickets from the conductor's ticket machine as consolation for his disappointment at not being allowed upstairs. This was a great responsibility and attracted envious glances from other small boys on the bus as Daddy told him, "You look after these tickets for me just in case the ticket inspector wants to check them."

The bus pulsated with excited children. Our conductor spent his time running up and down the stairs to make sure they didn't misbehave but it was just good-natured excitement on their part. Although there were lots of people waiting at the bus stops along the way, the driver sailed past them as the bus was now completely full. As the city centre appeared in the distance, the excitement reached a crescendo and the noise from the top deck was nearly enough to blow the roof right off. As the bus stopped in the main shopping area, there was a sudden mad rush as everybody tried to alight at the same time.

The flustered conductor had to stand well back to avoid being squashed as masses of exhilarated children stampeded off the bus. He shouted, "Hold your horses now. Where's the fire?" But nobody took any notice of him in their eagerness to get off.

There was a weak sun shining now and most of the snow had melted into dirty slush in the gutters. Excited crowds of shoppers hurried up and down every street, dashing in and out of the big stores laden down with heavy bags. All the shop windows were brightly decorated for Christmas, and we stopped and looked in the windows, completely mesmerised. I was so enthralled by the sights in one of the shop windows that I never noticed the family move off, leaving me behind. Turning to put my hand in Daddy's, I discovered with a shock that instead of Daddy there was a stranger standing beside me. Just as I was about to start crying, Daddy appeared, looking for me.

I gulped back the tears: "I thought you had gone and left me and I would never see you again." Daddy gently laughed as he told me, "Don't be silly. We wouldn't leave you behind. How could we forget our little Suzy? Dry your eyes now and we'll catch up with the others." We quickly caught them up a few doors along the street. Mammy rolled her eyes: "Try to keep up with the others and don't get lost again." After that I held on to Daddy's hand and made sure I kept everyone in sight for the rest of the trip.

In the store we raced past the glass counters of perfume and make-up in an effort to be the first to reach Santa's Grotto, with Mammy and Daddy following more slowly behind. I stumbled on the steps but was up again in a flash and tried to keep up with the others, yelling at them, "Wait for me, wait for me!" But they didn't take any notice and ran ahead, eager to be first in line.

I stopped in awe at the entrance to the toy department. It had been transformed into a wonderland. The twinkling fairy lights and sparkling snow made it seem truly enchanted. Behind big fluffy snowdrifts were reindeers pulling a sleigh full of Christmas presents, and the shop assistants were dressed as fairies and elves.

The sight of the enormous Christmas tree made me catch my breath. It was covered with twinkling fairy lights of many colours and laden with sparkling balls, tinsel and beautiful ornaments. Nobody could fail to be enchanted at this wonderful sight, especially the littlest ones who thought the Grotto really was Santa's house. It was the most beautiful thing I had ever seen and I thought it was magical.

The boys pushed and shoved to get into the queue to see Santa and were told off by one of Santa's elves: "Stop pushing. Santa doesn't see little boys who push and shove!" Daddy told them to be gentlemen and move back to let the girls go first. They weren't too pleased about it but did as they were told with very bad grace. We grinned at their furious faces, which made them even more annoyed.

The long line of excited children shuffled slowly forward and eventually we reached the front of the line, entering the Grotto one by one. When it was my turn, I was pushed forward by one of Santa's helpers. Santa held my hand: "What's your name little girl?" I whispered my name but was feeling shy and kept my eyes down.

The big jolly Santa smiled down at me. I remember he had a kind voice as he leant in to speak to me. "I'm sure you've been a great girl now Suzy. I'll be round to your house on Christmas Eve, sure I will. Now what would you like for a present?" I was overwhelmed with shyness and couldn't think what to say. He took a small package out of a big tinsel-covered box on the ground beside him and handed it to me. Then somebody gently pushed me out of the Grotto.

At the back exit all the parents were waiting. I met up with Mammy and Daddy. I proudly showed them my present: "Look, what I got from Santa." I was caught up in the spirit of it and told them what Santa had said and showed off the cheap little gift he had given me as though I still believed he was real.

When all of us had seen Santa, Daddy gave each of us a small amount of money to spend on toys and candies. We went down the street to Woolworth's store where we could get lots more toys and candies for our money than in any other shop, especially the department store, and we spent ages choosing exactly what we wanted.

Callie and I walked along behind Mammy and Daddy, admiring our purchases. The little ones were overawed as they thought they had just met the real Santa Claus. For once they were quiet and not arguing, trying to be good in case Santa heard that they had misbehaved and decided at the last minute not to visit them on Christmas Eve!

To finish off the day, we had a meal in a restaurant in O'Connell Street. Fast-food restaurants hadn't been invented then and it was a rare treat for us to eat out. This was an especially memorable occasion as it was the last time we would be together in public as a complete family.

Chapter Eight

O'Connell Street is probably one of the most famous streets in Irish history. It was where the uprising (known as the Rising) of Easter Monday 1916 took place, when a band of Irish Republicans (the IRA) seized the General Post Office and other buildings, raised the tricolour and proclaimed an Irish republic. In the battle that followed, the overwhelming forces of the British Army defeated approximately 1,000 Irish Republican volunteers. They held out for a few days but were eventually forced to surrender. Their leaders were tried and executed, became martyrs and heroes of the Republican movement and were later immortalised in song.

Part of the Post Office was destroyed by fire during the battle and was later rebuilt. Even today the bullet marks from the battle can be seen on the original stone pillars at the front of the building that still stands in O'Connell Street.

In the middle of the wide avenue stood Nelson's Pillar. The monument had been constructed to commemorate the Battle of Trafalgar and honour Lord Horatio Nelson. It was similar to Nelson's Column in London's Trafalgar Square and thus was viewed as an insult and a symbol of British sovereignty over the Irish. When it was blown up by the IRA in March 1966, the head of the Nelson statue was rescued from the wreckage and is now displayed in Trinity College in Dublin. The column was eventually replaced by the Dublin Spire, which stands 120 metres tall.

We never missed the annual St Patrick's Day fancy dress parade with the colourful decorated floats that meandered down O'Connell Street towards the River Liffey. Everybody proudly displayed little sprigs of shamrock, the Irish national emblem, on their clothing. Little did we know, that day in O'Connell Street, that very soon the River Liffey would play a significant part in our lives.

After the excitement of seeing Santa and doing our shopping in Woolworth's, we were all starving. We soon perked up, though, when we entered the restaurant opposite Nelson's Column. It was more of a Mom and Pop café really and not at all fancy by today's standards but we were still a little overawed by our surroundings. This seemed the epitome of luxury to us. Callie was thrilled to bits at the elegance and sophistication of it all. If only her friends could see her now. "I'll read the menu to you all," Callie said, opening it with great assurance as though it was something she did all the time.

The waitress hovered by our table with her pad waiting to take our order: "Would you like something to drink before you order your food?" Everybody ordered different coloured fizzy drinks but just couldn't decide what to eat, though. Joseph decided to order whatever Daddy recommended: "Daddy, what should we order?" Daddy looked over the menu and picked out something he knew we all liked. "What about chicken? That sounds nice. You'd like chicken, wouldn't you?" An excited Joseph shouted, "Yes Daddy!" "Me too!" chimed in Imelda, her eyes wide and her mouth salivating at the huge list of food. Anthony copied Daddy, of course, and ordered exactly the same as him.

It really was a special treat to dine in these glamorous surroundings. The waitress brought us our fizzy drinks in tall glasses with coloured straws and the bubbles fizzled up my nose when I sipped mine. It was the first time I had ever tasted

French fries and I loved them. And for dessert I choose ice cream. My ice cream was served in an elegant silver dish with three scoops of ice cream: vanilla, strawberry and chocolate. The top was decorated with a cherry and a fancy fan-shaped wafer and there was a slim long-handled spoon to eat it with. All around came the buzz of conversation and laughter from the other tables, but we didn't talk much as we were busy savouring the food and, if the truth were told, we felt a bit intimidated by our surroundings.

"This is the best dinner I ever had," I said and I meant it. It wasn't the food so much but the restaurant, the waitress, in fact the whole experience, which was something I wasn't used to but really loved. "What, better than my cooking?" said Mammy in mock horror. I quickly tried to backtrack: "No, no, I didn't mean that." Mammy started laughing as she tried to reassure me: "I know you didn't. I was only joking." The others laughed at me as I blushed.

Daddy whispered something to Mammy, excused himself and got up from the table. I was worried about him: "Where's Daddy going?" But Mammy once again hid his pain and agony from us and told us everything was okay: "He's just got something to do. Don't worry, he won't be long."

What we didn't know was that he was in so much agony that he went into a nearby bar and drank a brandy to try to ease the agonising pain he was suffering, although he was a teetotaller and normally never frequented bars.

We were mostly quiet on the bus journey home because we were all pretty much exhausted. Most of us were fast sleep as soon as our heads hit the pillows. There were no complaints about going to bed from anyone that night.

Before I drifted off to sleep, I relived the whole day in my mind. All in all, it was one of the best days I ever had, one I have remembered all my life. Mammy and Daddy must have decided to make this last Christmas outing special for the children, knowing the tragedy that was about to befall us, and in our childish innocence we didn't suspect that this was almost the end of our happy and idyllic childhood.

Chapter Nine

Soon after our trip to see Santa on Christmas Eve, Callie and I helped Mammy to do the shopping for our family of eight. In the decade just after the end of the Second World War, life was much more basic for most people compared to the abundance of things we have today. Even in Ireland, which had been neutral during the war, it was still a time of austerity, as the devastating economic impact had been felt there as well as elsewhere in Europe.

We, too, like the British people, had to show ration cards when buying some of the foods that were still scarce even in the early 1950s. Ordinary people didn't have cars, fridges, home telephones or washing machines, all the things that are taken for granted today.

The average family considered television, which was broadcast only in black and white then, a luxury only for the rich. Even supermarkets hadn't yet been invented. We had to buy our food from individual shops: the grocer, the butcher, the greengrocer, the baker and the confectioner.

Mammy, Callie and I headed off to the Vernon Avenue shops early in the morning. We trailed from shop to shop buying the Christmas food. Loaded with heavy bags, we staggered to the bus. When we arrived at our stop, Mammy said to Callie, "These bags are very heavy. Do you think we should wait here while you go ahead and get Anthony to help?" Callie agreed and ran to get Anthony who helped us carry the bags of goodies from the bus stop to the house.

There were delighted "Oohs" and "Aaahs" when we un-packed, especially at the sight of the huge luxury Christmas cake, with icing in the form of snow. Little figures and fir trees decorated the top. It was wrapped round with a big red bow. Imelda, especially, was impressed by the size of the cake and her eyes opened wide at the thought of how much of it she could eat!

On Christmas morning we were awoken while it was still dark by the noise of excited shouts from Anthony and Joseph, who were already awake and ripping the paper off their presents to get at the treasures inside. "Look what I've got," yelled Joseph, so loud the whole street could probably hear him.

The boys had both received roller skates and couldn't wait until everybody was up before trying them out. They immediately rushed down the stairs and started skating up and down the hallway in their pyjamas, making so much noise that they woke everyone up. Mammy came out of the bedroom. "Who's making that awful racket? Anthony, don't you know what the time is? You're going to wake the whole house." But the boys were just too excited and carried on skating as Joseph shouted, "Look what Santa brought me."

But by now it was too late as we were all wide-awake anyway and eager to open our own presents. We were thrilled when we saw our gifts in their beautiful wrappings. There were delighted exclamations: "Look what I've got," and "Look what Santa's left me!"

Callie had received a beautiful watch and felt very grown up as she strapped it on her wrist and told us the time. I loved my beautiful new doll with her blonde curls just like mine and wanted to show her to my friends; it was too early, however, although most of the other children in the street were also up as the lights in all the houses testified. The little ones proudly showed Mammy and Daddy what Santa had brought them and both of them pretended to be amazed with Daddy exclaiming, "Santa must have thought you were very good to give you such wonderful presents."

Later on, when the boys were tired of skating, we all had a go, holding on to the furniture to avoid falling over. "Daddy, tell them to stop; they'll break my skates," said Joseph, who was very upset that everyone else was monopolising his favourite present. "Come on now, that's enough. You've got your own toys to play with," said Daddy.

At Christmas Mass at St Gabriel's church we saw all our friends and discussed what Santa had brought us. We promised to meet up later to see each other's presents. Callie and I then spent the morning helping Mammy to cook Christmas lunch. I peeled potatoes and brussels sprouts and Callie stuffed the big chicken after first gingerly taking out the giblets. The Christmas pudding was put on to boil for a few hours and the dining table was laid with the best china and cutlery.

I took great pleasure in helping to decorate the table for the great feast. We put a Christmas cracker in each place.

Everybody's eyes lit up when they saw the results of our morning's work and were greatly impressed with the size of the enormous chicken. After saying grace, we ate till we were stuffed fit to burst, some more than others. We were all so full that none of us could manage the Christmas pudding until later.

When the Christmas dinner was over we helped Mammy to clear away and did the washing up and were then free to play with our toys again. I called on Jean, my best friend from a few doors down, to show her my doll. "Look what I got from Santa," I exclaimed proudly as I showed Jean the doll. I even let her hold it for a few seconds! Lots of children were out playing in the street while their parents recovered from the early start to the day and the big Christmas lunch. Baldy O'Hare, who considered himself to be a cut above everyone else because his father had a car, had received a bicycle from Santa and was riding up and down showing off, ringing his bell to try to attract everybody's attention. Nobody was impressed because they all had their own presents.

For me, nothing could compare with my precious, beautiful doll that Mammy had brought from London especially for me. I proudly showed her off to anybody who cared to look.

Chapter Ten

Shortly after Christmas, Daddy's condition had begun to deteriorate so much that the doctor was forced to make frequent visits, eventually visiting the house daily. It had reached a point when he had become too weak even to make the journey up the stairs to bed.

"Who's going to help me move a bed downstairs for Daddy?" asked Mammy. Immediately we all volunteered to help as she instructed us, "Anthony and Callie, you bring the bedstead and Joseph and Suzy, try and manage the mattress." We struggled down the stairs, manoeuvring the heavy bed and mattress as best we could, bumping and banging against the walls but eventually managed to get the bed into the room. Mammy made it up with clean sheets and blankets for Daddy. We watched with pride as Daddy climbed in to rest in comfort. Exhausted, he sank back on the pillows. He barely had the strength to talk but smiled and said, "Thanks everybody. This is great." We beamed back at him, feeling very proud of ourselves. Anthony took up his usual place by his father's side as he dozed off and we trooped out of the room.

The room always felt stiflingly hot. Even from the doorway we could feel the waves of heat emanating from the coal fire that burned almost all day and night to keep Daddy warm in the cold winter weather. Because he had lost so much weight and was really just skin and bones, he now felt the cold more than ever. He would shiver if even a whisper of a draught wafted in when the door was opened. The skin on his hands was like tissue paper and so thin that the blue veins stood out and could clearly be seen all over his body. His face was pinched and deathly white. There were dark shadows under his eyes and his arms were covered in big black bruises from the injections given by the doctor and which he tried to hide from us. Every movement had become excruciatingly painful for him and he needed continuous pain medication.

During the night Mammy and Callie took turns watching over him. After a mostly sleepless night, in the morning Callie would tiptoe into the room ahead of Mammy to check on Daddy, afraid that he might have died since they last tended to him. Mammy's usual courage deserted her for a fraction of a moment. "Callie, please go in first. I just can't face it," she whispered as they stood hesitantly by the door, putting the weight of the world on Callie's shoulders.

With a knot of apprehension gripping her stomach, Callie gently turned the doorknob and silently pushed the door open. She stopped for a moment in the half-light, listening intently to see if Daddy was still breathing. Satisfied that he was still alive, she entered the room and called softly, "Daddy, are you awake?" He stirred from a restless and painful sleep and struggled to sit up. She kissed him gently and Mammy cleaned away the blood that had trickled from his mouth in his sleep and stained his bedding. They changed his sheets and pillowcase so that we wouldn't see the blood and be frightened when we came to see him, and made him as comfortable as they could for the start of another long day of suffering.

When we came down for breakfast, Mammy put a finger to her lips, motioning for us to be quiet and not to disturb Daddy, as he needed to rest. Normally we were very noisy in the mornings, but now we tiptoed around getting ready for school and later, just before we rushed out the door to catch the bus, we gathered in the dining-room doorway to say good morning to him. In the dim light we didn't notice just how very ill he had become because the deterioration had been a gradual process. Even so, Mammy tried to hurry us so that we wouldn't realise how bad his condition really was. She wanted to protect us from the shocking sight of his bruised and wasted body as much as possible.

As we crowded around the doorway, Mammy urged us, "Say hello to Daddy and be quick now. You'll miss the bus if you don't leave straight away." We all chimed in together, "Hello Daddy." He would give us a weak smile and say, "Have a good day. I'll see you later." Before he became ill, every night Daddy had left six copper pennies on top of the big clock on the mantelpiece in the dining room for our bus fares to school and sometimes a bit extra to buy some small candies on our way home. When the weather was good, we walked to school and spent our bus fare on extra candy on the way home. But now it was Mammy that gave us our pennies in the mornings. This should have been a sign to us of how sick he was, that he didn't even have the strength to count out the pennies, but we were just too young to understand then.

However, we couldn't help but be aware that the atmosphere in the house was different now. Daddy and Mammy spent a lot of time talking together. Her eyes always seemed to be red-rimmed and she looked very sad. She was still trying to protect us from the gravity of the situation; when we asked her what was wrong she would try to reassure us, preparing us for the worst while at the same time doing her best not to alarm us.

Then came the day Mammy had been dreading and a day we were unprepared for as she sat us all down to tell us, "Daddy's not very well. He'll have to go into hospital for a little while." I was distraught: "When's he going? What hospital?" Mammy didn't know all the details but was honest this time and told us what she knew: "I'm not sure but it'll probably be quite soon. The doctor will decide when the time comes and then we'll know for sure."

Fear struck my body and my stomach clenched in knots: "Mammy, I don't want Daddy to go away." Mammy did her best to reassure me and the younger ones: "I know, Suzy, but he'll be better off there for a little while. They can do more for him in the hospital."

Shortly afterwards he was admitted to hospital. It happened while we were at school. The doctor visited and immediately called for an ambulance to take Daddy on his last journey to the hospital. When we arrived home from school, Callie opened the front door with her key and we all ran to the doorway of the dining room to say hello to Daddy. Surprised, we stopped short at the open door and looked at the empty bed.

"Mammy, Mammy are you here?" shouted Callie but there was only an empty silence. She found a hastily scribbled note on the kitchen table from Mammy to say that she had gone to the hospital with Daddy. Shock and apprehension gripped us because we hadn't been expecting it so soon. I burst into tears: "Callie, where's Daddy? What's happened to him?" We crowded round her, and the little ones clung to her as she tried to calm our fears. She tried to be brave and not show that she was also worried as she told us, "Don't worry. Mammy'll be home soon and we'll find out then. I'm sure everything will be okay then."

When Mammy arrived home a short time later we anxiously rushed to hear the news. Holding herself together emotionally so as not to frighten us, she said, "The doctor says that Daddy needs some special treatment and they're keeping him in the hospital for a little while." Our innermost fears were allayed for the moment and we relaxed a little. The atmosphere of relief was almost tangible, but I was desperate to know when we'd see Daddy again: "When can we go and see him, Mammy?"

Mammy hesitated before telling us, "Not just now but you can in a day or two when the doctors have made him feel better." A few days after he was admitted to the hospital, we went to visit Daddy and were shown to his bed in the ward by a nurse in a starched white uniform with a big round watch pinned to her chest. The atmosphere in the ward was intimidating and we felt very subdued as we cautiously approached Daddy's bed. Propped up with the starched white pillows supporting him, he gave us a weak smile while valiantly trying to pretend to us that there was nothing wrong but looking so ill and fragile that we were very scared. Mammy told him, "They've all been really good and have been helping me out and doing their chores." How heartbreaking his thoughts must have been. They both knew there was nothing more the doctors could do for him; he was dying and would soon be leaving us forever, so Mammy was just trying to take his mind off his pain with talk of the everyday things we did at home.

We chatted away to him for a while, telling Daddy of all the things we'd been doing and how school was. Anthony boasted about his schoolwork, telling Daddy, "The teacher says I'm the best!" while Callie added, "Suzy made another great apple pie!" I couldn't help myself and blurted out, "I wanted to bring you some but there's none left! Sinead and Imelda ate it all!"

Daddy smiled as best he could and then there was the quick pitter-patter of the nurse's footsteps on the floorboards indicated that it was already time for us to leave. She smiled at us before whispering something in Mammy's ear. Mammy nodded to her before turning to us: "Say goodbye to Daddy now. The nurse needs to get the patients ready for the doctor."

We stood in line to kiss him goodbye and were then quickly ushered out of the ward by Mammy and Callie. As we went out of the door, the nurse bustled around setting up the equipment for his blood transfusion. I was fascinated and wanted to know what was happening: "Mammy, what's happening? What are they going to do to Daddy?" Mammy tried to explain to us what was happening, but to shelter us from the reality of what was happening, she downplayed what Daddy's treatment was going to be: "The nurses have to make sure that all the beds are nice and tidy and the patients have their temperature and blood pressure taken for when the doctor comes around to see them."

But I wasn't satisfied with that answer and demanded to know: "Will he be coming home soon?" I'm sure Mammy knew the real answer but she tried to remain upbeat for our sakes: "I'm not sure when. It's up to the doctors." Mammy and Callie knew that he wouldn't be coming home ever again.

We were never to see him in person in the ward again as he had now been moved to the intensive care unit. The only way we could see him was through the high-up hospital window where he stood behind the glass with a nurse supporting him for a few minutes, waving down to us as we stood shivering in the freezing grey concrete courtyard with the icy rain lashing our upturned faces.

When we arrived at the hospital, Mammy stationed us in the cold concrete square facing the windows of the wards that overlooked the quadrangle. She gestured to Callie: "Callie, mind the others for me. Wait here until I come back and don't move. Daddy's going to come to one of the windows up there to see you. I won't be long." She turned to enter the hospital. "Mammy, don't forget these," I said, remembering the little notes and cards we had made for Daddy. She turned and quickly grabbed them from my outstretched hand before rushing into the hospital. The rain had gotten heavier and we were in danger of getting soaked, so we moved into the shelter of some doorways where we anxiously scanned all the windows overlooking the courtyard so as not to miss a sight of Daddy.

I was shivering and my teeth were chattering but I almost didn't notice the cold in my intense desire to see him. We weren't sure which window to look at because we didn't know where he was going to appear, so we constantly scanned them. Even Imelda and Sinead weren't arguing for once. Callie tried to keep our spirits up: "Daddy'll be coming to the window in a minute." Callie then pointed up towards the windows: "Look, there's Daddy. Up there, look, at that window on the second floor. The one on the corner."

We shouted and waved up at him, jumping up and down with excitement. We screamed really loudly: "Hello Daddy, here we are Daddy!" He spotted us below and blew kisses. After a few brief minutes he gave a weak wave goodbye and turned away from the window. The nurse took him by the arm and they both disappeared from view as she helped him back to his bed. Exhausted by even the smallest effort and with his remaining strength depleted by his short trip to the window, he needed to return to his bed to recover. We were so happy to have seen him but felt somewhat cheated and disappointed that it had been for such a brief time.

As his condition got worse Mammy had to invent excuses why we couldn't visit him: the doctor was coming around to see the patients or the nurse was taking their blood pressure and temperature; we were too late and visiting time was finished; even that all the patients were having their afternoon nap and couldn't be disturbed because the doctor would be cross if Daddy was woken up.

Eleven-year-old Anthony wouldn't accept the fact that hospital regulations prevented him from visiting the intensive care unit to see his father. He made the journey to the hospital every day instead of going to school. Nothing mattered to him except his daddy. He sat patiently all day on a chair in the corridor outside the intensive care unit as if willing Daddy to live. The staff couldn't help but notice his presence and when they asked him what he was doing, Anthony boldly told them, "I'm waiting to see my father. I can wait all day." They eventually took pity on him. They sneaked him into the ward for a few minutes to see his beloved father once more before he died.

Mammy continued to make her daily visits to the hospital while we were at school. When she arrived for one visit in early February she received some terribly distressing news. A nurse took her aside. She told Mammy, "I'm so sorry but your husband has passed away. His body is being prepared to move the mortuary. Would you like to see him now before he's moved?" Devastated by this, Mammy composed herself and went with the nurse to see his body. She had an awful shock at the sight of the dead person lying in the bed. It wasn't Daddy – they had got the wrong person. He was still barely alive, still clinging on in the intensive care unit. Despite her distress, Mammy had to quickly pull herself together in order to see him. He finally died the next day and she had to go through the awful agony for a second time.

On a quite ordinary day that February of 1958 our little world was cruelly shattered when we were told the heart-breaking news that Daddy had died. Mammy met us at the door on our return from school to tell us. Her face looked so bleak and we could see that she had been crying. She had a neighbour standing with her to give emotional support.

We knew immediately. I cried, "Oh, God, oh, God, oh God." We were inconsolable with anguish. They tried their best to comfort us but there was nothing anyone could say or do that would assuage our grief. Sinead and Imelda clung to Mammy for comfort, then wandered aimlessly through the house weeping and calling, "Daddy, Daddy." Callie ran out to the yard and was violently sick. Joseph and Anthony were stunned into silence at the terrible news. They looked like they were turned to stone, their faces white with the awful shock. I could feel the tears gushing uncontrollably down my face. My legs felt shaky and almost gave way beneath me. I collapsed onto a chair.

Later on, I reacted in my usual way to bad news and lost my appetite completely. Mammy became concerned about me but I just couldn't eat anything. Over the next few days she and Callie offered me food but I wasn't interested in eating, even though they tried their best to persuade me: "Suzy, you must eat to keep your strength up. Here, please, please try some of this." When we awoke every morning the shocking truth hit us anew – we would never see our adored father again. Never would we meet him at the bus stop on his return from work, nor spend summer days together at the beach or go for walks in the fields and woods with him. His loss was devastating and there was nothing we could do to ease the terrible agony. We were utterly bereft.

Chapter Eleven

On an icy winter's day in the middle of February 1958, the funeral service was held at St Gabriel's Church, the big parish church just up the road from our house. Our family, dressed in our best Sunday clothes, sat in the front pew of the lofty, echoing church. The polished wooden coffin with brass handles was placed on a stand in front of us. It was topped with a big wreath of flowers and lighted candles in tall candlesticks surrounded it at the four corners.

I must have been numb as I felt no emotion at the sight. Somehow it didn't seem real to me: I just couldn't imagine that my father was in that wooden box. The pews were packed with people in black clothing, some of them sobbing loudly.

After the lengthy church service, which passed in a daze, the pallbearers, who included Daddy's two younger brothers, carried the flower-decked coffin out to the big black hearse. Local people stood and watched as the cortège moved slowly away from the church and glided along the grey rain-swept streets in the direction of the cemetery atop the Hill of Howth on the northern side of Dublin Bay. Along the route, bystanders made the sign of the cross and bowed their heads in respect as the hearse passed slowly by. The procession of cars followed the hearse along the coast road to Sutton Cross and then climbed up the steep hill to the cemetery overlooking the bay. The priest conducted the burial under a bleak grey sky as our father was laid to rest on the hill facing Clontarf, while seagulls soared gracefully overhead, oblivious to the sad scene below.

We children didn't attend the burial service because it was considered too distressing for us to see our father's coffin being put in the ground. Instead, we were sent to stay with neighbours until the mourners came back from the cemetery. That was the day I saw television for the first time in my life and it remains forever etched in my memory. I guess the neighbours thought letting us watch television would take our minds off what was happening at the burial service. In a way they were right: to this day I remember that the first programme I ever saw on television was the movie *The Third Man* starring Orson Welles.

After the burial service, the mourners came back to our house and it was soon full of people with solemn faces, all dressed in black. Relatives and complete strangers clucked over us: "You poor things. What's going to happen to you now? God help you."

As it later turned out, they weren't offering us any help. We were definitely on our own and never saw most of them again after that. Maybe they expected 'God' to provide the help they spoke of because it certainly wasn't coming from any of them.

They were full of platitudes: "Your Daddy's in heaven with God now," and "Your Daddy's an angel now." As if that was any consolation. And they couldn't – or wouldn't – answer the questions we had: "Why did God have to take our Daddy up to heaven? We needed him. Why didn't he take someone else instead?" Nobody explained why and we were left with these sad unanswered questions.

A few of them were so overcome with emotion they didn't know what to say but instead pressed money into our hands. That was their way of showing sympathy. Later, when they had all gone home and we were finally alone in our grief, Callie took us out for a walk. She told us, "Mammy needs a rest." Mammy was certainly exhausted from the trauma of the day. Our walk took us to the shops at Vernon Avenue where we spent the money we had been given by the mourners. I doubt that anybody had any enthusiasm for shopping but we went through the motions anyway, and I bought a book with my share of the proceeds.

It was only later, when the last of the mourners had left and we were alone, that we grasped the enormity of our loss. We would never see Daddy again – he was gone forever.

Later, when the younger children were in bed, Mammy, Callie, Anthony and I sat huddled close together for comfort, discussing what to do next about our predicament. "We're on our own now and we'll have to pull together to get through this," said Mammy, determination etched in her face. Callie, who knew the truth of the situation we were in, was desperately worried: "What are we going to do, Mammy? How on earth are we going to manage?" Mammy tried to reassure her: "Don't worry. I'm sure we'll think of something."

Mammy had always been extremely resourceful and was confident that she would find a way through our present problems. Anthony, who was just 11 years of age, quickly assumed the role of man of the house: "I'll look after you Mammy. I've got some money saved. You can have it." Mammy smiled sadly at him and gave him a hug. This time he didn't shrug her off with the embarrassment of a prepubescent boy.

I cried myself to sleep that night, exhausted but unable to sleep for hours, tossing and turning for most of the night – and if I'm honest many more nights after that too. During those long stressful months, Mammy's hair had turned completely white. Although she still had a young face, her hair was completely drained of colour.

A month later I had my tenth birthday. I cried when Mammy produced a bottle of Lucozade along with a box of chocolates and told me, "Happy Birthday, these are from Daddy." His visitors had given them to him and he had saved them for me, knowing that he wouldn't be alive on my birthday to give them to me himself.

Later that day after we'd celebrated my birthday, it was time to celebrate Daddy even though he was now gone from our lives. He was gone but most definitely not forgotten so we planted some forget-me-not flower seeds on his grave as a token of our love. In the language of flowers their meaning is "True love, hope, remembrance, memories".

Chapter Twelve

By some awful oversight, Daddy had died without any life insurance cover, leaving Mammy with six children under the age of 12 years to support from her small widow's pension. That news was bad enough, but much, much worse was to come. Mammy had discovered that because Daddy had not made a will, his estate was legally required to be held in trust until the youngest child reached the age of 16 and the house couldn't even be sold until then. At that time Sinead, the youngest, was just five years of age. The mortgage on the house was also unprotected by insurance but still needed paying until the end of the term – approximately 12 more years.

A few months earlier, Daddy's colleagues from the Guinness Brewery at St. Joseph's Gate had organised a collection to send him to the Catholic shrine at Lourdes, where an apparition of the Virgin Mary was reputed to have appeared to some peasant children. It was believed that bathing in the spring waters would cure the desperately ill people who made their way there hoping for a miracle. He was to be accompanied on the trip by Mammy and they hoped for a miraculous recovery for him. Those kind friends had also collected enough money to hire a woman to look after the children while they were away, but Daddy became too ill to travel such a long way and died soon after.

When he died, these caring men decided to use the fund to help support our family. One of them cycled out to our house every Friday with money for Mammy. He did this faithfully every week until the fund was exhausted.

Meanwhile, Mammy was still in desperate financial straits and had to do something drastic soon if we were to survive this further blow. She now had six children to support and no money coming in apart from her widow's pension, which had been appropriated to pay the mortgage, so her finances were at rock bottom. That was when she came up with the idea of engaging a woman to look after us while she sought work as a secretary in Dublin.

There was an employment agency in the city that she had used previously when she was working and needed nannies/ housekeepers. Mammy made a trip into town to see them but they had nobody suitable available. As she left the agency she met a woman at the bottom of the stairs. It transpired that the woman, who was called Maureen, was a housekeeper looking for a job. They ended up going to a café for a cup of coffee while Mammy interviewed Maureen for the job of looking after us. Her references appeared to be in order and she was a friendly person, well dressed and clean. It was mutually agreed that Maureen would work for a trial period.

Maureen duly arrived at our house the following day. Giving her time to settle in and to see how we all got on with her, before she looked for secretarial work for herself, Mammy spent a few days showing her our routine. Maureen was a motherly type of person who liked children and we all got on well together. She was a happy, chatty type of character, although sometimes she appeared lost in thought. We felt quite comfortable in her company and enjoyed her cooking.

It appeared to be a good arrangement and Mammy was pleased. She was confident that things would turn out well. That night she said a prayer of thanks to God. She told Callie, "Things are looking up. It won't be long now before we're back on our feet, please God." Callie gave a smile of relief: "I know we'll be okay Mammy."

Mammy hoped to be able to get a good job soon now that the domestic arrangements had been sorted out. She had the Pitman Gold Medal in shorthand, was an experienced legal secretary and had never had any difficulty getting work before. During the Second World War, she had worked in the War Office's Liaison Office in Dublin, helping to facilitate the passage of Irish volunteers who wanted to join the British Army to fight Hitler.

Also, at that time British factories and industries were in desperate need of workers because their employees had been called up to fight in the armed forces and those who remained were mostly women, boys and old men. There were plenty of jobs available for Irish men and women who wanted to make the perilous journey across the water separating Ireland from the UK, avoiding the German U-boats that infested the waters of the Irish Sea and the English Channel.

Mammy loved poetry, especially William Shakespeare's sonnets, and was extremely well read. Another favourite was the *Rubaiyat* of Omar Khayyam. When she was brushing my curls she would teach me poetry, which we both loved. Sometimes she quoted Elizabeth Barrett Browning's love poems. Other times we had a singsong instead although Mammy and Daddy constantly encouraged us to read. We had our own bookcase full of children's books and I always had my head stuck in a book.

When the weather was good we spent most of our time outside playing with our friends and visiting their houses. Jean, my best friend, had been born with a cleft palate, which had been operated on when she was small and she was left with a lisp. Her great ambition was to be a ballet dancer and she had lessons every week. She had an older sister who was a nurse in London and we sometimes discussed visiting there when we were older. As it happened, Jean later became a professional ballet dancer in London.

In the dark winter evenings or when it was too wet to go out, we would listen to the radio or play games. We always found something to do and were never lonely or bored and, because we had so many friends and siblings, there was always someone to play with.

A few days after Maureen's arrival, Mammy, Callie and I sat at the kitchen table. Through the window we could see the others playing in the back yard. Anthony, Joseph and Sinead were kicking a ball around and Imelda was standing watching them. We could hear their shouts and laughter as they played.

Chapter Twelve

We were drinking tea and eating the freshly baked scones that Maureen had made earlier which were still slightly warm from the oven. I split mine in half, spread it with butter and strawberry jam and sandwiched it together. As I bit into it, the jam oozed out: "Mmm, these are lovely." Maureen was pleased; she smiled at me as she stirred her tea, telling me, "Eat up, girl, there's plenty more where they came from."

All of a sudden she gasped and dropped her spoon. The door to the pantry, which normally stuck and had to be prised open with a knife, started opening and banging shut as though the wind were blowing it, although all the doors and windows were closed and there was no draught anywhere in the kitchen.

Maureen was wide-eyed, shaking with fright and her face had turned white as a sheet. She looked at the door and then made the sign of the cross: "Jesus, Mary and Joseph, God bless us and protect us. There's a ghost in this house, so there is. Someone's going to die." Maureen then moved her chair so that she couldn't see the cupboard door from where she was sitting.

Mammy's expression was one of shock. She was completely aghast at the housekeeper's outburst and turned to look at Callie and me to see our reaction. We were puzzled and frightened at this unexpected and alarming turn of events. Mammy gave Maureen a warning look and said to Callie and me, "If you two are finished, go out and play with the others. I want to talk to Maureen." As we went into the garden, Callie whispered to me, "Don't tell the others what Maureen said." I nodded and pretended that nothing was amiss.

After that episode and their chat, everything appeared normal between Mammy and Maureen and Mammy reassured us there was nothing to be scared of. The next morning, as usual, after we had left to catch the bus to school with Callie escorting us, Maureen and Mammy were left alone in the house.

As Mammy later told us, "Maureen began behaving very strangely. She said that she couldn't sleep in her bedroom anymore because she felt uneasy there. During the night she had been woken by unearthly noises, she said. Somebody had come into the room riding a horse but she couldn't see who it was as she was completely paralysed in the bed and couldn't move any part of her body. She had bad dreams all night and had to come downstairs and make a cup of tea early in the morning."

Mammy was very worried now and was rapidly becoming concerned, especially after yesterday's outburst. What was the matter with Maureen? Was she unstable? Had she made a mistake employing her?

Later, Mammy gave Maureen some money and she went off to the shops to buy food for the evening meal. After a short while she returned and told Mammy, "I don't feel very well." But she couldn't be specific about what was wrong with her. She appeared to be dizzy and looked very pale. Mammy suggested that she visit our doctor and gave her the address of the surgery and directions on how to get there. Maureen set off up the road to see him.

After she had been gone for a long time, and with evening drawing near and the darkness setting in, Mammy became worried, especially after the odd things she had said and the fact that she hadn't been feeling very well that morning.

Chapter Twelve

She said to Callie, "I wonder what's happened to Maureen. It's very strange that she hasn't come back. Do you think she's all right?" Callie replied, "I really think she's a bit strange, Mammy. Do you think she's all there?" "I don't know. I'll have a serious word with her when she gets back," said Mammy, looking very worried.

Mammy sent Callie to the doctor's surgery the next day to enquire whether they had seen Maureen, but they had no knowledge of her. A couple of days later, early in the morning, the milkman knocked at our door and showed Mammy the daily newspaper. He pointed out an article on the front page about the death of a woman by drowning in the Liffey in the centre of Dublin. He asked Mammy, "Isn't that the woman who was working for you? God rest her soul." Mammy was stunned when she read the description of the victim: "I'm sure that's Maureen. She went out to see the doctor and never came back. I was wondering what had happened to her."

In the event it transpired that a couple of evenings previously, two boys walking by the River Liffey had witnessed what happened. They saw Maureen climb over the wall of the quay on to an iron ladder that led down to the water. She stood on the top of the ladder for a moment, blessed herself and then started climbing down towards the dark water. Watching her descent down the ladder into the river, one of them shouted to her, "Hey, missus, don't go down there, you'll fall in the water." "Mind your own business," she replied. Concerned, one of them said to the other, "I'll wait here and watch her while you go for the Gardai (police)."

The other one ran off to find some policemen who were patrolling a short distance away.

Maureen continued her descent into the dank, grey water. The boy who had remained again pleaded for her to wait while his friend got help, but she didn't take any notice of his pleas. By the time the police arrived she had disappeared into the murky water and couldn't be seen in the darkness. The police rushed along the quay in a desperate search for her, with only weak moonlight and their torches to guide them. Eventually they spotted her lifeless body floating in the water and quickly pulled her out, but they were too late: she couldn't be resuscitated and was pronounced dead at the scene.

After Mammy had recovered from the shock of reading the newspaper article, she went to the phone box and contacted the police. They asked her to come to the station that same day to make a statement, and later on she was requested to attend the inquest to give evidence. Maureen's son also attended the inquest and in his evidence to the Coroner stated that Maureen was an alcoholic. It transpired that she had been drinking in a pub all afternoon before her death and that was why she hadn't been feeling well when she left our house the next day to do the shopping – she had been suffering from withdrawal and desperately needed a drink. Maureen had spent the housekeeping money Mammy had given her on alcohol and was probably afraid to come back to our house.

The Coroner recorded a verdict of suicide.

Chapter Thirteen

The suicide of our housekeeper was another appalling blow for Mammy. Frantic with worry, she didn't know which way to turn or what to do next. Now she couldn't be sure that we would be safe while she was out working and didn't know what to do to resolve our desperate situation. Although she depended on Callie such a lot, Mammy felt she couldn't burden her with the enormous responsibility of helping to care for us, as she was only 12 years of age herself.

There was no question of Callie not being capable, as had been proved while Mammy was away in London, but it would be too hard on her to have to do it permanently and besides it would affect her schooling. She was very bright and was expected to attend university later. They were very close. Mammy's pet name for her was 'Callie the Brave'.

Mammy wasn't without her own bravery either. Daddy had always said to us, "Your mother's a great woman. She's got the heart of a lion." They were well suited and really loved each other. He was a very kind, strong, silent type of character. He admired Mammy and supported her ambitions for all of us.

All her courage and considerable inner resources were now called upon to try to make a decent future for her young family. Mammy, Callie and Anthony sat for long hours discussing what to do about our awful predicament. We younger children were kept unaware of just how serious the situation really was, although there was an undercurrent in the house that we couldn't quite understand. Whispered conversations stopped when any of the younger children came within earshot.

Some close neighbours, Mr and Mrs O'Neill, called to the house to see Mammy. They offered their help and Mammy gladly accepted it as she thought they meant well. Who could blame her? After all the trauma of the past few months, she probably wasn't thinking clearly and perhaps that was the reason for the unfortunate choices she now made to help her out of this terrible dilemma.

These people were members of a religious organisation called the St Vincent De Paul Society. The society was affiliated to a religious order that looked after children. Mammy made the agonising decision to ask them to care for us while she went to London for a while. She could do temporary work there, giving her more time to see us and deal with any domestic emergencies that might arise than if she were in a permanent job. There was also more work in London than in Dublin and it was better paid, even when the cost of frequent return trips back to Dublin from London were taken into account.

Mammy had previously encountered problems trying to get work in Dublin. She had already applied for jobs and had been refused because she was a woman alone with six children. Employers didn't want to take her on because of the risk that she might need frequent time off for domestic reasons. She was considered to be a liability in Dublin, but the market was larger and more flexible in London. She could work as a temp while she looked for something more regular.

The advantages of doing temporary work in London would mean that she could take time off when necessary. Mammy intended saving as much money as she could, visiting us in Dublin whenever she was able, and then setting up home in London for all of us as soon as possible. In the meantime, she expected that we girls would be safe and cared for by the nuns of the Catholic Church, and the boys by the Christian Brothers. Like most Irish people at that time, she thought they were the kind and caring people they portrayed themselves as to the public.

So, that was how we three girls came to be standing in the unfamiliar surroundings of the orphanage that spring day in 1958, feeling extremely scared and uncertain of what the future held for us. The reason Callie hadn't come with us to St Vincent's at that time was because she was staying at home with Mammy for a little while longer to help with the task of packing up the house and also as comfort for Mammy until she left for London within a few short weeks.

We three felt so alone, totally bewildered and lost. Entering an alien world expecting to be cared for, we were instead to be abused and exploited by the representatives of the Catholic Church.

Their doctrine of love for their fellow men didn't extend to the pitiful little souls in their care, as we were very soon to discover. Our crime, and that of most of the other children in the institution, was that we were fatherless and vulnerable – in other words: perfect victims.

Chapter Fourteen

The orphanage and Catholic Church dominated and dictated the lives of the mainly poor, working class people of the district. It wasn't long after the end of the Second World War when jobs were very scarce everywhere in Europe, especially so because of the millions of soldiers that had returned from the war seeking work. Competition for jobs was extremely fierce. The majority of families in the locality were Catholic and extremely large, as women were expected to continue giving birth as long as they were able, no matter whether they were capable of doing so either physically or financially.

You would have expected that the orphanage and attached school would have been a more imposing building considering the prominent part it played in people's lives, but it was completely unremarkable with no particularly distinguishing features. It was a redbrick, warehouse-like structure, situated in a small street in a run-down, bombed-out inner-city area of Dublin, just a few minutes' walk from the city. The narrow side street was just off the main approach road to the wide avenues of the city centre with its department stores and restaurants, but they might as well have been a million miles away.

Hitler's Luftwaffe had bombed part of the area around the orphanage during the Second World War. Although neutral Dublin escaped the mass bombing that England had endured, some bombs were dropped by the German air force, hitting the densely packed houses of the working class districts of the city. In 1941 high-explosive bombs were dropped on the North Strand area where the orphanage was located. Around 300 houses were damaged or destroyed and many people killed. Some suspected that the bombing was deliberate, possibly in revenge for the decision to send fire engines to aid the people of British-controlled Belfast in Northern Ireland following major bombing by the Germans.

When we arrived at the orphanage in the late 1950s, the deep craters where the bombs had exploded remained unfilled, and debris from houses and other buildings that had been destroyed in the air raids littered the whole area. The dusty wreckage stretched for miles around the orphanage and was a boy's dream of a place to explore. Unaware of the danger, which may have included unexploded bombs, hordes of children played among the mounds and hills of bricks and rubble, scrambling over what had once been houses, shops and pubs, sharing their playground with rats, cats and stray dogs. The debris held a great fascination for them and they spent most of their leisure time exploring the ruins, and building dens from the shattered bricks and bits of wood and glass.

My first coherent memory of the orphanage and the people was 'the meal'; the terror I experienced at the hands of one of the nuns comes back instantly when I think of that day. The memory is still vivid after 50 years and the feelings of shock, the terror, the panicky feeling and the tightness in my chest fill me with dread when I think of it.

Newly arrived in the orphanage and knowing nothing about the rules and regulations of the institution or how to be an orphan, we were escorted by the nun from the parlour to our supper in an austere dining room known as the refectory. On entering the enormous wood-panelled, high-ceilinged room, our ears were immediately assailed by a cacophony of noise. There appeared to be hundreds of chattering, noisy children seated at the tables. It was completely overwhelming: the noise, the crowds and, most of all, the complete strangeness of it all.

One of the nuns barked at us, "Over there!" and pointed at us to join the end of a long line of children that was wending its way past a serving table. We tagged on to the end of the line and tried to look as inconspicuous as possible so as not to attract attention. Conscious of being the focus of much interest from the other girls, Imelda tried to hide behind me, while the normally extrovert Sinead was abnormally subdued. We followed the example of the children in front of us and took a bowl from the big pile on the table. Shuffling along behind the other girls, we eventually arrived at the head of the queue.

There I met for the first time an extremely tall nun called Sister Concepta. The enormous headdress perched on her head added to her towering height and dominated everything around her. She appeared to be as tall as the ceiling and was standing there with a big scowl on her face. It later transpired that this was her customary expression and accurately reflected her personality. 'Unpleasant' was the only word to describe her and she was one of the nastiest, scariest and most sarcastic people I have ever met in my life.

During all my time in that institution I never saw her smile at any of the children, let alone say a kind word to them. It appeared that she didn't grasp the 'concepta' of being a nun – she wasn't a Christian, neither humble nor good, nor any of the other descriptions usually applied to nuns.

Never having been in such close company of nuns, my notion of them was that they were kind, happy people who only wanted to do good deeds for others. What a misconception that turned out to be.

The nun stood at the mid-point of the serving table. In front of her was an enormous iron pot and she held a big ladle in her hand. Her expression wasn't very friendly and I tried to avoid looking into her face as she snarled, "Bowl," at me and then, as I held it out, she slopped some horrible greasy stew into my bowl. It consisted of big lumps of gristly grey meat that could have come from any animal, as well as potatoes and carrots. I was revolted at the sight of the unappetising fat and gristle swimming around in greasy water, but tried not to show it so she wouldn't notice me and I kept my head well down to avoid catching her eye.

After being served, I waited at the end of the table until my sisters had gotten their meals. We found space to sit at the nearest table that had enough room for the three of us. All around us at the other tables, children had the same disgusting bowls of stew in front of them. One fair-haired girl sitting opposite us was obviously not looking forward to eating hers, judging from the look of revulsion on her face as she sat staring at it.

The nun rapped the table with the ladle and shouted, "Grace!" Instantly there was a hushed silence as the children clasped their hands and bowed their heads in prayer to thank God for their food. From the sight and smell of the food, it was apparent that God didn't think the children deserved very much. In fact, he must really have hated them. When grace was finished, the tumultuous sounds of the children's voices and the clatter of cutlery rose up once more and filled the air.

I kept my head down but nobody appeared to take too much notice of us, as they were more interested in their food. Later, we were to learn just how important food was to them. We sat there trying to eat the revolting slop, except for one girl who watched our plates with eyes like a hawk. "I'll have your bread if you don't want it," she said to me and, as I wasn't in the least bit hungry, I gladly handed it over to her. Sinead also held hers out and the girl wasted no time in leaning forward to grab it. Somebody else looked hopefully at Imelda's bread but she was eating it – she never had much trouble with her appetite.

The only edible bits of the stew were the vegetables, and I ate some slivers of carrot. I just wasn't hungry as I was so upset by the separation from my mother and the rest of my family that I couldn't manage more than a few mouthfuls. Even if I had been starving, there was no way I could've even attempted to eat any of the revolting grey fatty meat. Just the thought of it made me want to retch. Noticing that some of the other girls had taken their plates up to the serving table and scraped the remains of their meal into the waste bin on the floor at the side of it, I decided to do the same with mine as I couldn't face eating any more of it.

I began emptying the contents into the bin but was startled when Sister Concepta suddenly shouted at me, "Girl! You there, STOP!" Recoiling in fright, I almost dropped my bowl. She leaned down from a great height and screeched, "What do you think you're doing? We don't waste good food here. Who do you think you are, madam? Get back to that table and finish your supper."

Never having experienced such aggression before in my life, I was so shocked that all I could do was stand there for a moment, fearful and unable to move, my mind trying to absorb what I had just heard. The hostility emanating from Sister Concepta really scared me. She had a look of triumph on her face and a strange gleam in her pale blue eyes. This was an expression I came to recognise over time. I don't know whether it was down to madness or evil, but it frightened me and I didn't dare disobey her then or in the future.

Sister Concepta must have known that she had scared me but didn't appear to care, as she had achieved her desired effect. She watched as, terrified, I crept back to the table observed by all the other children, some of whom laughed at this great entertainment. Being an extremely shy child, to be the focus of so much attention was sheer torture for me. Reaching the table where my sisters sat, I was aware of sympathetic looks from them, but they were now also very scared. I put my head down and attempted to eat a little bit more of the stew but it was cold and congealed on the plate. I couldn't force it down: my throat seemed to have constricted with fright and was so dry that I just couldn't swallow anything.

My tormentor seemed to enjoy her little game of threatening to force-feed me. This was a completely different experience from the children's home when I had refused to eat the tapioca. Unlike the staff in the home, this nun was completely terrifying. I was made to sit there for what seemed like hours shaking with fear and trying not to cry as I sensed that she wouldn't approve. I occasionally managed to slide a morsel of the stew down my dry throat as the nun stalked up and down the room, her intimidating footsteps ringing in my ears.

As she came by my table, she stopped and snarled, "Have you not finished yet? I'm keeping my eye on you missy. Think you're too good to eat our food, do you?" I shivered with fear. My terrified little sisters were too scared to say anything. They kept their heads down and forced themselves to eat, even though I could see they felt sick too. Gradually, most of the other children finished their meals and left the refectory along with Sinead and Imelda. My sisters looked back at me with pity. The other girls didn't seem surprised or have any sympathy for my predicament. It was obviously normal behaviour on the part of the nun.

I was left all alone at the table trying to finish my meal. Although I thought about trying to hide the meat in my pocket, it was more than likely that she would frisk me before I left the refectory. That left just me and a few other girls who were also having difficulty eating, under the malevolent gaze of Sister Concepta. She occasionally walked past their tables to check on them too. They would hunch down over their plates and try not to draw attention to themselves, probably glad that most of her attention was trained on me.

Later, when she returned to check that the girls had cleaned the refectory to her satisfaction, she discovered that I was still sitting at the table in the now almost empty room. "Are you still here? Get out of my sight," she snapped. Turning to one of the girls sweeping the floor, she yelled, "You, take her upstairs and show her what to do."

I was so frightened that I can't even remember what the girl's name was or even what she looked like. She took me up to the dormitory and showed me where to wash and get ready for bed. Too scared to say anything, I just followed her and did as she told me.

My two little sisters were in the beds next to mine at the far end of the dormitory. They were also in a distressed state but I was in no position to console them as I was unable to control my own tears. I wanted to go home to my mother. Sick with terror and scared of the nuns after the events of the day, I wondered how we were going to manage to live in this horrible place and prayed to God to help us. The tears welled up again. "God, please help us," I prayed. But it turned out God wasn't listening to my prayers.

There was no such thing as privacy or dignity for the children: we had to undress by the side of our bed with everybody looking at us. Naturally, being new, we were objects of curiosity. Some of the girls were already in bed and stopped chatting to look at me with inquisitive eyes. As I wasn't used to taking my clothes off in public, I tried to undress without any of them seeing my body, but was aware of countless eyes staring at me from all sides. Hot with embarrassment, I wished I could have been anywhere else but there.

Without showing too much of my body, I somehow managed to change into the nightdress which had been given to me, and climbed wearily into my bed. My sisters were asleep, or pretending to be. The mattress was rock-hard and the pillow felt like a stone. I couldn't get comfortable no matter which side I lay on.

Being almost completely new to this particular environment, even though we had experienced some communal living in the children's homes a few years earlier, we were helpless and at the mercy of everybody, particularly the cruel nuns. It was a shock to discover that they weren't kind and caring. I prayed again to God to help us and to get us out of this awful place. Of course this changed nothing, as their God obviously didn't hear me and didn't know or care what his representatives on earth got up to.

When all the children were in bed, the nun who was supervising us came back into the dormitory and turned off the lights, plunging the room into complete darkness and leaving us alone and unsupervised for the rest of the night.

After what seemed an age, most of the girls had drifted off to sleep and the room was quiet, but I was still awake tossing and turning. My inability to sleep, despite being totally exhausted, gave me plenty of time to examine my surroundings. The dormitory was only in semi-darkness, as the faint moonlight

Chapter Fourteen

coming through the bare windows illuminated my surroundings. There were two long rows of army-style beds with grey, scratchy, woollen blankets and thick white cotton sheets smelling of soap. They may also have had some starch in them as they felt very stiff. The beds were all neatly made with the end corners tucked in. Each row consisted of about 15 or more beds. The floors were of bare polished wood, the walls were painted either cream or white and the windows were without curtains or blinds of any kind.

I wondered who the girls in the other beds were. One or two of them had acknowledged me but there hadn't been any time to get to know anybody, even if I hadn't been so shy. Although I was worn out from the trauma of the day and was desperate to get some sleep, I found it impossible, as I was frequently disturbed by the sounds of the children in the dormitory crying or shouting in their sleep.

Eventually I fell asleep, only to be awoken in the middle of the night by a loud noise, my heart thudding wildly with fright. Not sure where the noise had come from and unable to get back to sleep again, I lay there for hours thinking and wondering what the next day would bring. I missed my home and family and the comfort of familiar surroundings. My sisters were fast asleep in their beds next to mine. Still upset, I shed more silent tears.

Finally, as dawn arrived and the sky lightened, the birds began their chorus and I fell asleep. It seemed like only a few moments later that I was woken by the lights being switched on and the noise of the other girls as they started chattering and banging around as they got out of bed and began preparing for the new day.

I was exhausted by the events of the previous day and my fitful sleep, and felt anxious about what this new day would bring. For a start, we didn't know what to expect or how to do anything for ourselves in this unfamiliar environment. We got out of our beds and sat on the sides, lost and waiting for somebody to tell us what to do. Sister Concepta strode into the dormitory, looked at us sitting there, and barked crossly to one of the other girls, "Orla Murphy, you look after the new girls; show them what to do and mind you're quick about it."

Orla, a thin, acne-faced girl of about 14, with long straggly hair, scraped back to one side with a bobby pin, sullenly showed us the routine and we struggled to cope as best we could, feeling totally disorientated. She grudgingly showed us how to make our beds in the institutional way, looking on impatiently as we struggled to follow her instructions: "Hurry up and be quick now and I'll show you where to get washed when you've finished that."

Her curt attitude showed that she wasn't happy with having to teach us the ropes; I wasn't too surprised as it was so early in the morning. When we finished the bed-making, she took us to the washroom. We had each been given a face flannel, toothpaste and toothbrush and a comb, which we kept in a wash bag in our unlocked bedside lockers. Orla told us in a sharp voice, "Get washed and dressed as quickly as possible or you'll be in trouble with Sister Magdalena."

We had no idea who Sister Magdalena was, but we were scared enough already without having to worry about another nun.

Orla then snapped, "When you've finished washing come back to the dormitory and I'll tell you what to do next." Then

Chapter Fourteen

she left us alone in the washroom and went back to get herself ready for Mass.

On one side of the room were dozens of hand basins, with toilets in separate cubicles on the other. There were pools of water on the floor from where the children had washed earlier, and it was extremely slippery, so we took great care not to fall and injure ourselves. We washed our faces, cleaned our teeth and brushed our hair and were ready in record time as I anxiously urged the others: "Oh God, come on, be quick Sinead, stop dawdling and hurry up. We'd better get back to the dormitory soon in case that girl goes downstairs. We won't know what to do if she goes and leaves us and then we'll be in trouble with the nuns."

That made them speed up. Sinead wasn't in any mood to be hurried but the thought of the nuns brought a sudden spurt to her steps. We quickly made our way back to the dormitory and were relieved to see that Orla was still there: "Okay, if you're ready now we'd better get going as we don't want to be late."

We obediently followed her down to the chapel for daily Mass. It was miles away across the other side of the playground and it seemed to take forever to walk there through the endless corridors. Orla rushed us along and when we lagged behind her she told us, "Hurry up!" We were almost running in an effort to catch up with her. She kept anxiously turning round to urge us not to be late for Mass: "Come on, come on, hurry up or you'll be in for a caning from Sister Magdalena." Her threat made us quicken our steps even more and we quickly caught up with her.

We eventually reached the chapel and nervously followed Orla to a pew at the back, trying to be as inconspicuous as possible. Even so, people looked curiously at us as we made our way past them to our seats. The atmosphere in the chapel was hushed and expectant, with not a sound or movement to be heard, apart from the odd suppressed cough or the rustle of a nun's rosary beads. The air smelled of a mixture of polish and stale incense. Behind the highly polished wooden railings, the white marble altar was decorated with freshly cut flowers and tall white candles.

Nuns occupied the front pews and their big white head-dresses almost blocked our view of the altar. All the children sat in the back pews in complete silence, except for the occasional sniffle, with the big girls keeping an eye on the restless younger ones to make sure they didn't disturb the service. The priest entered from behind us, dressed in long embroidered vestments and swinging an incense holder as he led a procession of altar boys up the central aisle. One or two of the teenage girls took great interest in what was happening; they were especially interested in the altar boys, but most of us were just too tired to care.

At that time of the morning the strong smell of incense as it wafted around the chapel was most unpleasant and made me feel sick. I held my breath to try to avoid inhaling it. Arriving at the altar, the priest and the altar boys, dressed in white smocks over long black garments, genuflected in front of the big crucifix with the figure of Jesus on it. They made the sign of the cross and then dispersed to their assigned positions. Mass began with the priest chanting in Latin and the congregation giving the appropriate responses, almost like zombies. The altar boys assisted the priest by handing him the items to be used during the service.

I tried hard not to fall asleep while the extremely boring ceremony dragged on and on. At certain points during the performance we were required to kneel down on the wooden supports in front of us. They were very hard on my bony knees, so I was glad to get back on the wooden seat again when the rest of the congregation sat back up.

The only people who appeared to show any interest in the ritual were the nuns, who gave it their rapt attention. None of the children appeared to care, especially at that unearthly time of the morning. Another hour in bed would have been of more benefit to us. After a while I felt my eyes drooping and knew I was in danger of nodding off. I struggled to stay awake as I could see Sister Concepta in the pew in front of me and was scared that I might attract her attention. After an interminable time, we had to go up to the altar rails to receive communion, a thin wafer that was placed on our tongues and dissolved instantly, making me long for food. My thoughts turned to breakfast.

It was now at least 14 hours since I had been forced by Sister Concepta to eat my revolting supper; I was so hungry by now that I hoped the boring service would be over soon and we could get something to eat. At long last it came to an end and we followed the rest of the chattering children as they filed out of the chapel and along the corridor to the refectory for our first meal of the day. Although I was extremely hungry and desperate for something to drink, I was also feeling nervous because of the traumatic events of the previous evening.

After that ordeal with Sister Concepta, I was dreading my next encounter with her and hoped that maybe she wouldn't be serving breakfast. Some hope. When we finally arrived in the refectory, there she was again behind the table. I kept my head down in order to avoid attracting her attention as we lined up for another unappetising meal.

She didn't appear to pay me any special attention as she ladled a portion of porridge into my bowl. I was relieved and swiftly moved away from the serving table. My sisters quickly joined me and we sat down to examine our food. This time the meal consisted of porridge, not porridge with milk as most people like it, but a nasty grey sludge with great big lumps like stones in it. It had a taste unlike any porridge I had ever tasted, salty, watery with half-cooked grains and chewy lumps. As soon as it entered my mouth I felt an impulse to spit it out, but as there was nowhere to put it, I tried to swallow it. A girl called Eileen noticed that I couldn't eat it and said, "If you don't want that I'll have it."

I was amazed but grateful and immediately passed it over to her. My sisters looked hopefully at her. Sinead asked, "Do you want mine, too?" Eileen took Sinead's bowl of porridge and polished it off in a few minutes. Then she looked at Imelda's plate with an enquiring look and Imelda pushed it across the table. It really must have been bad if Imelda couldn't eat it. She had never been known to turn down food. I made a mental note to sit at this girl's table in future.

Some of the other girls looked hopefully at our bread. Maggie asked, "Do you want that bread?" I told her, "Yes, I do." She was disappointed but I was starving hungry and managed to eat the bread even though it was liberally covered in stinking margarine. We also got a cup of pale watery tea from a big urn, which we drank out of tin mugs.

It seemed that the people in the kitchen didn't care what slop was served to us. They obviously considered anything to be good enough for us, whether we liked it or not. It wouldn't have occurred to them that we'd perhaps been used to good food before entering this place. But we didn't have any choice: eat it or go hungry. There was nothing else to eat and no way of obtaining any other food for the majority of the children, most of who didn't have regular visitors or access to money. Of course the nuns didn't share our food but ate in their own dining room in the convent.

In the first few months we rapidly lost weight, and for the remainder of my time there I was extremely underweight and malnourished, as were a lot of the children who existed on such poor food. Once, a nun excused me from carrying heavy packages because I looked "too frail to carry such heavy things". We were all astounded: it was unheard of for any of them to be concerned about whether a child was fit enough to do whatever work was required of them. I wasn't suffering from any eating disorder – just a lack of nourishing food. It showed how bad our diet was, that she actually noticed something was wrong. It would never have occurred to any of them, of course, to check my state of health.

Before leaving the refectory we had to line up while the dreaded Sister Concepta force-fed us a dose of cod liver oil from a huge bottle, which she ladled out in big spoonfuls whether we wanted it or not. When it came to my turn, she glared at me as I tried to avoid her gaze. She made sure that my large spoonful was full almost to overflowing. I made a face and gagged when she roughly pushed the spoon into my mouth, forcing me to swallow the stinking stuff. It tasted fishy and oily and I was tempted to spit it out. That was a signal for her to give me a second dose for being stupid enough to let her know that I didn't like it. "That'll teach you to be ungrateful, missy," she sneered.

She obviously had not forgotten the events of the previous day and was still determined to punish me. My sisters didn't dare show any reaction after seeing what happened to me and received just the one dose of cod liver oil. Sister Concepta certainly taught me a lesson that I would never forget. I was careful never again to make the mistake of showing her that I didn't like anything she gave me, whether it was food or anything else.

However, I made sure to show emotion when she whipped me with her cane; to remain stoical only resulted in a further beating until the tears came to my eyes. Only then would she be satisfied that she had received the proper response and turn to her next victim. This was the beginning of an entirely different sort of education for us: an education that was essential to enable us to survive in this harsh new world.

Chapter Fifteen

After breakfast, Orla came looking for us and took us along a warren of corridors to the sewing room. Two women, a nun and another grey-haired old woman dressed in secular clothes who appeared to be her assistant, occupied this room. Her assistant was sitting at an old-fashioned sewing machine and looked at us with interest, giving us a fleeting smile before putting her head down and continuing with her work. These two women looked after the nuns' habits and priests' vestments and made any necessary repairs or alterations. The nun also supplied the orphans with school uniforms upon their arrival or when they had outgrown their current ones. Her assistant was the only secular person we ever saw working in the convent or orphanage, apart from a few schoolteachers in the day school.

The nun was tall and thin and looked even taller with her enormous headdress. She had a stern and unfriendly air about her and didn't even look us in the face when she spoke to us. We could have been invisible for all she cared. Opening a big cupboard, we saw shelves full of navy uniforms. Pointing to me, she said, "You, come here."

She issued us with a bundle of clothes. Although these were new when they were given to us upon our arrival, during the rest of the time we spent in the orphanage the gymslips were never washed. On Wednesday afternoons we were each given a nailbrush and spent the afternoon scrubbing any dirty marks off the garments. All our other dirty clothes were sent to the laundry somewhere in the vast building, to be washed by the staff.

After receiving our uniforms, we went back up to the dormitory to change for lessons and Orla showed us where to store our old clothes. She was slightly friendlier and a bit more relaxed now she'd eaten her breakfast. All the corridors were deserted as we ambled along beside her. "What's your name and where you from?" she enquired. As I was the oldest, I answered, "I'm Suzy, this is Sinead and Imelda, and we're from Clontarf."

Orla then asked me, "Why are you here?" I decided to be honest, even though what happened with Daddy was still raw. I tried not to show that I was still upset as I told her. "Because our daddy died and our mammy is going to London to work." Orla either didn't notice or chose not to say anything about my trembling lip as she said, "London, that's a long way away. Why doesn't she work in Dublin?" I had no answer for that, which quickly put a stop to Orla's questioning.

This building was the biggest I had ever been in, ever bigger than the children's home we had been in a few years previously. It had long wood-panelled corridors and highly polished floors.

There were seven flights of stairs leading up to the roof. We had only ever lived in a suburban house apart from our short time in the homes, and this place seemed enormous to us. The orphans' part of the building contained two big dormitories, a basement kitchen, the refectory and a big wood-panelled room where we played in the winter or when the weather was bad. There were enough bathrooms and washrooms for all of the children, who numbered around 50 or so and maybe more at times.

The convent where most of the nuns worked, ate and slept was in another part of the building. There was also a day school on the premises that catered to outside pupils as well as the orphans. This was in a separate part of the orphanage and was reached through a maze of corridors. Then there was the chapel for daily Mass, which we had to attend every morning during the week without exception, except for Saturday, when the priest had a rest to prepare his sermon for Sunday, his big day of the week.

I savoured the freedom from this ritual on Saturdays, as I am sure did most of the children. We also had to attend another meaningless service in the evenings, called 'benediction', when we said the rosary. This involved endless prayers: Hail Marys and Our Fathers. The recitation droned on and on hypnotically. On warm summer evenings it lulled me into a trance and I almost fell asleep. Apart from the monotony of having to say the same prayers over and over, we were tired from the long days, having been up since dawn, and had to fight to stay awake. Sometimes an unfortunate girl did fall asleep and was punished later by the nuns for this outrageous insult to God.

It didn't matter whether we could sing or not, but we were compelled to join the choir anyway. This 'choir' was composed only of the orphans, and we were required to perform in the big old church just along the road on Sundays for the edification of the public. One of the nuns taught us the hymns and made sure we didn't take any opportunity to shirk. I was forced to become a member even though I couldn't sing in tune or hold a note, but that didn't matter at all as we didn't have any say in the matter. If you were an orphan you had to sing.

We weren't allowed to say no to the choir, to be a member of which was considered a great honour by the nuns, although I didn't notice them sitting in a freezing cold church for hours on end singing meaningless songs. There was no pleasure involved in this exercise at all. Just like everything else there, it was just another chore. In the winter the church was so cold and draughty that it was an ordeal to sit on the hard pews hour after hour with chattering teeth pretending to sing, while being totally uninterested and wishing we could be anywhere else. Why was everything about religion so difficult?

Orla took us to the day school, passing along deserted corridors full of classrooms from which the murmur of children reciting lessons could be heard. After knocking on the door of one classroom, Orla pushed Imelda and Sinead through in front of her and said to the teacher, "These are the new girls."

Imelda and Sinead both turned and looked at me. It broke my heart to see them looking so frightened and not knowing what to do, but I was powerless. I stood in the corridor just staring, as the classroom door slammed shut with my sisters looking forlorn and lost on one side and me on the other. We were only a few feet apart but it felt like an ocean with the door firmly shut between us. There was nothing I could do but turn away and follow Orla.

Chapter Fifteen

We then walked along more corridors until we came to my class. I was dreading the introduction to my teacher and classmates. This was a daunting prospect for me as I was very shy. When I was little, I was so shy that if anybody spoke to me, I would cover my face with my hands because I thought they couldn't see me. At least Sinead and Imelda were together, but I was left to face this ordeal alone.

As I entered, what seemed like hundreds of eyes stared at me and I could feel myself blush bright red. Orla pushed me forward towards the teacher: "Sister Josephine, this is the new girl." She didn't think to tell Sister Josephine my name but just turned and walked quickly out of the room; she had no more interest in me now that her task was done and she was rid of us. The teacher asked my name, along with my Gaelic name of *Siobhan Breatnac* and marked it in a register. She then pointed out a desk for two people, where a girl of about my own age was sitting: "You can sit there. Kathleen, you show her what to do."

Kathleen smiled at me. She was a pretty little girl about my age with beautiful shiny brown hair. I was glad to sit beside her, as she was the first person who had shown any friendliness since my arrival, apart from the smile we had received from the old woman in the sewing room. I immediately warmed to her and smiled back as I sat down.

The desk was an old-fashioned wooden one with a hole for an inkwell cut into the wood. The surface of the desk was scratched and the varnish had long since worn off parts of it. My chair, like all the chairs in the schoolroom, was extremely hard and uncomfortable.

The class was a mixture of day girls and orphans. Most of the pupils who attended the school were local girls who lived in the little terraced houses in the narrow streets surrounding the orphanage, with a few girls from the wider area of the North Strand and Fairview. The orphans made up about 30 per cent of the pupils.

The children from the small row of houses opposite the orphanage played games in the narrow street after school and at weekends. How we envied them their freedom, impoverished as their lives were. We watched them from the windows as they played hopscotch and ran up and down the street, playing hide and seek, skipping and other street games. They, in turn, pitied the orphans and for most of the time were nice to us because of our situation, having no illusions about our lives in the orphanage. In school they also experienced the harshness and cruelty of the nuns.

The fathers of most of these children were manual workers, unemployed or even petty criminals and all extremely poverty-stricken. Despite their poor living conditions, the parents of most of these poor families loved their children and tried to do their best for them. Daily life was an extremely grim hand-to-mouth existence for most of them. It was even worse when the breadwinner was also a drunk and squandered his wages in the pub on a Friday, sometimes coming home in a drunken state to beat his terrified wife and children.

In despair at yet another pregnancy, women sometimes resorted to dangerous back-street abortions, which sometimes resulted in tragedy when the women died from complications caused by infection from dirty and unsterilised instruments. When these women died, they often left behind large families, who were then taken into care and shuttled off to the orphanages because the fathers were unable to cope or simply abandoned them.

Although my new teacher, Sister Josephine, had a plump, cherubic face and looked kind, appearances turned out to be deceptive. She was just like the rest of the nuns – pure evil. Both the day girls and the orphans, were on the receiving end of her treatment. I noticed that she kept her cane within reach on her desk in front of the blackboard and it was obviously not just there for decoration.

It was the middle of summer and the air in the room was hot and oppressive, without even a hint of a breeze despite the window being wide open. The teacher would often doze off during the lesson. She would suddenly stop talking and her eyes would gently close. This was a signal for the girls to start chatting to each other. After a short nap, she came to life with a sudden start, grabbed her cane and rushed down the aisles between the desks, hitting out indiscriminately at us in an attempt to restore order. We had to shield our faces in case the cane injured our eyes. She then returned to her desk and resumed teaching as though nothing had happened.

As I sat down at my desk, Sister Josephine didn't bother to introduce me to the class or tell me the names of any of my new classmates. Instead she just opened her book and said, "Now, where were we?" At long last the mid-morning break arrived and we were let out from the classroom into a dreary, grey, concrete courtyard enclosed on all sides by tall buildings. This bleak place contained, beyond some iron railings in the middle of the square, a graveyard for the nuns who had lived and died in this desolate place over many decades.

I was very surprised at the sight of it, but also curious, as I had never been in a graveyard before. Looking through the railings I could see that some of the graves were very old and were sinking slightly into the ground, probably as a result of the coffins disintegrating and the earth on top sinking down.

Around the inside of the railings were some shrubs, which were full of leaves at this time of the year. It was most bizarre to see a graveyard in the middle of a playground, but the children milled around taking no notice of it as it was just part of the scenery to them. After a while I came to accept it too and almost forgot it was there.

There were two playgrounds, one for the day-school pupils and another for the orphans to use after school hours. Our area contained a seesaw, which was the only piece of play equipment there. Later, when the day girls had gone home, we used their playground.

The many buildings around the square consisted of the convent, orphanage, day school and chapel. In one corner of the square, beyond the graveyard, was a laundry. We never met the people who worked there but were told they were young girls and women, probably from the area around the orphanage and working for a pittance. The nuns could undercut local businesses by using the older orphans as unpaid labour.

Chapter Fifteen

It looked and felt like a prison, and there was no way out for us. A door in the wall led to the road outside, but it was kept locked and the wall was too high to climb over. Even if we had been agile enough, there were no handholds or footholds to climb up.

After a while I noticed my sisters standing together in the corner, looking lost and upset, and went over to join them. "I don't like it here, I hate my teacher and I hate the nuns. I want to go home," said Sinead. "Shh. Don't let anybody hear you. I hate it too, but there's nothing we can do about it. We can't get out of here," I whispered. Imelda just stood there looking incredibly sad and pathetic. She shed silent tears that trickled slowly down her face and dripped from her chin. I put my arm around her and tried to comfort her: "Please don't cry."

The loneliness washed over me and I felt very homesick as we huddled together in the corner. The hot sun was burning my fair skin. My arms were rapidly turning bright red and I could see that the others were suffering too. We were very thirsty, but I didn't know where to get a drink of water and was too shy to ask. Eventually we found a shady place and moved out of the hot sun for a while, but our throats were still dry and parched. "That's better, now all we need is a drink of water," I said. "We'll have to ask someone where to get it from."

We asked a girl, one who didn't look too threatening, and she showed us a drinking tap in the cloakroom. Relieved that we had found some water, we let it run until it was cold and took turns to gulp it down until we were full to bursting and then spent time in the toilet relieving ourselves one by one while the others kept guard. Feeling refreshed again, we returned to the playground.

We stood and watched the other girls playing, longing to join in. The playground was full of children whose ages ranged from five years up to the leaving age of about 15 or 16. Some girls were skipping and playing games while others just stood around watching.

My new friend from class, Kathleen, spotted us and came over: "Do you want to come over and play with us?" She pointed to a group of girls on the other side of the playground. "Yes, these are my sisters, Imelda and Sinead, can they play too?" "Sure," said Kathleen

We followed her across the yard to where her friends were playing. They stopped what they were doing and looked at us with interest: "This is Frances, this is Rose, and this is my sister Patsy."

They seemed to know my name. Kathleen must have told them. "Hello Suzy. What are your sisters' names?" enquired Patsy. "This is Sinead and this is Imelda." We joined them in a game of hopscotch; they had scratched the squares and numbers on the grey concrete with the little stones they had collected from the nuns' graveyard. Engrossed in the game, we almost forgot our depressing surroundings, but all too soon a nun appeared and called to us to line up and come back inside for the next lesson.

At lunchtime, the day girls were let out of the school to go home for their midday meal. We were ushered inside to the refectory for our main meal of the day, which was something stodgy and, as usual, unappetising and completely unmemorable.

Chapter Fifteen

After lessons had finished for the day, I met up with my sisters again and we sought out the new friends that we had made in the morning. They were happy to see us and didn't mind us tagging along with them. We were not used to being locked up and the lack of freedom was frustrating, but we didn't feel quite so alone now that we had made friends. If it hadn't been for these girls I don't know how we would have survived. They showed us the routine and with their help we gradually began to find our way in this strange society.

The nuns were not concerned whether we settled in or not and made no attempt to get to know us. They appeared to have no empathy with our situation and didn't offer us any help or show any concern. We were just thrown in at the deep end and left to survive as best we could; it was only thanks to the help and kindness of the other girls that we survived the nightmare of those first few weeks.

Chapter Sixteen

The nuns with day-to-day charge of us were Sister Magdalena and Sister Concepta. They wore elaborate white winged headdresses of some starched material, which soared above their heads and looked like Japanese origami birds, along with long black robes with wide sleeves and a white bib at the front. They had a string of rosary beads and a bunch of keys around their waists. They were nicknamed God's Geese or the Pelicans by the general public, although some might say they looked like vultures. They swooped along the highly polished corridors with their skirts swishing. The jangling and clattering of their keys and rosary beads as they hurried along alerted the children to their coming.

We lived in fear of them, in particular Sister Magdalena. She was quite good-looking: tall and slim, with beautiful dark long-lashed eyes and a pretty mouth. In the outside world she would probably have attracted many male admirers. However, her pleasant looks belied her malicious nature – she was a real devil. Completely two-faced, she revealed her brutal side only to the children. She showed only sweetness and light to people from outside the orphanage. Inside the walls, and out of sight of the public, she was a bully who enjoyed inflicting untold cruelty on the orphans. She had a vicious and spiteful temperament.

When the nuns gave an order it had to be obeyed instantly and without question. They took all their frustrations out on the children in their care. We seemed to be the only outlet for their anger, but the release was only temporary because they were still unhappy and bitter after they had vented their fury. While the children would be able to leave that place one day, the nuns were trapped there until the day they died. They were in a prison of their own making, from which they could never escape, and they took it out on the poor, defenseless children.

The children would be left with life-long traumas from their ill treatment at their hands. I wonder if the nuns ever became resigned to their fate or whether, somewhere deep inside, they harboured a secret hope that they, too, would one day escape from that awful place.

Sister Concepta, in particular, seemed to enjoy making the children's lives miserable and took great pleasure in any misfortune that befell us. She would say, "It's your own fault. Don't expect any sympathy from me. I always said you were useless." The children had long since learned not to expect any compassion from either of them; that would indeed have been a miracle. Sister Magdalena's favourite taunt was a sneering "You'll never amount to anything." Like her, perhaps? What had she amounted to – a child abuser and monster, how much more shameful could one be?

Even though we had by now settled in slightly after that first traumatic period, we were still homesick and desperately sad at

Daddy's death. We missed our mother and our other siblings from whom we were now parted, but no compassion, care or affection was shown to us by the nuns, and we soon learned not to expect any. They appeared to have no childcare skills or training, they disliked us and were just not interested in our problems. We were just a nuisance to be tolerated and, when they were in a bad mood, to be used as punch bags to vent their frustrations on. We tried to avoid attracting their attention, as this meant becoming a target for them.

As the eldest of the three, I was also responsible for my sisters, even though I was completely distraught myself and just ten years old. I found it very hard to be the one who had to be strong and protect them. When we cried, the nuns would snap, "Pull yourselves together," before they pulled out a cane. Or if we cried at night, the other girls would tell us, "Stop crying. If the nuns hear you, you'll get the cane."

We usually had advance warning that the nuns were on the rampage when we heard their furious advance along the long corridors, keys and rosary beads jangling. Everybody tried to keep a low profile when they were on the warpath. Eventually we came to distinguish each nun's particular footsteps, not just Sister Concepta or Sister Magdalena's but all the nuns. We could predict who was approaching and what sort of mood they were likely to be in. When we heard Sister Magdalena storming along the corridor with her beads clacking wildly, we knew this was a signal to hide.

With hearts pounding, we frantically grabbed Imelda and any of the younger children who were too slow to react. We all scattered, trying to find somewhere to hide until the danger had passed. Anyone unlucky enough or not quick enough was grabbed and pulled into her office. Howls of anguish from the unfortunate victims escaped through the closed door as they were caned within an inch of their lives with the big stick that she kept in a cupboard on the wall.

When she was in a particularly vicious mood, it wasn't an unusual sight to see Sister Magdalena grab a small child by the hair and drag her into her office for a caning, often with the terrified child begging, "Please sister, please, I promise I won't do it again, sister," even though they didn't know what they had supposedly done to warrant such a beating.

It made my stomach churn with fear because I knew it was only a matter of time before I got on her wrong side. Eventually my turn came. My heart nearly stopped with terror when she grabbed me from behind. I hadn't heard her coming along the corridor and was startled when she appeared and grabbed me in an arm lock. In a rage, she dragged me into her office. She quickly informed me of my crime. She told me, "I've seen you biting your nails, it's a disgusting habit." As I stood quivering in front of her, she took the cane down from its cupboard and advanced furiously towards me like one possessed. Her eyes glittered and showed the excitement she felt at the pain she was about to inflict on me.

Like a sadist, she appeared to enjoy her power over her helpless victims. I could hear her harsh breathing at she came nearer. She appeared to lose complete control as she lashed out violently. Anticipating the pain that was about to be inflicted, and in a vain effort to avoid the cane, I instinctively cupped my hands. "Hold your hands out straight," she screeched.

Trembling, I closed my eyes to avoid seeing the cane as it swung towards me with a swishing sound. The pain was agonising and I snatched my hands away.

"Look at me. Don't you dare turn away from me," she said, as she paused to get her breath back before resuming the beating, turning to thrash my legs and then back to my hands in a violent frenzy.

The beating continued until her rage abated and she came to her senses. She stopped hitting and shouted, "Get out of my sight!" The sting of the cane on my hands and legs and the hot throbbing pain lingered for hours afterwards. My sisters tried their best to comfort me. "Poor Suzy," they said.

With tears streaming down my face, I tried to ease the agony by holding my hands in cold running water. Imelda went to the nuns' graveyard and picked some dock leaves. Nettles flourished among the shrubs and dock leaves grew nearby. We used the dock leaves for rubbing on our stings and, bless her, she thought they might help my poor swollen hands.

I felt so degraded and helpless after the beating from Sister Magdalena but I learned a harsh lesson. In future I vowed to be more alert and never to allow myself to be caught by the old witch again. Most of the time I was successful in evading her, but on one or two occasions she caught me, resulting in another violent beating. I hated her with all my being and wished her dead many a time, as did most of the girls.

Like a cat stalking a mouse when she was looking for an unsuspecting victim, Sister Concepta was equally as violent as Sister Magdalena. She was very sly and held her beads and keys so they didn't make a noise. Unfortunately for her, we could recognise her footsteps as they made a sound all of their own on the bare floorboards.

It was humiliating to be beaten, particularly when we had done nothing wrong, but just because one of the nuns was in a bad mood and would strike out at anyone in their path. I soon began to notice that they only picked on the young children, or those who were new to the orphanage and therefore slow to react when the nuns were looking for victims. It seemed to me that they were very selective about who they caned. They didn't dare hit any of the bigger children. Some of them were almost as big and as tough as them and wouldn't have thought twice about hitting them back; but the young children and the newcomers were easy targets. They were either too small or too scared to fight.

The nuns knew what they were doing was wrong as they took great care not to leave any evidence. Red welts on the skin from the canes were usually hidden beneath long socks or under sleeves. They tried not to mark faces, although on occasion they would leave a mark when the victim turned away and the cane inadvertently caught the child's face. It was only years later as an adult that I realised how cowardly the nuns' actions were. They deliberately only picked on the younger and weaker children, as all bullies do.

But it wasn't just the children living in the orphanage who were left shrinking in terror from the threat of a cane. Back then, corporal punishment was allowed in schools and the nuns took full advantage of it. They didn't beat the local children as badly as they beat us, but they often got several lashes across their hands for talking in class or some other minor infraction.

It was no surprise that a lot of the nuns' bullying attitudes rubbed off on some of the children. The nuns were excellent teachers in the art of sadism and the bullies copied them and preyed on the weaker children, just as they had seen the nuns do. Those children without parents or older siblings to protect them were at the mercy of both the bullies and the nuns. The people running the establishment didn't seem to be accountable to any official body, although by law they should have been subject to state regulation.

Many of the children were from broken homes with perhaps a father in prison and the mother penniless and unable to cope with the burden of so many children; others were from deprived backgrounds, or had been completely orphaned. Still more were referred through the courts, because their parents were not considered, in the eyes of the Catholic Church, to be morally fit to care for them. They were taken from their parents and put in the hands of the nuns and priests until they reached the age of 16.

We were lucky in that we had had a warm and loving home with caring parents and a happy early childhood before encountering these monsters. Unlike some of the other children who had been in the institution all their lives, we knew that not every adult in the world was an abuser of children and that our mother still cared for us.

Chapter Seventeen

Mammy paid an unexpected visit to the orphanage on a day not usually designated for visiting. Sister Concepta instructed one of the girls to take us to the parlour, which was in the convent area of the building. We were in the middle of a maths lesson when the girl knocked on the door of my classroom. The teacher told her to come in and she gave her a message from Sister Concepta. I was called to the front of the class and trembled as the nun said to me, "Go see Sister Magdalena."

My sisters were waiting outside the classroom and we apprehensively followed the girl along the corridors, wondering whether we had done something wrong, not knowing what to expect and what was going to happen to us. My stomach was churning with fear. When we arrived at the door to the parlour, the girl said, "Knock and when she answers, open the door and go straight in."

She then scuttled off as fast as she could until she was completely out of sight. We were left standing nervously in front of the door. The others stood behind me for protection and it was left to me to timidly knock on the door. Sister Magdalena's voice boomed through the thick wood: "Come in."

Mammy and Callie were sitting on the sofa with Sister Magdalena. She was all smiles and appeared to be very nice and friendly: "Ah. Here they are now, Mrs Walsh. I'll leave you in peace for a while." She exited the room but left the door wide open. We were conscious of her menacing presence outside, listening to everything that was being said. Terrified of making her angry, we were aware that we would be at her mercy after Mammy had left and would be in serious trouble if we complained about anything.

Mammy hugged us all and said, with tears glistening in her eyes, "I've got to go to London again to earn some money. Callie's going to be here with you." We were distraught and begged her not to go. "Please, Mammy, please," I whispered. "Please don't go. I'm afraid you'll never come back." She tried her best to reassure me: "I came back from London the last time, didn't I, Suzy? And I'll come back again soon. Don't worry. I won't be gone forever. It won't be long before I see you again. I'll be back for the Christmas holidays and you can come home then for a visit. I wouldn't go if I didn't have to. It will be better for us in the end if I do."

In her own way Callie tried to comfort us as well: "Mammy's right. If she stays here we won't have any money. What'll we do then? All starve to death?" But I wasn't comforted or reassured. I was deathly afraid of Mammy leaving and never coming back and being left with the nuns forever. I wailed, "What if we never see you again Mammy?" She told me not to be so silly, adding, "Of course you know you will."

She reassured us over and over again that she would come back to see us as often as possible and take us home for visits when she was able to get a few days' holiday from work. It wouldn't be long before we saw each other again. In the meantime she would keep in contact by weekly letter.

Our reunion was interrupted by the arrival of Sister Magdalena, who stood in the doorway and smiled at Mammy, an indication that our time was up. We parted company with lots of hugs and kisses and tears. Sister Magdalena showed Mammy to the front door. When she had gone, we felt that our hearts would break and we shed more tears. But Sister Magdalena didn't care, and as she came back into the room, she snapped, "What's all this noise? Stop your snivelling and get out of my sight."

The transformation in the nun's attitude was totally unexpected and Callie was shocked at the sudden change. She stared at her in amazement, not quite comprehending what she had heard. Callie had no previous experience of the nuns and their attitude to the children, whereas we had now come to expect nothing else. From the expression on her face we could see that she was horrified. However, we knew better than to say anything and quickly obeyed the nun, mindful of her lack of sympathy and with memories of the cane in the cupboard on the wall of her office.

We quickly dragged Callie out of the room and along the corridor before she had a chance to say something that might make the situation worse. Sister Magdalena watched, unmoved and uncaring, as we left the room. She firmly closed the door behind us and we were left to make our way back to the orphans' quarters, wiping our tears and stifling our sobs.

When we were well out of Sister Magdalena's sight and hearing, we stopped and told Callie all about the nuns and how they really behaved towards the children. I said, "They hate us and beat us, for nothing." Sinead piped up, "They're mean. I hate it here." Callie was very shocked but it was too late now to say anything to Mammy as she was already on her way home to prepare for her journey to London. Without a home telephone, or access to a phone at the orphanage, there was no way to contact Mammy: we were locked in this prison with no way out.

Callie was furious. I couldn't tell if she was mad with the nuns or with us: "You should have said something when Mammy was here." I tried to defend our behaviour, tried to explain to Callie how much trouble we would've been in if Sister Magdalena had heard us say anything bad: "We couldn't, *she* was listening outside the door, and we would have been in trouble."

At least we had the consolation of having our big sister with us in the orphanage now. I was so happy that she had arrived because she was so friendly and easy-going, and everybody liked her. Since we were little she had been my heroine and I always tried to emulate her in everything I did. I had always followed her around like a little shadow and she sometimes got annoyed with me because she couldn't go anywhere without me trailing along. Because I was extremely shy, I admired her ability to socialise with everybody. My ambition when I grew up was to be just like her: outgoing and friendly.

Callie automatically took on the role of our protector and surrogate mother and although we desperately missed Mammy we felt a little bit better now that we had someone to care for us and fight our battles. It was a great relief for me to share the massive burden that had been getting me down so much. I was no longer the sole protector of my little sisters in our daily battle to survive.

The institutional food hadn't become any more palatable with time and mealtimes were not something that we ever looked forward to, we dreaded every meal. The food was so bad that we devised a scheme to try to make it a bit more bearable. Some of the children were unfortunate enough to have lived in the orphanage almost from the day they were born, and were not too fussy about their food because they didn't know any better. They ate almost everything they were given without question.

When we offered them some of the food that we had the most difficulty eating, they were happy to eat it for us, as they were always hungry. Because they never had enough to eat and there was no way for them to get any other food, they were actually glad to have most of ours. Being new, we couldn't force ourselves to eat the disgusting slop, but they seemed keen enough to eat anything that was left over. They often said when they spied a particular bit of food that we were having a difficult time eating, "If you don't want that, pass it over, I'll have it."

One speciality was something they called 'gruel' a thin watery porridge that we called 'slop'. This was sometimes served for supper and if we didn't eat it we went to bed hungry. Occasionally we were served something called 'brawn' which was jellied pig's head.

There was one delicacy the girls weren't keen to eat for us, however, and that was the dreaded black pudding. This black pudding (or blood sausage) was the stuff of nightmares. It was made from pigs' blood with big lumps of fat liberally distributed throughout and was usually served with watery, lumpy turnips. I think it was even worse than the cold, lumpy, gluey breakfast porridge. It stuck to our teeth and covered our gums and made us want to vomit. When the horrid black pudding was on the menu everybody tried to hide it in their pockets for disposal after the meal, sometimes down the toilet or anywhere they could find to hide it, even bribing the day girls to smuggle it out for later disposal. It was almost impossible to find anywhere to hide it in the orphanage.

Sometimes, while we were pretending to look for stones to mark the hopscotch patch on the concrete, we managed to dump it in the graveyard when nobody was looking, hoping that the birds would eat it. Unfortunately, when the weather was bad, we weren't allowed out in the playground and had to try to be more inventive in our methods of disposal. As most of the children were unable to eat this vile stuff, we sometimes witnessed new girls rushing to the toilet during lunch and being violently sick.

On April Fool's Day, some of the girls decided to play a trick on us. They told us, "The toilet's blocked with black pudding. Sister Magdalena is hunting the culprits and she's going to punish them!" As we had disposed of our black pudding in the toilet that very day, we sat in the classroom all afternoon feeling sick with terror, hoping that we wouldn't be identified as the culprits and get a lashing from Sister Magdalena. We turned our pockets inside out and shook them to make sure that no evidence remained. After classes, we were finally let into the secret that we were April Fools. How the other girls laughed: "Who's a stupid April Fool then. Ha, ha, ha."

We didn't care that we were the butt of their laughter, just very relieved that Sister Magdalena had not discovered what we had done with the black pudding and that we had avoided another beating from her or Sister Concepta. We relaxed after our day of fear. The weight of the world had been lifted from our very scared shoulders.

For the rest of that day, every time the other girls saw us they started laughing again, but we now joined in, enjoying the joke out of sheer relief at not having been found out. It was one of the few times we were able to laugh and experience something even remotely resembling a normal childhood that included fun and games, even if they were at our expense.

Chapter Eighteen

Some of the children, including Sinead who had never been a bed-wetter at home, wet their beds every single night. The nuns didn't consider this a symptom of their distress, but more a deliberate act of annoyance. The nuns shamed these unfortunate children in front of all the others by screaming at them, "Wet-the-beds!" These were mainly younger children, although a few of the older ones had not yet learned to control their weak bladders and lived in daily fear of Sister Magdalena and Sister Concepta finding out. The stress inflicted on those poor children and the sleepless nights they suffered trying to control their bladders must have been terrible.

They were embarrassed in front of the other children by being forced to sleep in 'wet-the-bed-nighties'. These were ragged old summer dresses long since discarded by the bigger girls. The garments were about five sizes too big and would have looked comical, if they hadn't been so tragic, as the children tried to manoeuvre their way into bed without tripping over the long folds of material. They were obviously designed to humiliate the children and to discourage them from wetting their beds, but they never had the desired effect. A kind word and some concern on the part of the nuns would have helped but they didn't seem to know the meaning of compassion. Instead they made the problem a hundred times worse for these stressed and scared children.

I was terrified that Sister Magdalena would one day catch me wetting my bed and I would become a 'wet-the-bed'. Thankfully, I never did, and I made sure not to drink anything in the evening before bed. My first thought on awakening every morning was, "Is my bed dry?" I felt around to make sure and then relaxed for a minute before making my weary way out of bed for another fraught and anxious day.

A lot of the children were very disturbed, even violent at times, especially the ones who had been in the orphanage for a long time. This wasn't their fault because they had never received any love or kindness, and the behaviour of the nuns convinced them that aggressive behaviour was normal. We tried to avoid being physically attacked by the worst bullies but were not always successful. In addition, most of our possessions were stolen. It was the law of the jungle and we would need a lot of cunning to survive.

Us new girls were seen as softies and suffered both at the hands of Sisters Magdalena and Concepta, and some of the bigger girls. Then, like a light being switched on, it gradually occurred to us that we had bargaining power in the form of the candy and chocolate our mother brought with her on her visits from England. These goodies were coveted by the other children and became a bartering tool for us.

True to her word, Mammy made frequent visits to see us in Dublin, leaving London after work on Friday evenings, catching the train to Liverpool and the overnight ferry from there to Dublin. She spent Saturday night in Dublin and left again on Sunday evening, travelling overnight on the ferry, snatching some sleep on the ship and train and arriving exhausted in London just in time for work on Monday morning. She did this about every couple of months but in the summer and at Christmas she was able to stay a little longer and we could all spend a few days together at home. Later, when her finances improved, she caught the 'milk flight' from London. This was the early morning plane that carried the daily newspapers to Dublin from London.

During all this time we never told her what was happening behind the doors of the orphanage. Of course, we couldn't bear to think of the repercussions if the nuns found out we'd told on them, but also we didn't want to worry Mammy. We knew she had to go to London and work and there was nowhere else for us to go. If we'd told her and she had taken us away from the nuns, she would have lost her job in London and the money it brought her. We didn't want that on our conscience, so we agreed to keep quiet in the hope that Mammy would soon have earned enough money for us to be able to go home for good.

And so our new life gradually unfolded. We started learning the ropes and gradually began settling in. Meanwhile, Sinead – 'the defiant one' – wasn't afraid of anyone and would take on the bullies, frequently scrapping with them. "Just wait until my sister Callie comes, she'll get you," she'd say. They didn't believe her. "You're lying. You haven't got a sister called Callie.

Where is she then?" they taunted her. One day 'Big Sister' arrived and was met with a long list of names from Sinead to whom she was required to mete out retribution. With a mixture of diplomacy and the fact that she was twice their age and size, 12-year-old Callie saw the bullies off.

Later some of them changed sides and became good friends with Sinead. This was not unusual since allegiances changed all the time; sometimes the girls would have rows and team up with someone else, or new girls arrived and they became friendly with them. It was a constantly changing social scene.

Sinead was still a rebel who wouldn't accept authority and didn't like being told what to do. She could never grasp the fact that Sister Magdalena and Sister Concepta had total control over her life. If she didn't like her food, she would hide it in her clothing; after meals she'd throw it onto a low roof in the playground or into the shrubs in the cemetery because those were the only places where she could get rid of it. Unfortunately she didn't realise that the playground was overlooked, and one day one of the nuns saw her disposing of her food.

When Sister Magdalena found out, she dragged Sinead to her office and once again caned her within an inch of her life. From then on she made sure that Sinead ate every scrap of food at every meal; somebody stood over her to make sure that she wasn't hiding it, even if it meant that Sinead had to stay in the refectory all day until it was finished. Sister Magdalena regularly beat her with the big cane for her willful refusal to be cowed, but she continued to defy her. It was a constant battle of wits. Sister Magdalena often said to her, "Don't think you can best me, I'll see you in hell first. I won't even leave the priest's share of you." (By "priest's share" she meant her soul.)

The cane would lash poor Sinead, while she defiantly held back the tears that Sister Magdalena wanted to see flowing down her determined little face. She would never give in and Sister Magdalena was equally determined that she would submit to her will. It was an ongoing battle of wills that Sinead could never hope to win.

After yet another beating, Callie would plead with Sinead, who was covered in old multi-coloured bruises on her legs and hands from previous beatings. "You've got to stop annoying her. She's going to kill you one day if you keep on. Please, please stop it, do what she says," she begged, with tears in her eyes.

One day, after Sinead had received yet another thrashing from Sister Magdalena, Callie became very concerned for her welfare and contemplated running away with her. The nun on duty had seen Sinead struggling to eat her dessert of tapioca, which she loathed. There was no way to dispose of it and it was time to return to school for the afternoon session.

Sinead was gagging and retching in her attempt to eat the slop. She was sent to see Sister Magdalena for a caning, which Callie had been forced to watch, another cruel form of punishment from the nuns. Afterwards they both walked back to lessons crying. Callie cursed the callous, vicious nun and vowed to get back at her somehow.

Callie was very upset in class all afternoon and unable to concentrate on her lessons. After school they both stood at the back gate while Callie planned how to abscond with Sinead.

She was terrified that Sister Magdalena would seriously harm her one day very soon, as the beatings were becoming more frequent and more violent. They discussed the best way to escape from the nuns. Sinead suggested, "Let's just climb over the wall tonight," but Callie reluctantly came to the conclusion that she couldn't leave Imelda and me behind to face Sister Magdalena's wrath.

Callie knew that the nun would take her revenge out on us even though we would have played no part in their escape: we would be victimised because they had escaped her clutches. Besides, there was nowhere to run to and when they were found and returned to the orphanage, Sinead would be in even greater danger.

There was only one person they could turn to. Our grandad. But he was in his eighties and very frail. Since Daddy's death, his health had deteriorated significantly. He had come to our house one day to ask Mammy if she would look after him when our aunt Sue, his daughter, who had lived with him along with her husband and two children for many years, emigrated to Australia shortly after Daddy's death and left him behind. It was obviously impossible for Mammy to help as by then she'd made plans to work in London.

Although Grandad had two sons still living at home with him, they were too wrapped up in their own lives and too selfish to care for him. He was eventually admitted to hospital as he was considered to be in danger. He had been found in a church, disorientated and unable to remember where he lived. During one visit home, when Mammy was able to stay in Dublin for a week, we were taken to see Grandad in hospital. He was in a ward with a lot of other old men, one of whom was dying. We could hear the death rattle of the dying man behind the closed curtains that surrounded his bed. Grandad told me, "I treasure that Christmas card you sent me. I keep it under my pillow." He then lifted up the corner of the pillow and showed me the crumpled, dog-eared card he'd lovingly kept close. He died a short time later.

One of our uncles came to tell us the sad news. That was his one and only visit to us in all the time we spent in the orphanages. Our uncles, Daddy's brothers, had no interest in us and never even visited our brothers in their institution about a mile away from their house. Mammy was an only child whose parents were dead, and she had no other close relatives.

Even if we'd had lots of relatives, the nuns would have discouraged them from visiting us as they wanted complete control over our lives and didn't welcome outsiders. They made people so unwelcome that they eventually stopped visiting. Some of Callie's friends attempted to visit her but were told that she couldn't see them and not to bother calling again. This was also what the nuns had told our brothers when they had called to see us earlier.

Callie knew that we were trapped in this prison with these monsters, people who appeared to take a perverse pleasure in making us suffer. She was so worried, and finally decided to tell Mammy on her next visit about the punishment inflicted on Sinead in the hope she would be able to do something about the situation, perhaps by talking to the head nun.

Chapter Eighteen

At least we had the comfort of knowing that Mammy hadn't abandoned us, unlike a lot of the other children who were unloved and unwanted by anybody. These included some of the children who were particularly disliked by Sister Magdalena and were selected for special punishment by her. There was nobody to care about them. They never had any visitors or mail and were deprived of any kind of normal family life. What anguish they must have experienced and how it must have affected them emotionally. All alone in the world, they would remain at the mercy of these people until they reached an age when the Church would no longer receive payment from the government for them. They would then be thrown out into the world to make their own way in life, discarded because they had served their purpose and were of no further use to the Church.

Completely institutionalised and having had very little contact with the outside world for most of their lives, they were cast adrift to fend for themselves, lacking the social skills necessary to survive in an unfamiliar and sometimes hostile world. They were condemned to a life of menial work because of their limited education and were vulnerable to any predator who chanced upon them.

A lot of children from Irish institutions emigrated to England, where some had family links, in an effort to get as far away as possible from the influence of the Church and begin a new life. Most were lucky enough to survive, some with the help of relatives. They eventually made decent lives for themselves, despite the shameful neglect and lack of preparation for their future by the nuns and priests. A lot of the children had never even handled money or travelled on public transport by themselves and didn't know how to shop for food or clothes.

Some didn't have the inner resources to cope and succumbed to drug addiction, prostitution and alcoholism, or ended up living on the streets. Others had experienced sexual abuse at the hands of the priests and nuns and there was no counselling or psychotherapy available to help them. They had to deal with the devastating emotional and psychological effects of the abuse all by themselves.

Some of the older girls in the orphanage were used as unpaid out-workers for a commercial factory making rosary beads. The nuns received payment from the company for the children's labour, money that was never passed on to the girls. Callie did this work for a time but I somehow escaped it, maybe because I wasn't considered agile enough. It was time-consuming work and needed nimble hands. Anybody who was clumsy was excluded from this job, as the nuns couldn't afford to waste time on workers who didn't produce perfect products. This was just one enterprise operated by the Catholic Church, which didn't miss a trick when it came to making money.

Many of the children in orphanages would have been, in the eyes of the Catholic Church, 'born of sin', meaning that they had been born out of wedlock. That also made them sinners in the eyes of the Church. They were seen as the offspring of people who had strayed from the Catholic religion and they therefore carried the sins of their parents. These children were therefore of no value in the eyes of the Church and had no human rights. It wasn't surprising that most of the children suffered from low

Chapter Eighteen

self-esteem and a feeling of worthlessness that resulted in a life-long sense of inferiority that blighted their lives.

The nuns truly believed they would be rewarded in heaven when they died, despite their abuse of the innocent children and babies in the orphanage. They also taunted the pupils in the day school, belittling them for their perceived lack of intelligence, attributed to their poor working-class backgrounds.

One particular nun frequently told the girls. "You're stupid and useless, just like your parents." This was the prevailing attitude of the so-called Sisters of Charity and Sisters of Mercy to the poor and destitute. Many of the children threatened to come back and kill the nuns when they grew up. I could understand exactly how they felt as I regularly had a few fantasies about it myself. We all did.

Chapter Nineteen

Sister Magdalena slept in a wood-panelled cubicle just outside the entrance to the younger children's dormitory. There was a curtained window in the wall looking out onto the room, from where she kept an eye on everything the children said or did. Sister Concepta slept in another room elsewhere in the vast building, most probably with the other nuns in their 'cells', as their bedrooms were called; in a sense this was a very appropriate word as they were in a prison of sorts, serving a life sentence which didn't end, even in death.

After lights out in our dormitory and when the nuns had retired to their prayers and recreation, we were left completely alone in the dark for the rest of the night without any supervision. These few precious hours without the company of the nuns were extremely exhilarating and we savoured every moment of our freedom.

From under our mattresses we brought out our 'Maggie' dolls, which we had made from odd scraps of material we had acquired from somewhere. I can't remember why we called them Maggie dolls. They were very basic creations, just small scraps of cloth stuffed with bits of fabric and a few strands of wool for hair. We drew the features on the faces in ink. The dolls were not very pretty but served us well for entertainment purposes.

Because we had no other toys and no play equipment, apart from the seesaw in the playground, our Maggie dolls served as substitutes. They became props for our nightly puppet show, which was organised with great skill and enthusiasm by Callie. We eagerly looked forward to these shows, as they became our way of relieving the frustrations of the day.

The scripts were worthy of the greatest playwrights, and we put on silly voices to imitate the nuns. If any girls had been beaten or humiliated during the day, we singled out the particular nun responsible, making fun of her and belittling her. We enjoyed making fools of the nuns, especially the most hated ones such as Sister Concepta and Sister Magdalena. We would make the Maggie dolls 'stomp' across the dormitory floor before imitating the Sister with such phrases as: "Time for your beating!" and "You're useless, get in line." Although we didn't realise it then, it was probably a form of therapy for us.

In the darkness, we sometimes frightened ourselves with our stories and found it difficult to sleep after a particularly scary story. There was a big wooden door at the side of our dormitory, behind which a flight of stone steps led straight down to the playground. It was probably a fire escape of sorts. Lying in our beds, we imagined that we heard footsteps coming up the steps and were extremely scared that someone was going to come into the dormitory during the night and attack us.

Because the nuns' graveyard was in the playground just outside our dormitory, we also imagined that ghosts of dead nuns would come up the stairs to haunt us. Naturally we couldn't express our fears to Sister Magdalena or Sister Concepta as they were completely lacking in understanding. We would probably have been punished for being awake and talking when we were supposed to be asleep, although the nuns were never concerned whether we had a good night's sleep or not. Our comfort and welfare were the last things they cared about.

It seemed to me that however deprived the day girls in our classes were, at least they had their freedom and families and homes to go back to at the end of the day. Unlike us, they only had to endure the company of the nuns for part of the day. After lessons had finished and the day girls had departed for home, we dragged our reluctant feet back across the playground to our part of the building where we were set to work cleaning and scrubbing, supervised by Sister Magdalena with her big cane. Her presence was always threatening and I was scared stiff of her. I kept my head down and worked even harder when she was around. Visions of her cane swam in front of my eyes and I didn't want to risk a beating.

I had never done such heavy manual work before, having only helped my mother with the cooking or done little chores around the house. This was completely different – it was sheer hard manual labour and the work seemed to be backbreaking and was never ending. The whole building was spotless, but the nuns constantly told us, "This is filthy, do a better job you lazy good-for-nothings."

Chapter Nineteen

In all my time in that place, I never once heard a nun praise any child for anything or compliment anybody on any achievement. They didn't seem to pay the same attention to our schoolwork, and it didn't matter to them whether we were progressing in our studies or not. They didn't seem to have any concern for our futures after leaving the orphanage.

Every Saturday we had to polish the enormous dormitory floors, one chore that we actually enjoyed. We tied rags around our feet and slid up and down the full length of the room, buffing the floor until it shone like glass. Occasionally, for some unknown reason, we had to scrub the floor to remove all the old polish and then re-polish it completely. Why this was necessary I don't know but then lots of things didn't make sense in that place. We sometimes got splinters in our feet when polishing the floor and they had to be dug out with a sewing needle.

We seemed to spend our 'free time' scrubbing every object in sight. When there was nothing left to clean they found other things for us to do. I have memories of working outside in the convent yard in the freezing winter weather, sweeping the paths in the graveyard or washing the headstones, before a nun called me in to have a drink of butter-milk – sour milk with lumps of butter floating in it – even though it made me feel sick. There was nowhere to dispose of the foul stuff, and I was forced to drink it, retching, as the nun watched me to make sure I finished it, all the while seeming to enjoy my discomfort.

In the cold winter we all suffered from bleeding chilblains on our hands from scrubbing the front steps and cleaning the windows in the freezing conditions. We didn't receive any medical treatment for this condition and were just expected to suffer until the warm weather arrived in the spring and they got better. Never before or since have we suffered from chilblains.

The other girls were very inventive and over the years had worked out some clever scams to save time and effort. After meals, hundreds of plates had to be hand-washed and dried. They had devised a system whereby they only dried the bottom and top plates in the pile and stacked them in the cupboard. All the children knew this and at mealtimes wiped their own wet plate on their sleeve before joining the queue for their food.

The nuns controlled the children by intimidation, instilling fear either by caning or threats. There was an atmosphere of fear about the place and even the little toddlers and babies were aware that it wasn't a good idea to attract the attention of the nuns. Some of them were terrified of the nuns because they had been beaten by Sister Magdalena or Sister Concepta and knew never to expect anything good from them, not even a kind word. Some tried to hide when they saw the nuns approaching. One particular baby was terrified, and cried whenever she saw anybody dressed in black; she had come to associate that colour with fear.

The nuns constantly criticised, physically and verbally abused us, and threatened: "You're all going to burn in hell because you're all such wretched sinners and deserve nothing better." Each week we went to St Agatha's church up the road to confess our sins and beg for forgiveness from God for being bad. I tried to be inventive when I made up the sins I had supposedly committed during the week; I didn't believe I had committed any and thought it stupid to have to make up lies.

Chapter Nineteen

Seated opposite the priest in the dark, stuffy confessional, I waited while he attended to the sinner on the other side. The confessional consisted of three compartments, the middle one for the priest and one on either side of him for the awful wretches who had transgressed since last week. While the priest attended to the other person I sat waiting for my turn and pondered my sins: should I say I lied again? Should I confess to unholy thoughts maybe, whatever that might mean? When the priest had finished dealing with the sinner on the other side, he turned and slid open the window on my side of the box.

Through the grille separating us, I recited the sinner's prayer to the shadowy figure: "Bless me father, for I have sinned. It is a week since my last confession." He performed his part of the ritual. Then I confessed my sins to him: "I told a lie." He would then ask, "Anything else?" And I would tell him, "No." Sometimes I would tell him that I had had bad thoughts; nothing specific, though, as I don't think he would have liked to hear my thoughts about the nuns!

He gave me a penance for being such a terrible sinner. I was to say some prayers, perhaps three Hail Marys or two Our Fathers. Then he absolved me of my sins. He closed the window and that was me cleansed for another week and I left the confessional box without a stain on my sparkling clean soul. At least if I died during the night I would be guaranteed a place in heaven along with the nuns. Wasn't I the lucky one?

In the meantime, I did my penance to purify my soul, just in case I ended up in hell. Also I was free to commit some new sins because I would be absolved of them the following week.

I was repentant every week because I had told him a lie the previous week about the non-existent sin I had confessed to him then. It was quite a good system.

But I was not totally out of the woods yet. To be absolutely certain of gaining admittance to heaven, I would also need to have received the last rites from the Catholic Church before I died. I didn't really understand why I should need them if my soul was clean from confessional. It was all very puzzling. Just in case the priest recognised that I had committed the same sins the previous week and thought I hadn't been sincere in my repentance, sometimes I tried to vary them. He might tell one of the nuns that I was not repentant enough and I would be in hell on earth then, never mind having to wait until I died.

Anything I said in the confessional was supposed to stay secret but you just never knew. The priest might let it slip when he was chatting to one of the nuns, and I didn't want to miss out on going to heaven because I had told a little white lie. That would have been the ultimate insult, to have endured hell on earth with the nuns and then have to burn in another hell forever with the other sinners and the devil, while they were having a grand old time in heaven sitting at the right hand of God for all eternity.

It was very confusing, though, that all the bad nuns and priests who made us suffer would go to heaven, while we would go to hell for telling a lie. The only people who would burn in hell, of course, were the orphans and the poor. The nuns deemed themselves and the priests to be excluded from any punishment in the hereafter and could be as evil as they wished here on earth. Come to think of it, maybe hell was a better alternative after all.

Chapter Nineteen

In the eyes of the Church, only nuns and priests were guaranteed entry to heaven by divine right; even the middle and upper classes would have a hard time getting in. They had to work hard for their ticket to the Promised Land by being good Catholics, not rocking the boat, and giving lots of money to the collection at Sunday Mass. The nuns told us that it was easier for a camel to get through the eye of a needle than for a rich man to get to heaven. Did this also apply to the hierarchy of the Church? What about the Pope and the cardinals in Rome and the bishops in their palaces, who lived in great luxury with servants to cater to their every whim? Or did they have special dispensation from God to bypass the system?

One of my day girl classmates suffered greatly both at the hands of the nuns and the secular teachers because she was left-handed. They constantly punished her for this affliction because they considered that she had the devil in her. They labelled her a 'ciatog' which is a derogatory Irish name for someone who uses their left hand instead of their right. The nuns made her life a misery by trying to make her write with her right hand on the blackboard in front of the whole class and told everybody, "Look at her, she's stupid." I am sure she dreaded coming to school as much as we hated being there as they took every opportunity to belittle and humiliate her.

They constantly denigrated the local children's families, sneering at their deprivation and poverty-stricken lives and seeming to take a delight in humiliating them as much as they did us. They branded the poor 'feckless and useless' but they didn't seem to realise that without them and the orphans, they would be out of a job. When any of the day girls met a nun in the street they were expected to bow to them. If they didn't observe the formalities, they would be caned in school next day as punishment and a reminder of just who was in charge.

We orphans didn't fare any better, of course, and bore the brunt of their frustration and ill will 24 hours a day. The effects of this constant stress took their toll on the children. It wasn't unusual to wake up in the middle of the night and see children walking in their sleep, wandering around the dormitory like ghosts. I was no exception. On one occasion I remember standing by the side of my bed and seeing another girl sleeping there. What was she doing there? I shook her indignantly and said, "What are you doing in my bed? I'm cold. Get out." She woke up with a start and said, "I'm not in your bed. Leave me alone or I'll tell Sister Magdalena."

Then I woke up and realised with horror that I was at the other end of the dormitory from my own bed. I was very confused and stumbled back in the darkness. It was freezing cold and I realised that I had been sleepwalking. Usually I woke up standing by the side of my bed not knowing what was happening. I didn't know whether I had just got back, where I had been or whether I had just got out of bed.

Chapter Twenty

Now we were able to teach Callie how to avoid some of the pitfalls we had encountered when we had first arrived in the orphanage. With our help she eased herself into the system more quickly than we had. She also helped us in our fights with the bullies. They soon backed off when they realised how tough and fearless she was. It was good to have her fighting our corner and we began to relax a little. Life didn't look quite so bleak now.

Callie, with her big heart, also took on what should have been the nuns' job of caring for the young children and babies. She was only a 12-year-old child herself, but tried to mother them all and protect them from the nuns' worst excesses and brutality.

One of the little girls, called Anne, was considered creepy by the other children, as she would attach herself to anybody who encouraged her and tell them, "I saw my daddy sticking a knife in my mammy." She followed Callie around and told her the story of how her father had stabbed her mother. We didn't know whether her mother was alive or dead but she never received a visit from her parents and she had no other visitors either. This poor child never received any comfort from the nuns and was left all alone to cope with the effects of her terrible tragedy. She was left to get on with her new life all by herself and was frequently punished by the nuns for telling stories and annoying people.

Many a time Sister Magdalena dragged this little child into her office and we all knew what that meant. There was no need to listen for the sounds of the cane and the child's cries, as it was obvious from the nun's attitude what was about to happen. It seemed heartless of us not to intercede on her behalf but there was nothing we could do. We all disappeared as fast as we could in case the nun wasn't satisfied with just the one victim.

Frances, another disturbed child of about six years of age, constantly pulled the hair from her head and ate it. She also ate hairs from the hairbrushes when she was cleaning the bathroom. Sister Magdalena frequently beat her for this as she considered it "a filthy habit". This compulsive habit is considered to be a sign of stress and there is a medical name for it: 'trichophagia'. Eventually, Frances needed to have an operation to remove a ball of hair from her stomach as it was causing an obstruction. The cause of the stress, however, was never treated.

One day, Sister Magdalena instructed Callie to bring a toddler, two-year-old Louise, to her office. With Callie watching and warned by the nun not to interfere, she took her cane down from the cupboard, pulled the little child's pants down and used all her strength to hit her, leaving a big red welt on her bottom. As the child screamed, "No, no!" she took this as defiance and gave her another blow.

She then told Callie, "Pull up her pants." As Callie gently tried to pull the little girl's pants up without hurting her, Sister

Magdalena added, "Take her upstairs to bed and don't you dare, under any circumstances, comfort her. I'll know if you do and you'll get the same." Callie had no idea what crime the two-year-old child had committed that warranted the violent punishment inflicted upon her, but then Sister Magdalena didn't need an excuse to vent her anger.

She seemed to feel no shame at her vile treatment of the children; none of the nuns ever exhibited any embarrassment and didn't seem to realise that they had done anything wrong. Although not all of the nuns were abusers – they didn't all physically take part in the ill treatment – most of them were weak characters and did nothing to help the children or tried to stop the abuse. They condoned it by not intervening and were therefore guilty by association.

If any of the children became ill or had a nightmare during the night, it was left to the other girls to help them, as we didn't see any of the nuns again until the next morning. Because Callie had become known among the children as a kind and caring person, the little ones especially looked to her for comfort. One night a small child called Kathleen woke Callie in the middle of the night. Everywhere was dark and hushed. It was probably about one or two o'clock in the morning and everybody was in deep sleep. She had found her way down from her own dormitory in the pitch black and now stood beside Callie's bed and shook her awake: "Callie, please come with me to the toilet, I'm afraid of the dark."

Callie reluctantly roused herself and got out of her warm bed. She took Kathleen by the hand and they found their way out of the dormitory and into the washroom in the dark. The whole building was kept in complete darkness all night, probably to save money, and it was scary trying to find the way in the pitch black of the night. For this reason we tried to avoid going to the toilet in the middle of the night, but the fear of wetting the bed and facing the wrath of Sister Concepta or Sister Magdalena in the morning was far more terrifying than the fear of any ghost or bogeyman that we might encounter on our way. We quickly learned to conquer any fear of the darkness, but it was preferable to have company if possible when we had to go to the bathroom in the night.

The bathroom was located outside the dormitory and was completely deserted at that time. Kathleen, like a lot of the children, was very small and couldn't reach the light switch, but she was expected to find her way around in the dark without even a glimmer of light to guide her. When Kathleen had finished, Callie, after waiting patiently in the freezing cold, was now wide awake. She had to return Kathleen to the little children's dormitory upstairs where Sinead and Imelda also slept.

Sinead was a bed-wetter so Callie decided that as a precaution it would be a good idea to take her to the toilet too. The two of them crept up the stairs and along the corridor past Sister Magdalena's room.

Silently moving past the nun's door without waking her, to their horror they heard a floorboard creak. They came to a sudden stop and stood completely still, almost turned to stone and with their hearts in their mouths, expecting that at any moment the door would be flung open and the tyrant would rush out and grab them. But all they heard was her loud snoring, which didn't miss a beat. Although Callie was terrified of waking Sister Magdalena, she was even more afraid of the consequences of Sinead wetting her bed and getting another beating from the nun in the morning, so they cautiously continued into the dormitory.

Reaching Sinead's bed, Callie gently shook her and told her, "I'm going to take you to the toilet but you can't make any noise." Sinead immediately understood how important it was not to alert Sister Magdalena. It didn't take her long to get used to being woken every night and going to the toilet in the darkness. As it became routine, the operation took less time and Callie decided that she couldn't leave the other little bed-wetters to face punishment from the nun in the morning either. She and Kathleen then took all of them to the toilet to relieve themselves.

During all the nights that Callie and Kathleen performed this act, Sister Magdalena never woke up, nor did she ever notice that her charges were absent from the dormitory. They could all have been stolen during the night and she would never have known, or probably never even have cared, except that she would have been in trouble because one of the money sources had disappeared. In fact, Callie was lucky that Sister Magdalena never woke up, as she would have been severely punished for being out of bed and wandering around the building in the middle of the night.

In the beginning, when Kathleen roused her in the middle of the night, Callie struggled to wake up, but as time passed and it became a regular occurrence, her arrival at Callie's bedside would instantly waken her from whatever depth of sleep she happened to be in at that moment. After a while it became normal for her to spend half the night wandering around the building tending to the other children.

Gradually, we had become absorbed into the system and were soon replaced by fresh arrivals. They became the 'new girls' and bore the brunt of the nuns' bad temper. Although we felt sorry for them when they first arrived and knew they were as bewildered and upset as we had been, we also felt slightly superior as we had now adapted to the system and they were just at the beginning of the process. Most had no siblings to comfort them.

It was dreadful to be alone in that unfamiliar and hostile environment and have to grieve for their dead or absent parents without any compassion being shown to them by the nuns. Their mother or father, or in some cases perhaps both parents, may have only just died, but the nuns didn't offer them any sympathy or comfort. They were thrown in at the deep end and had to learn to sink or swim. Who knows what might have happened to them if it hadn't been for the help given to them by some of the other girls?

However, eventually they too became initiated into institutional life and finally learned to stand on their own two feet. It was still extremely painful and heart-breaking to witness them being sadistically bullied by some of the older girls or the nuns when they were in a state of deep depression and despair. Like us, they must have been left with deep emotional scars from

Chapter Twenty

the trauma, an experience that probably resulted in life-long psychological and emotional damage. It is not known just how many lives the priests and nuns damaged over the decades, nor the long-term consequences suffered by the children because of it.

Chapter Twenty-One

Sister Magdalena didn't just dislike Callie: she hated her with a vengeance. We never knew exactly why she took such a dislike to her. It could have been because all the little children loved Callie and went to her for comfort, or because she was so pretty and popular with a lot of the other girls. Callie was what is known as an 'Alpha female' and possessed a natural authority that people responded to. That is possibly the reason for the nun's hostility towards her. Maybe she sensed a rival in Callie.

Sister Magdalena, probably out of spite, assigned Callie the hated and back-breaking task of cleaning the seven flights of stairs leading up to the roof. This job, on weekday mornings, after Mass and breakfast but before lessons, involved dusting the banisters and sweeping the steps.

At weekends, as well as the sweeping and polishing, she also had to scrub and polish each step. On the lower steps she constantly had to stop what she was doing and move aside to let people pass by. The bullies thought it a great laugh to run up and down the stairs while she was cleaning them, trying to knock over her cleaning tools and tormenting her. Sometimes

Chapter Twenty-One

they tried to stamp on her hands as they ran past but she was too quick for them.

No passing nun could resist the opportunity to stop and tell her how it should be done. Sister Magdalena would creep up behind her and run her fingers along the banisters to check for dust, all the while threatening Callie: "Make sure you clean them properly. God help you if I find even the slightest speck of dirt, you'll be for it."

Callie knew that this was no idle threat and made sure that every step sparkled. She had already been a victim of the sadistic nun, having suffered an injury to her neck when Sister Magdalena pulled her by her long hair and jerked her head back, because she wasn't quick enough to move out of her way on the stairs. Callie had been in agony but was told to "stop malingering" and get on with her work.

The injury was only discovered many years later when Callie had an X-ray after a car crash. The doctor treating her told her that she had a very old injury to her neck, probably received when she was young, and asked her if she remembered having had an accident. She remembered all right, but it was no accident.

On this particular Saturday she was thoroughly fed up. Sister Magdalena had given her a hard time at the bottom of the stairs and she had shed a few tears on her way up at the unfairness of her life. By the time she reached the top step she was dejected, resentful and was having murderous thoughts about the nuns. How she longed for something bad to happen to all of them. Hot and tired, she felt like crying and wished she could be anywhere else but there. As she sat on the landing for a little while to rest her weary body and fritter away some time before taking her tools downstairs and joining the queue for her unappetising meal, something caught her eye.

At one end of the landing was a door. Callie had noticed it before but was always in a hurry to finish and get back downstairs and hadn't taken too much notice of it. This time, though, her curiosity was aroused and she took the opportunity to explore what lay beyond it. There was nobody around, so, warily, she put her ear to the door and listened for movement on the other side; there wasn't even a whisper, just the sound of her own breathing. Even so, she cautiously opened the heavy door, not sure what she would find. It didn't occur to her that if anybody had been inside the room, they would probably have come out to see who was making all the noise as she clattered her way up the stairs, and would have probably told her off for making such a racket. Inside the room all was dark and quiet, so she switched on the light.

In the weak glow from the low-voltage electric light bulb, she saw spread out before her an enormous attic running the entire length of the orphanage. Callie was amazed at the size of the room. It was so big that she couldn't see the other end from where she was standing. Venturing deeper into the dimly lit attic, she could see that the dusty room contained furniture and some big wooden trunks set back against the walls and packed behind the big wooden beams that rose all the way up from floor to ceiling.

She shivered with the cold and a little bit of fear. In that eerie place she felt slightly spooked, all alone in the total silence, but she was curious enough to overcome her initial fear. Inquisitively, she approached one of the trunks. At first she was reluctant to lift the lid, afraid that she might find the mummified body of a dead nun inside. However, her curiosity got the better of her and she nervously opened the first one.

As she raised the lid and the riches inside were revealed, she gave a gasp of delight. To her amazement, it contained a treasure trove of old costumes from past school plays. There were beautiful dresses, hats, feathers, jewels and black patent shoes with fancy buckles. Dazzled by the beauty laid out before her, Callie could hardly contain her excitement and immediately wanted to tell us what she had found. Excitedly, she opened more and more of the trunks and saw that they also contained colourful, sparkling treasures.

Ecstatic at the thought of what we could do with all these beautiful objects, her mind began working overtime. She thought of the plays she had organised at home with the neighbourhood children in their parents' garages, when we made our own costumes and she wrote the scripts. This was wonderful!

It was so exhilarating that she could hardly contain her joy. Full of new energy, she wanted to fly downstairs to tell us what she had found, but had to wait impatiently until her work was finished and she had put her cleaning equipment away. Hurrying down the stairs, she found the nun in charge and asked for permission to leave. The nun asked Callie the usual questions: "Are you sure it's finished? Have you done it all properly? Did you go all the way to the top?" Callie dutifully replied, "Yes Sister." She was only then given permission to leave: "Okay, you can go now."

She hurried off to find me in the dining hall to tell me the exciting news. "I've got something great to tell you," she whispered, trying to contain her excitement. "What?" I demanded to know. But she couldn't tell me right there: "Let's find somewhere quiet later and I'll tell you all about it." I was intrigued and could hardly wait to hear her secret.

We finished our food as quickly as we could, left our plates on the pile for washing and casually walked out of the refectory. The fact that I finished so quickly was unusual for me, as I normally spent ages chewing every horrible mouthful. Nobody seemed to notice my unusual speed this time. We found a place away from everyone and Callie excitedly told me about her incredible discovery: "You'll never guess what's at the very top of the stairs."

I had no idea what she had found and she excitedly told me: "A big attic full of trunks filled with lots of lovely dressing-up clothes." Now I was excited too: "Can we go and see them? Now?" But Callie quickly dashed my excitement: "No, not just now we can't, we don't want to get caught by the nuns. We'll go later when they're at evening prayers. It's a big secret so don't tell anybody else because you know we'll get into trouble if they find out."

I had an agonising wait before I could see this exciting place. It's not easy for a ten year old to have patience, especially for something as big as this! Later, when the nuns were in the chapel saying their evening prayers and the children were at recreation so nobody was around to see us, Callie took me up for a quick look. She had decided to tell only a few trusted friends about our exciting find. She made them swear on their mothers' graves that they would never tell a living soul.

Although she could be a bit bossy at times, she was also our unelected leader and the children liked and trusted her. They agreed not to tell anybody about our secret because if it got back to the nuns, it would mean not only a caning from Sister Magdalena but banishment from our gang. We had by then become a close-knit group, as we knew that there was safety in numbers. To be ostracised would be unbearable, as any girl who had no friends would be without protection and at the mercy of the bullies and the nuns, with nobody to look out for them.

Callie took each of them up to the attic over a period of time, so as not to expose our secret to any of the nuns or the other children. We didn't want to arouse the suspicions of anyone who might then be tempted to tell the nuns what we were up to in order to curry favour. The sneaks were well-known and we tried to keep well out of their way at all times.

When our friends saw what Callie had found in the attic, they realised that if anybody outside our circle ever found out, that would be the end of our secret; the nuns would lock the door and we would be forbidden from ever setting foot up there again. Sister Magdalena or Sister Concepta would also probably vent their anger on us for daring to do something that they didn't approve of.

We devised a plan for our visits to the attic. Creeping up the stairs one by one when the nuns were in the chapel saying their evening prayers, we took it in turns to be the lookout posted at the door. The lookout lay on the landing keeping watch through the banisters down the many flights of stairs, in case any of the nuns decided to make the long climb to the attic and catch us in the act of actually being children. The lookout's job was also to keep track of the time so that we wouldn't forget to go back downstairs in time and miss the nuns as they returned from the chapel. For this, Callie gave the lookout her precious watch.

The attic was so high up in the building that the nuns rarely went there; also they couldn't possibly hear us because it was so far away from the ground floor. Still, we took our shoes off and tried not to make too much noise. We learned to keep our voices down and almost whispered when we wanted to say anything.

A code word was devised like in an Enid Blyton story. Our code word was 'beads', a reference to the rosary beads worn around the nuns' waists. They rattled and gave warning when any of the enemy were approaching. We spent many happy times dressing up in the beautiful outfits. And if we heard the code word 'beads' we ran to our designated hiding places until the danger had passed.

Dressed up, we thought we were princesses or movie stars. Although the clothes had picked up the overpowering smell of the mothballs that had been packed in the trunks to protect them, we didn't care, and after a while we didn't even notice the rank odour. In our long dresses and fancy hats with feathers, we thought we were the epitome of glamour and felt really beautiful. We carried beaded handbags and wore elegant high-heeled shoes of many sizes, none of which fitted very well. The only thing missing was make-up but even so we still felt incredibly beautiful.

One of the girls, Margaret, coveted a pair of battered old fairy wings and a tutu that she found in one of the trunks. She searched inside and found a crown and a wand. The wand was almost bare, with just a few strands of tinsel hanging from it, but as she twirled and pranced around, her eyes shone and she became the fairy of her imagination. This was her favourite dressing-up outfit and she always grabbed it first. Although in my eyes she didn't look much like a fairy as she was a bit plump, wore grey woollen socks up to her knees and had a pudding basin haircut, it was the fact that she felt like a fairy that mattered. She would always ask, "God, I love this dress. Don't I look nice in it?" We didn't have a mirror so she couldn't see what she really looked like, but we all agreed that she did indeed look beautiful. "Yes, you look gorgeous," we told her every time.

My favourite dress was a pink ball gown with lots of frills and flounces. It really made me feel like a princess as I twirled around. I searched through the trunks and found some shiny jewels, a necklace and a bracelet combination in garish colours to complete my ensemble. I imagined that I was going to a wonderful ball and would dance with a prince, just like Cinderella. I loved the feel of it. It was made of a shiny material and was so soft and silky against my skin.

Callie, with her long dark curls and beautiful face, really did look like a princess and I gasped when I saw her. When we were playing up in the attic, time passed in a blur and we almost lost track, but all too soon it was time to go back downstairs. The lookout heard the nuns coming back from prayers and alerted us, so we reluctantly put everything back in the trunks, making sure that the room was left tidy and with nothing out of place, before making our way downstairs.

One day a nun was seen climbing up the stairs when she should have been at prayers in the chapel. The lookout did her job well. When we heard the alarm we scattered to our hiding places. The nun came into the attic, switched on the light and stood looking around. She spied our 'coach' – an old wooden wheelchair, which had probably been there for decades because it was made from wood and extremely antique-looking. We used it as our transport to push each other up and down the length of the attic, pretending it was a carriage.

We held our breath and hoped we wouldn't be caught but she was only interested in the wheelchair and didn't realise that anxious eyes were spying on her from dark corners. She tested the chair by sitting in it and wheeling it up and down for a few paces, all the while muttering and sighing to herself. Then she wheeled it out of the attic and switched off the light, banging the door shut behind her. We hadn't found a key, but we later made sure that the door couldn't be locked while we were inside by stuffing something in the keyhole to block it.

The nun left the wheelchair on the landing, probably for later collection by some of the bigger girls, and went off downstairs. We gave a collective sigh of relief as we heard her footsteps disappearing in the distance. Not wanting to risk being discovered, we waited a little longer until her steps became very faint, before daring to come out of our hiding places and hurriedly taking off our costumes.

Callie rushed us: "Quick, she's gone, but she might come back to get the wheelchair. Let's go down now, one by one, so nobody sees us." We silently sneaked down the stairs, conscious of our narrow escape but pleased that our security system had worked and that our secret was undiscovered.

We were extremely disappointed to be deprived of our carriage. Now our only mode of transport was some old wooden crutches with padded leather armrests which we turned upside down and used as stilts, but they didn't have quite the same elegance as our carriage and were unwieldy as we clumped up and down the attic on them.

Amazingly, neither the nuns nor any of our enemies ever discovered our secret world and we continued to enjoy many hours of innocent pleasure, dressing up and playing to our hearts' content.

We went up to the attic as often as we dared but only when it was safe to do so, not wanting to risk being discovered by the nuns and bringing the wrath of Sister Magdalena or Sister Concepta down on our heads. The short time we were able to spend in our secret world wasn't nearly enough, but it was an escape from the grimness of our real lives and allowed us to forget that we were prisoners in that awful place.

Chapter Twenty-Two

I was an extremely shy child and tried not to attract attention to myself. My way of adapting to this situation was to withdraw further into myself and live in a dream world. I hoped not to be noticed by the nuns and bullies and to avoid becoming a target for them but all the while listening, learning and absorbing.

I had one painful experience at the hands of a bully that particularly stands out in my memory. Mammy had taken us home for a short visit at Christmas and I had bought a little toy snake in Woolworth's. It wriggled all over my hand and everybody was fascinated by it. Unfortunately, one of the big girls, called Carmel, decided that she wanted it. When the coast was clear, she waylaid me and grabbed my hair from behind. Pulling hard on it and twisting my face round to hers, she said, "I want that snake. Give it to me or I'll bash you."

She was twice my size so I handed it over without a struggle and she let go of my hair. The snake had caught her attention and she was so engrossed by the sight of the little creature wriggling over her hand that she momentarily forgot about me. I managed to escape unnoticed as she played with the snake.

Chapter Twenty-Two

I was very upset at the loss of my little toy but learned a valuable lesson. In future I was careful to keep out of her way, and learned to hide my possessions so that they wouldn't be stolen. My scalp was sore for a few days and was a reminder of what I had lost.

Although I didn't realise it in the beginning, I possessed a valuable asset that would become very important during my time at St Vincent's. I was very good at English and my teacher often praised me in class for my homework. It embarrassed me when she singled me out, as I didn't want to draw any attention to myself and it would make me a target for the bullies.

This didn't go unnoticed, though, but not in the way that I expected. There was one particular girl who had great difficulty in that class and was frequently punished by the teacher for her inability to submit her homework on time. She struggled to make headway with her work and dreaded the lesson, often feigning illness in order to avoid it. One day she approached me and asked, "Will you help me with my homework?"

I was very surprised at her request because she hadn't been all that friendly to me before now, but I agreed to help her all the same as I saw what misery and humiliation she was forced to endure in class. I also felt sorry for her because of the torment she endured at the hands of the nuns because of her so-called 'affliction': she was left-handed. The nuns really were pathetic, ignorant people.

Word soon got round and I was asked by some of the other bullies to help them with their homework in return for laying off my sisters and me. They appeared to be grateful for my help, as it stopped them in turn from becoming victims of the teachers and being punished for being "stupid dunces".

In time I found myself becoming better able to cope with the trauma. We were gradually learning how to fit in and eventually became adept at paying lip service to the nuns: "Yes sister, no sister, three bags full sister," we'd say, while all the time feeling utter contempt and loathing for them. At the same time we were also becoming more successful in our efforts to avoid being made scapegoats by the nuns and being picked on by all and sundry. We had formed our own little gang with Callie as our leader. We had learned that there was definitely safety in numbers.

Shortly after we arrived at St Vincent's, the whole community made the journey, lock, stock and barrel, to the order's convent in Clontarf for a few weeks' 'holiday' during the long summer break.

The convent was a few minutes' walk away from the Bull Wall, the place where the Vikings had beached their longships on the beach at Clontarf. Clontarf is Gaelic for 'The Plain of the Bull'. The name comes from the rumbling sound made by the sea as it rolled over the sandbanks of Dublin Bay before the sea walls were built.

By a strange coincidence, this convent was also just a short distance from our family house where we had lived until recently. Although I had passed almost daily by the convent on my way to the shops to buy the newspaper, I had never taken much notice of it and had never seen any children playing in the grounds.

Now, although we knew the local children playing outside the convent walls, we were not allowed out of the grounds to join them. Once, I was caught talking to some of them through the gate, a group of both girls and boys. They included neighbourhood boys and some pupils from my school. Naturally they were curious about life in the orphanage and asked me lots of questions, like "Why are you always kept behind the high walls and the big iron gates? Why can't you come out to play with us? Can we come and play in there with you?"

Without warning, Sister Magdalena appeared and they all melted away. She grabbed me by the arm, shook me and screamed, "You hussy, get away from that gate. What do you think you're doing? You girls are all boy-mad, that's all you think about." I was astounded by her strange attitude. What was wrong with boys? I knew these boys, they were friends and people just like my brothers whom I had played with most of my life.

She was furious and shouted, "Get inside. NOW!" I quickly obeyed her. This place also felt like a prison even though we were supposed to be on holiday. I longed to be at home with my family and to be normal again. The other girls told me I was lucky not to have received a beating, because sometimes when a girl was caught speaking to any of the neighbourhood children, she was punished with a caning, probably to discourage the other orphans from wanting any contract with the outside world, especially with boys.

We were occasionally taken for a walk through the neighbourhood, but mostly we were locked up in the grounds of the convent watching the children playing outside and longing to be out there with them. It was very frustrating.

After a few weeks stay in Clontarf, we returned to the city centre orphanage, no more refreshed than when we had started out. It had not been a holiday for us, just a different prison in a different location but with the same old guards.

Chapter Twenty-Three

My two brothers, Anthony and Joseph, then aged approximately eleven and eight years of age, were incarcerated with the male representatives of the Catholic Church, the Christian Brothers, in an orphanage in the Glasnevin area of Dublin.

Joseph needed frequent medical care for his chronic asthma and we were desperately worried about him. Since babyhood we had been very protective of him and helped to look after him when he was unwell. We also missed Anthony, with whom we had many playful scraps and to whom Daddy used to say when he became too boisterous, "Don't hit your sisters, only cowards hit women." Both boys had inherited some of Daddy's best characteristics: his easy-going personality, his friendliness, his intelligence and love of family.

Anthony and Joseph had made a journey to see us when we were first in St Vincent's. They brought an orange for each of us as a present. The nun who answered the door told them, "No, you can't see them. Go away and never ever come back." They were too scared to try to come back to St Vincent's to see us ever again.

The only contact we had with them after that was when Mammy came to visit and took us home for a few days; later, when we were at St Joseph's, they were able to sneak into the grounds by a side entrance on Sunday afternoons. I also saw them when I visited Callie in hospital later on. Some of our friends from home also called to see us and got the same reception from the nuns. We couldn't understand why we were not allowed to see our brothers but were too scared of the nuns to ask.

Anthony and Joseph were so neglected and uncared for by the Christian Brothers that they were allowed to run wild through the streets of Dublin at all times of the day and night. This was the 'care' the Christian Brothers had promised Mammy they would receive. The very thing that Mammy had wanted to avoid when she left them in their care had happened: nobody knew or cared where they were most of the time and they were in great danger because they lacked any form of supervision. She had trusted these people to care for her children and they had betrayed that trust. Anthony and Joseph were actually in more danger from the Christian Brothers' neglect than from any perceived threat from outsiders.

Poor Joseph was particularly badly neglected. He was very ill at times from his asthma and had to stay in bed in the infirmary for long periods. While the other boys were at lessons, he was left alone all day in the ward with no company, no stimulation or entertainment and not even a book to read. The only time he saw a living soul was when his food was given to him. Sometimes this state of affairs lasted for weeks.

In the meantime, his education suffered: he didn't receive any schooling while he was in the infirmary. Despite this, he and Anthony later became very articulate and cultured men. This was not due to the influence of the Christian Brothers, but down to their natural intelligence and the teaching and example of our parents earlier in their lives.

In their orphanage, the Christian Brothers fed the boys mainly on bread and butter and jam for most meals, with barley soup and bread for their main midday meal. Although there was a farm attached to the orphanage, with cows and poultry, they never received any benefit from this, although they were forced to work as farmhands sometimes. Very occasionally they received a sausage and were given an orange at Christmas. No wonder they were always starving when we saw them.

Their food was just put on the tables on big plates and each boy had to struggle to grab what he could. Obviously the bigger boys had first choice and the younger ones had to make do with what was left. The boys called these meals 'sav-in's' because they all had to dive in like savages to try to get a fair share.

The boys looked outside of the orphanage for their entertainment and one of their favourite past-times was swimming unsupervised in the local canal. Fortunately Anthony and Joseph were good swimmers as Daddy had taught them well, so they didn't get into difficulties.

It was strange not seeing them every day and we missed them terribly. This sounds terribly heartless but we had our own problems to worry about and, anyway, there was nothing we could've done to help them. Since our arrival at the orphanage,

Chapter Twenty-Three

Imelda had been very withdrawn. We were becoming concerned about her because she didn't appear to be very well. Then she started having convulsions. The first seizure happened when we were at a party around Christmas time. A charity had arranged this event for the children of the orphanage. It was an annual event and the other girls told us that we would have lots of lovely party food and be given candies and a little present from somebody dressed up as Santa Claus.

Prior to the day, we were asked to write down what we would like for our present but were warned by the nuns not to be greedy and not to ask for anything big. There was great excitement on the day and we were really looking forward to it: it would be a break from our normal routine and there would be some decent food to eat. We were in a big room decorated with Christmas decorations, balloons and a big sparkling tree, seated at rows of long tables. The fancy party food had been served and we were enjoying eating something edible for a change.

I heard a thud and turned to look behind me. Imelda had fallen off her seat and was lying on the floor. People started shouting and rushing around. A crowd gathered around her and there was a lot of confusion for a few minutes until a woman took charge. Imelda was writhing around on the floor, and somebody noticed that she was in danger of swallowing her tongue. They put a spoon in her mouth to hold her tongue down to prevent her from choking.

An ambulance was sent for and Imelda was taken away on a stretcher to hospital for further treatment. We were extremely frightened, but nobody seemed to know what was wrong with her; we had to wait for many hours to find out, and it was only because of Callie's persistence that we finally learned anything.

After being discharged from hospital the following day, Imelda was taken straight to the orphanage infirmary. This was in a distant part of the building, well away from our quarters. Mammy had been contacted in London and was on her way to Dublin. The nuns had told her that Imelda was dying but she didn't believe them.

We were not told where Imelda was, but Callie found out she was in the infirmary and tried to sneak upstairs to visit her. The nun in charge caught her and demanded, "What do you think you're doing? How dare you venture upstairs? Get back downstairs and don't even think of coming up here again." But Callie was so worried about Imelda she stood up to the nun and insisted on seeing her sister.

The nun relented when she saw how determined Callie was and allowed her into the infirmary for a few minutes. Imelda was pleased to see Callie: she had been left all alone in the infirmary with nobody telling her what was happening, and she was extremely scared. They both cried when they saw each other.

It was only after Mammy arrived that Sinead and I were also allowed to see her. Up until then the nuns hadn't even considered that we might be worried about our sister.

When Mammy arrived she was shown straight to the infirmary. Imelda was the only patient there and was lying in bed in the hushed and darkened room surrounded by a crowd of nuns kneeling at each side of the bed. Mammy said that they looked like a flock of crows waiting for Imelda to die. It must have been extremely frightening for a small child to be surrounded by them, not knowing what was happening. Her recovery started as soon as she saw Mammy, whose first act was to open the curtains to let some light into the room. She asked the nuns to leave them alone.

The doctor told Mammy his diagnosis: "Imelda is pining for you. The best thing for her to get better is to be with you and not in this place." It was decided that to help her recovery it would be a good idea if Imelda went to live in London with Mammy. She started to improve immediately after she left the orphanage. We were envious, but understood that it was necessary for her health and were relieved that she was not dying.

Callie remembers that at one time, she too was a patient in the infirmary and it wasn't a good experience. She can't remember what was wrong with her, but she said that for most of the time she was there nobody came near her, except when a nun came to give her some food; she was extremely lonely and bored.

When they arrived in London, Mammy had to try to find somebody to look after Imelda while she was at work. At that time it was difficult to find childcare, especially for a sick child. It was even difficult to find accommodation as people could pick and choose to whom they let their property. They put up notices saying, "No blacks, no Irish, no children, no dogs."

One child-minder neglected Imelda and her health stopped improving. This meant that it was impossible for her to stay in London, so Mammy reluctantly decided that she would have to return her to the orphanage. I can't remember whether this was to St Vincent's or to St. Joseph's, which was our next destination.

This orphanage was at the seaside, in a little town called Dún Laoghaire a few miles from the city centre on the south side of Dublin Bay. This was very different from the dingy, run-down inner-city location where St Vincent's was situated.

I think Imelda's ill health contributed to our move: she needed the fresh sea air and a healthier climate than the city centre, which it was hoped would also help her condition.

By the time we left St Vincent's, we were no longer the soft suburban children who had arrived at the orphanage the previous year. We had acquired some of the skills necessary to enable us to survive in that alien environment and had developed a veneer of toughness that was to stand us in good stead in the future.

Just before we left St Vincent's, one of the girls ran away. She was caught in the countryside attempting to get back to her family home and was brought back to the orphanage by the police. They didn't believe her when she told them that she was afraid of Sister Magdalena and the other nuns and that was why she had run away. They took her back to her abusers who punished her severely as an example to the rest of us, and as a reminder of what would happen to anybody else who attempted to escape.

We were extremely relieved to be leaving St Vincent's. Although we would miss the friends we had made there, we had no wish ever to see any of the nuns again. It was exciting to be going to live at the seaside and we looked forward to the change, since we thought that nowhere could be as bad as the place we were leaving behind.

What pathetic, naive fools we were. How could we have been so stupid?

Chapter Twenty-Four

At first sight, St Joseph's appeared to be a much nicer place than St Vincent's when we arrived there one early summer's day. We were taken in by its location in the pretty seaside town of Dún Laoghaire. The surroundings were pleasantly middle-class, with fragrant gardens of flower beds, graceful weeping willow trees and manicured lawns, unlike the grim setting of St Vincent's in the narrow, poverty-stricken city streets and bomb sites of Dublin that we had so recently left behind.

Dún Laoghaire is a small coastal town about 7 miles (11km) south of Dublin city. It gets its name from the Irish translation, Dún – meaning Fort – of Laoghaire. King Laoghaire was an ancient High King of Ireland.

Later, when the English arrived, they named the town Dunleary. In 1821 it was renamed Kingstown by King George IV of England to honour his visit to the town that year. It retained the name of Kingstown through the Victorian era until 1921, one year before Irish independence, when the authorities changed it back to the ancient Irish name of Dún Laoghaire.

It is well-known for its ferry port from which passenger ships set sail about four times daily across the Irish Sea to Holyhead in Wales or Liverpool, the journey taking approximately 100 minutes. There are frequent train connections to London from both ports. This was another reason why Mammy had chosen Dún Laoghaire, so she could make frequent quick trips to Dublin to see us, sometimes staying in a guesthouse nearby.

The convent, with the orphanage building behind, stood in the middle of a suburban street full of family houses, and backed onto a golf course. The extensive property consisted of many buildings and acres and acres of land, including two big orchards that stretched far off into the distance. We glimpsed a beautiful rose garden at the back of one of the retirement homes. The whole setting was idyllic, and Mammy thought we would be happy there.

Inside the convent, we were shown by a girl to a reception room to await the arrival of the Mother Superior. The girl said, "The Mother Superior is called Miss Brophy." I thought I must have misheard: why was she not called Sister if she was a nun or Mother if she was the Mother Superior?

The room was pleasant and very well furnished, with highly polished furniture and floors. There were comfortable sofas, pretty curtains and ornaments scattered around the room. Adorning the walls were the usual religious pictures and a couple of shrines to the Virgin Mary and St Joseph decorated with vases of fresh flowers. Lit candles were placed in front of the shrines and there was a faint aroma of incense in the room, probably emanating from the nearby chapel. It was a warm day and the room felt quite stuffy. I wished I could open the window to let in some fresh air. We were all quiet, feeling a bit subdued at the prospect of settling into a new place and meeting new people.

The door swung open and in swept a heavy-set – almost mannish – loose-jowled woman who carried herself with an air of self-importance. I thought she was very old but she was probably around 50 years of age. Her grey hair was clipped back in a bun and she wore old-fashioned metal spectacles. She wore a tweed suit with a white blouse buttoned up to the neck and a brooch pinned under the collar. Laced-up black shoes completed the ensemble. Introducing herself as Miss Brophy, she lowered her heavy bulk into a chair.

Bestowing a big smile upon us, she bade us welcome and then, turning to Mammy, she said, "Oh, Mrs Walsh. What lovely children. Don't you worry mother, we'll take good care of them."

When she spoke, the loose skin under her chin hung down and swung and wobbled like a turkey. I was fascinated but tried to avert my gaze to avoid my eyes being drawn towards her neck. We didn't dare look at each other either because I'm sure we would have burst out laughing. Later Callie told me that she had wanted to laugh, too: "Did you see her neck? She looks like a turkey the way the skin on her neck swings." We all agreed that she did and that became her nickname – Turkey.

It was all very confusing. We had been told that she was a nun, but she wasn't wearing a nun's habit. Her clothes made her look more like a spinsterish headmistress. She was probably used to the confusion about her status and explained to Mammy that the religious order to which she belonged had been founded in 1790 in France during the turbulence of the French Revolution, when both the Church and religious life faced extinction. It wasn't safe to be conspicuous in the streets and the nuns didn't want to draw attention to themselves, so in order to avoid being attacked they dressed in secular clothing. They used their own names and lived in their own homes and that was why they were not called 'Sister'. After the revolution ended, they expanded their empire to England, and later to Ireland, where they established themselves in two locations, Dún Laoghaire being one of them.

Mammy was reassured by Miss Brophy's friendly manner and smiled back at her. She appeared to be a very pleasant woman indeed, and Mammy was happy to leave us in her care. Mammy was in a hurry to catch the ferry back to England for work and was sure that we would be okay. We were taken in too. How could we have been so stupid? Hadn't we learned anything from our previous experience at St Vincent's?

Like the nuns at St Vincent's, Miss Brophy's friendly manner changed abruptly as soon as Mammy left the convent. Summoning one of her minions, a nervous little woman who almost jumped out of her skin when Miss Brophy spoke to her, she instructed her to take us through to the orphanage. Then she walked out of the room without a word or backward glance at us, as though we no longer existed. Later, with hindsight, we realised that the nun hadn't meant a word of what she had said about taking care of us. She must have been mentally rubbing her hands with glee: "Four more workers, God was indeed good."

It didn't take us long to discover our true function in this place. The nuns weren't concerned about the children in their charge, either those who had been placed there by the authorities or by widowed mothers or fathers, as we were to discover before too long. This was a money-making venture.

The beautiful location disguised the harsh reality of our situation. Although no corporal punishment was meted out there, we were soon to learn that these nuns were no different from those at St Vincent's. They also had no compassion or feelings for the children they were supposed to be caring for. This headmistress was of the same tyrannical type as Sister Magdalena at St Vincent's, but ruled with psychological terror instead of a cane. St Joseph's was another prison for children, albeit the equivalent of an open prison compared to the maximum-security regime of St Vincent's. This time the nuns' weapons of discipline were sarcasm, humiliation and hard labour, which they enforced strictly in an effort to crush any resistance to their rule.

There was one important difference this time though: we were not the complete innocents we had been when we had first arrived at St Vincent's, having learnt our lessons well during our time in that place. Although our living conditions here were equally as harsh, we had become somewhat more adept in the art of institutional living and had a head start this time. Reminiscent of totalitarian regimes everywhere, we were each issued with a number by which we became officially known. In our gulag at the back of the convent, hidden away behind the genteel façade of the convent, the children lived the lives of slave labourers.

The girls ranged in age from infants to those over 16 who had stayed on to work for the nuns when the government was no longer legally responsible for supporting them. This, in effect, meant that the nuns no longer received payment for their keep. They worked for the nuns for what amounted to board and lodgings and a small amount of pocket money, but they were still prisoners and had to abide by the strict rules of the institution.

Normally, when they reached 16, they would be thrown out onto the street to fend for themselves. Here, some of them were kept on as 'employees' because of the chronic shortage of free labour; also they had become so institutionalised that they were probably afraid to venture out into the world all by themselves. Who can blame them when the very people who were supposed to care for them had shown such disregard for their welfare; whom could they trust?

Although they called it an orphanage, the stated purpose of this order of nuns was to 'train' children in the arts of domestic service, which turned out to be a euphemism for exploitation. These people were businesswomen and we were destined to join their unpaid, underfed and exploited workforce. The nuns were not interested in educating the children or preparing them for any meaningful future in the outside world, but only as domestic servants.

Any schooling we received was minimal and just enough to satisfy the authorities. They had no aspirations or ambitions for us and didn't encourage any talents we might have possessed nor envisage a future for us as wives and mothers; therefore they discouraged relationships with siblings or relatives or the opposite sex. It seemed that the nuns had no regard either for the opinions of the children's families either. As far as they were concerned, the families, if they existed, were never consulted in any decisions concerning the children. The nuns had total control over the children's lives and didn't welcome any outside interference. In fact, they actively discouraged contact in some cases for "the good of the children". It was only persistent effort by some families that enabled them to stay in contact with their children.

With the exception of a chauffeur called Patrick and a few secular day teachers in the school, no other civilians were employed by the nuns. Patrick was employed solely to drive them and members of the upper echelons of the Church in their luxury car. No public transport for them – how could they be expected to demean themselves by travelling in the company of the poor, whom they appeared to despise. After all, it was the children of the poor and dispossessed who they were exploiting, and they had only contempt for them. They appeared to believe that the sins of the parents had been passed on to the children and so they deserved to be punished for their parents' crimes.

The businesses run by the nuns consisted of two retirement homes for elderly bedridden ladies, a religious retreat house, a guesthouse for visiting dignitaries and a day school for girls from the locality. There was also a poultry farm that supplied fresh eggs and chickens to the various houses every day but none were given to the people who did all the work and needed decent food – the orphans. The children never received any of this bounty, something that would have greatly enhanced our diet and provided a valuable source of protein that was sorely lacking.

Although the orchards produced prodigious amounts of fruit, including apples, plums, gooseberries and blackcurrants, some of which were made into jam and fruit pies, the orphans didn't receive any of these either. The only way for us to get fresh fruit was to steal it from the orchards. Obviously the children didn't merit decent food in the eyes of the nuns, despite the fact that our labour was enabling them to earn money from their businesses. Whatever the nuns did with the money, it was evident that they were not spending any of it on us.

Again, as in St Vincent's, we were separated by age into different groups. It wasn't long before it became apparent that our quality of life didn't improve with our surroundings. As with the other nuns, it seemed that the vows of poverty and humility they took were once again transferred to the children and didn't appear to apply to them. They had the best of everything: food, clothing, carpeted accommodation and child slaves to do all their work.

Our quarters were at the opposite end of the scale from the nuns' comfortable accommodation. They were totally spartan, with just basic amenities. There were no easy chairs, no carpets, no curtains on the windows, and no recreation room. Everywhere was bare and impersonal with nothing to soften the dreary functional decor.

We were later to discover that we didn't have much recreation time anyway, so why would we need anywhere nice to relax? Any spare time we had, between getting up in the morning and going to sleep at night, was spent working in the orphanage, school, kitchens, laundry or any of the various retreat, retirement homes or guesthouses. The work was never-ending and at times back-breaking, especially when we didn't receive enough nourishment to give us the strength for such demanding physical activity.

Half of our accommodation had been utilised to generate even more money. On the first floor of the orphanage they had managed to squeeze in three classrooms for the day girls. There were approximately 50 girls living in the orphanage at any one time, but no provision had been made anywhere for us to rest when we had any free time, infrequent though that was. We were expected to sit at the desks in one of the classrooms in the evenings while the nuns were at prayers or recreation.

During the day there was nowhere for us to rest when the classrooms were in use, but it didn't matter as we were either at classes or working. The babies and toddlers were usually kept up in their dormitory if the weather was bad or out in the grounds if it was fine, with an older girl to supervise them. There was no such thing as a separate nursery for them.

When the nuns were at recreation we had to sit in the classrooms doing our homework and mending the children's clothes and darning their smelly socks before they were sent to the laundry. This was necessary so the garments wouldn't disintegrate completely in the wash. Some of them had been mended so often that only the previously darned patches held them together. The nuns made sure they got every bit of use they could out of them. It must have broken their hearts when they finally had to dispose of a garment because it was so worn that it couldn't be repaired anymore. Even then, they were used as rags for polishing or dusting. Nothing was ever wasted.

Chapter Twenty-Five

The day school that we attended was located across a grey concrete square formed by the orphanage, the school buildings and the retreat house. A narrow lane at the side of the convent led to this area. There were fields and two big orchards at the back of this side of the property, containing many fruit trees – apples and pears – and lots of shrubs with gooseberries and blueberries. We shared this playground with the schoolchildren and after lessons had finished for the day, it became our territory.

As at St Vincent's, no playthings were provided by the nuns for the children. The only toys we had were those given by relatives or made by the children themselves. As usual, we had to make our own entertainment. We jumped over benches and climbed up some trees at the side of the playground. If we managed to steal some chalk from the classrooms, we made hopscotch marks on the grey concrete; otherwise we used the old standby of stones to scratch lines and numbers. When we were in the playground we had to mind the babies and toddlers who were still too small for school and therefore unable to work for their keep.

Chapter Twenty-Five

By the time we started our daily lessons in the school, we had already been up since the crack of dawn, had attended Mass in the chapel and done half a day's domestic work. The day girls, who lived normal family lives, would have been woken by their mothers and had their breakfast served to them before being escorted to school with a packed lunch and wishes for a good day.

For me, school was a brief escape from the stress of living with the nuns. For a few hours I spent away from them each day I could pretend that they didn't exist, except, of course, if I had one of them as a teacher. My class teacher was Miss Ward, a young and pretty secular teacher. It was a relief to have someone normal teaching me. She was probably in her mid-to-late 20s and had a boyfriend. All the girls admired her and wanted to be just like her. Unfortunately for us, she got engaged and soon gave up work when she married. We were crushed to find that her replacement was a nun. Nobody wanted to be like her. Her teaching wasn't at all inspirational and she didn't appear to have any pride in her work or any interest in the girls.

The teachers' expectations for the day girls were that they would become wives and mothers after a short time spent working as typists or shop assistants. In the eyes of the Church, their true role was to be good wives and produce more Catholic babies to fill the churches, so perpetuating the system. But how were married women supposed to become pregnant? By Immaculate Conception perhaps, as sex was considered by the nuns to be something dirty and repugnant in the repressed Catholic society of that time. It was something that was only indulged in by the poor, who were deemed to be 'feckless' and immoral.

Orphans, on the other hand, didn't need careers or families: they were born to be skivvies and shouldn't expect to live fulfilling lives. The nuns weren't interested in seeing beyond the time when the girls would leave the orphanage and need to earn a living. They were in fact encouraging the cycle of poverty and deprivation, but that probably suited them – where would they be without the poor?

Girls who were academically gifted were not encouraged to aim for higher education and no vocational training was provided either. As far as the nuns were concerned, it didn't matter, because as soon as a girl reached the age of 16 they could wash their hands of her; she would no longer be their problem unless they could further exploit her by making her work for very little money.

As for artistically gifted children, any talents they had in that direction were considered to be a complete waste of time. I had decided I wanted to be a dress designer when I left school. The comics that Mammy sent me had cut-out dolls on the back cover with different outfits to dress them in. I cut out the figures and designed my own outfits for them, which I drew in coloured crayons. I kept my ambition secret, because to have mentioned it to anybody would have provoked only derision and laughter, not only from the nuns but some of the other girls too.

The school curriculum was religion-based and very biased against the British, against British Protestants in particular. They were portrayed as oppressors of the Irish people and especially of Catholics. We were taught that they, along with other non-Catholics, would burn in hell when they died because they didn't worship 'the one true god'.

I remember one occasion when the priest was testing my class on the catechism. When it came to my turn he asked me, "What is servile work?" Servile work was supposed to be work that shouldn't be done on a Sunday, which was considered a holy day. I replied, "It's work like scrubbing or heavy cleaning." He was flustered and embarrassed when he heard my answer, as he must have known that we did exactly that on Sundays in the orphanage, and it didn't matter whether it was a holy day or not. He hurriedly moved on to the next girl and asked her a simple question that only required a simple answer that didn't trouble his conscience.

History lessons focused on the Irish potato famine of 1846–1850 when as many as one million people died from hunger and disease. The famine began with a blight of the potato crop – the staple diet of the mainly peasant Irish population at that time – and left acre upon acre of farmland covered with black rot. The crops, which the farmers relied on to pay the rent to their British and Irish Protestant landlords, were destroyed by the fungus. People who ate the rotten harvest sickened and died. Entire villages were consumed with cholera and typhus. Landlords evicted hundreds of thousands of peasants, who then crowded into disease-infested workhouses. Some landlords paid for their tenants to emigrate, sending hundreds of thousands of Irish people to America and other English-speaking countries.

The population of Ireland had been around six to eight million before the famine. It is estimated that during that period three to four million either died in the famine or left Ireland to escape it. Most migrants ended up in North America, while others headed for Australia. Some emigrated to Britain where they had relatives. Although many found prosperity in their new lives in America, a number of the émigrés never even got to see land after sailing from Cobh in County Cork, the chief embarkation point in Ireland for the United States. Travelling conditions at the time were so bad that many perished during the transatlantic voyage and never made landfall. There were two ways to travel: either standard class or steerage. Standard-class passengers had berths and were allowed on deck. Steerage-class passengers were crowded together below deck and often were not allowed to use the deck. For many impoverished emigrants, steerage class was all they could afford.

Many on board were suffering from fever and, coupled with the crowded and unsanitary conditions on board the ships, disease spread rapidly. These ships became known as 'coffin ships', but because people were so desperate to escape from the famine, they were willing to take the risk of travelling on them. It is estimated that perhaps as many as 40 per cent of steerage passengers died either on the journey or immediately after arrival at their destination. Although the ships were regulated, some captains overcrowded them with as many passengers as they could cram in, in order to make as much money as possible.

The vast majority of the people leaving Ireland at that time were the landless and impoverished, those with no future in their own country and many without the skills necessary to create a life in the New World. They just wanted to escape the famine. Most were headed for Irish communities in New York or Boston to join family members who had left Ireland earlier. Ever since then the Irish have resented the British for not helping them in their hour of need, and we were taught this day in, day out.

In the years after the famine, scientists discovered that the blight was caused by a fungus they named *Phytophthora infestans*. However, it wasn't until almost 40 years later that they discovered a cure: a solution of copper sulphate was sprayed on the ground before the fungus took root. At the time of the famine, there was nothing that the farmers could do to prevent their crops becoming infected.

Our history lessons also dwelt on the struggle for independence from British rule, the Easter Rising of 1916 and the Black and Tans. After the abortive 1916 uprising, the British government sent reinforcements to Ireland to assist the Royal Irish Constabulary to keep order. These reinforcements consisted of the Auxiliary Division (the 'Auxis', exclusively made up of ex-army officers), and the Black and Tans.

In 1919, the British government advertised for men who were willing to "face a rough and dangerous task". Many former British soldiers had come back from the First World War to mass unemployment. Plenty of ex-servicemen were willing to sign up and were paid ten shillings a day. They received three months' training before being sent to Ireland, and the first unit arrived in March 1920.

Once in Ireland it quickly became apparent that there were not enough uniforms for all those who had joined up.

They therefore wore a mixture – some military, some Royal Irish Constabulary. This gave them the appearance of being dressed in khaki and dark police uniform. As a result, they were nicknamed the 'Black and Tans'. They were not popular with the civilian population, who were extremely hostile towards them and often accused them of brutality.

In class, we were also taught to sing Irish rebel songs such as 'Kevin Barry'. Kevin Barry was a student and Irish patriot who was captured by the British after a gun battle during the Black and Tan wars of 1919. He told the British on the eve of his execution in 1920, "Shoot me like a soldier, don't hang me like a dog." The British hanged him. He was just 18 years old at the time and just one of a group of IRA members executed in 1920–21 collectively known as 'The Forgotten Ten'.

The ballad was penned shortly after his death by an author whose identity is unknown. It is sung to the melody of 'Rolling Home to Dear Old Ireland'. Over the years it has been performed by many Irish groups, including The Wolfe Tones and The Clancy Brothers. The American singer Paul Robeson included it in his album *Songs of Struggle*, although this version tones down the anti-British sentiment of the original. Leonard Cohen performed the song in concert in 1972.

It has become one of the most enduringly popular of Irish songs and has been largely responsible for making Kevin Barry a household name. It was said to be so popular with British troops during the Troubles that started in the late 1960s that it was banned. It was one of many Irish rebel ballads removed from Raidió Teilifís Éireann (RTE) playlists during the Northern Ireland conflict.

This is the song dedicated to his memory:

> In Mountjoy jail one Monday morning,
> High upon the gallows' tree,
> Kevin Barry gave his young life,
> For the cause of liberty.
> Just a lad of 18 summers,
> And yet no one can deny,
> As he walked to death that morning,
> He proudly held his head up high.
> Just before he faced the hangman,
> In his dreary prison cell,
> British soldiers tortured Barry,
> Just because he would not tell,
> The names of his brave comrades,
> And other things they wished to know,
> "Turn informer or we'll kill you",
> Kevin Barry answered "No".
> Calmly standing to attention,
> While he bade his last farewell,
> To his broken-hearted mother,
> Whose sad grief no one can tell.
> For the cause he proudly cherished,
> This sad parting had to be,
> Then to death walked softly smiling,
> That old Ireland might be free.

Vow *of* Silence

Another martyr for old Ireland,
Another murder for the Crown,
Whose brutal laws may kill the Irish,
But can't keep their spirit down.
Lads like Barry are no cowards,
From the foe they will not fly,
Lads like Barry will free Ireland,
For her sake they'll live and die.

Chapter Twenty-Six

The nuns never encouraged us to read for pleasure. They considered any time spent not working as wasted, so no books were provided, apart from some religious ones (of course) and some encyclopedias that were kept in a bookcase in one of the classrooms for educational purposes and had probably lain undisturbed for many years.

However, I discovered some books by Enid Blyton tucked away unnoticed by anyone but me on the bottom shelf of a big glass-fronted bookcase. It was a mystery how they got there. They had probably lain there for many years and were of no interest to anybody but me. I was thrilled when I discovered them and hid them so that nobody else could have them. Whenever I had any spare time, which wasn't very often, I found a place where I wouldn't be disturbed and could read them, feeding my imagination with the adventures of *The Secret Seven* and *The Famous Five*. These were the only books that were available to me and I read them over and over again. Although we had lots of books at home, it wasn't a good idea to bring them to the orphanage as personal items usually disappeared, never to be seen again.

The Famous Five consisted of Julian and Dick, their sister Anne, their cousin George (who was actually a girl) and George's dog Timmy. They would go on bicycling adventures and their mothers would wave them off with picnics of ham rolls, egg sandwiches, chocolate cake and bottles of lemonade.

The Secret Seven was a secret society for children. Peter was the founder of the club with his sister Janet. All of the members had badges, and a password was required to enter their clubhouse. They solved all kinds of mysteries, shadowed suspects looking for clues and found themselves in all sorts of awkward and dangerous situations from which they usually escaped unscathed and victorious They also had a dog called Scamper. With the other club members, they solved many exciting mysteries.

I used to daydream that I was one of the gang and wished that I could have great adventures like them. The stories reminded me of when I had played with my brothers and sisters, roaming the fields and woods behind our house. I wonder if any other child later found my books in their hiding place after I left the orphanage and received as much enjoyment as I did from reading them.

But I didn't get that much time to indulge in my secret pastime, as we worked from early in the morning until we fell exhausted into bed at night. No job was considered too dirty or too heavy for us, even though we were just children, and the work would have been considered arduous even for adults. The nuns didn't give any consideration to whether or not we were physically capable of doing the heavy manual work. It wasn't important; as long as the work got done, that was all that mattered. School, as far as the nuns were concerned, was just an annoying interlude that interfered with the main reason for the children being in the orphanage: work. Education was not a priority.

Miss Boylan and Miss Coote were in charge of allocating the work. The bitterness and frustration they exuded revealed the unhappiness of their own lives. They must have entered St Joseph's while still in their teens, but by the time they had become disillusioned with their life there, it was too late to leave. It was all they could expect until the day they died. They were rarely allowed to see their own families. It was no wonder they were so bitter and twisted.

Miss Coote had a myopic look as a result of the spectacles that she wore. Her black hair was styled in a bun and her grey suit completed the look of a kindly, old-fashioned schoolteacher; her appearance was very misleading, however, as there was nothing even remotely kind about her.

Her colleague Miss Boylan was very plain-looking and in the outside world would charitably have been described as a 'wallflower'. She was small, thin and grey-haired. Neither of them had any charisma or human warmth when it came to dealing with the children. Like the nuns in St Vincent's, they presented a very different face to the public. In fact, this description seemed to apply to all of the nuns in St Joseph's, perhaps to nuns everywhere. They could switch on their other face at will but couldn't be bothered to make any effort with the orphans. It was too much trouble for them, and they didn't appear to have what would be called 'people skills' these days.

There was a desperate need for domestic workers in all of their moneymaking establishments, as well as in the convent and orphanage, but the nuns didn't employ any outside help: they would have had to pay them. The children were the only workers and even our contribution wasn't enough to cover the never-ending work that needed to be done. This meant that we were permanently overworked. Needless to say, as soon as possible after our arrival, we were ordered to start work by the nuns. In their eyes we were there for no other reason than to work, and we had no choice in the matter. They supervised our every waking hour and made sure that we worked like galley slaves from morning to night. I'm surprised they even allowed us time to go to school.

At first I was assigned to work in the retreat house, where I made beds, washed up and cleaned and set tables for meals. This was in addition to my other jobs of cleaning the school after lessons, helping in the kitchen and looking after babies and toddlers, as well as washing up after our meals in the refectory. There was hardly a single moment when I wasn't working.

Once again Callie assumed the role of nursemaid to the younger children: they instinctively gravitated towards her, as they seemed to sense her kindness. She, in turn, loved them all and took great care of them. After supper each evening, Callie had to supervise these little children in a school room, which was full of desks but no play equipment, while all the other children and nuns were at rosary and benediction in the chapel. She looked after them until their bedtime when the other children came back from the church service. She escorted them upstairs to their dormitory to be washed and changed for bed. When they were all settled for the night, Callie hand-washed all their white summer socks for the next day.

On Saturday mornings she also had to wash their hair, but no shampoo was supplied for this purpose. The carbolic soap that was used to wash the floors also had to be used for all our bathing and hair washing. So, in addition to her other work, Callie was also a nursery nurse charged with looking after the little children and babies. The nuns were lucky that Callie was conscientious and actually took care of the children, unlike others, who, following the nuns' example, sometimes ill-treated them.

The nuns spent as little money as possible on the children, even though they were being paid by the government to care for them. In addition, they were also profiting from their unpaid work. There was no such thing as time off or proper breaks. We didn't deserve any consideration – that's what orphans were for. It was only when I had to look after the babies on Sunday mornings while everybody else was at Mass that I was sent down to late Mass in the church in town, and took the opportunity to enjoy some free time.

Since nobody else came to the service with me, I realised that I was free for a while. I didn't bother with Mass but instead went for a leisurely walk along the sea front until it was time to go back to the orphanage. It was so peaceful by the sea and I looked forward to my regular Sunday morning breaks.

The rest of the time our days were full and we rarely had a moment to ourselves. We cleaned, scrubbed and polished constantly, helped in the retirement homes, washed up and cleaned the refectory after every meal, cleaned the dormitories every day and polished and scrubbed every floor in the place at weekends, as well as cleaning the bathrooms and toilets. I was also delegated to work in the nuns' kitchen, cooking and lifting heavy pots and dishes from the cooker and cleaning and washing up after the nuns' meals. It was like a regular adult full-time job, but all this work was done in our spare time, before and after attending lessons during the week and all day at weekends.

Some of the older girls worked in the laundry: a hot, steamy place with dangerous clanking old-fashioned machinery that was always breaking down. The nuns had no concern for the safety of the children in that highly dangerous place. Many a time, the girls received minor burns or scalds, but these accidents were considered part of the job. Luckily for the nuns, they never had a major tragedy on their hands, and none of the girls were ever badly injured or even killed by the unsafe conditions.

At lunchtime, after quickly eating my own 'meal' in the refectory, I had to go straight to the kitchen to help serve the nuns their lunch. After washing up, I returned to lessons. I was then free from working in the kitchen until the next meal needed to be prepared. Obviously this took more time than the allocated lunch hour, but my teacher was aware of the reason for my late return to class and didn't say anything. After lessons had finished for the day I had to clean the classrooms too

Although we attended school with the day girls, socialising with them wasn't encouraged by the nuns, as we might have become discontented with our lot and hankered after a family of their own if we found out what kind of life the day girls had.

Chapter Twenty-Six

At the end of the day they went home to their families and normal life, while we resumed our role of slave labourers.

After classes had finished for the day and the day girls had left for home, I then began my job of cleaning the classrooms, supervised by one of the nuns. She sprinkled used tea leaves on the wooden floors, ostensibly to trap the dust but more likely to make sure that every bit of the room was swept, as she later checked to see whether any leaves were left behind. When this job was finished it was time to start work in the kitchen again to help prepare the evening meals for both the nuns and the children.

Later, some of us had to mind the younger children and babies. Again, as at St Vincent's, there were no paid staff or helpers, so we did all the work.

Chapter Twenty-Seven

St Joseph's was a lot different to St Vincent's in layout. For a start, it was more open because of the separate buildings and the extensive grounds at the back of the property, so we had slightly more freedom there. We were different people now too, a lot more cunning and a lot less naive than when we had first arrived at St Vincent's. Having learned our harsh lessons in survival well, we knew how to bend the rules to suit our purposes. It didn't take us long to find our feet and discover the possibilities in our new environment.

When we had time, we set out to explore the buildings and grounds. The large estate concealed some things that hadn't been apparent at first. There were lots of places where we could be out of sight of the nuns for periods of time. Apart from the warren of buildings, there were fields and orchards, which stretched a long way down the back of the property and spread out over many acres.

The nuns couldn't possibly know where we were and couldn't monitor our movements all the time. This gave us scope for manipulating situations to our advantage. We had also discovered the use of reverse psychology. If we really wanted something, we pretended that it was the last thing in the world that we desired and then we would probably be allowed to have it. On the contrary, if we didn't want to do something we begged to be allowed to do it.

Sometimes this method backfired on us, but more often than not it worked in our favour. We got to know how to read the moods of the individual nuns and knew when to keep out of their way. It was best not to approach them when they were in a bad mood, but to ask for favours when they were in a good one, which wasn't very often.

We were learning new survival skills all the time and becoming ever more resourceful, although living on our wits wasn't a natural way for us to behave. Our innocence had been taken away from us and we were becoming different people to the children who had left their suburban life just a short time ago.

Not only did the children have to endure the stigma of being orphans: it was impossible for people to be unaware of our status because of our unkempt appearance and shabby hand-me-down clothes. The nuns didn't seem to consider clothes to be important for the children, probably because most of the time we were in school uniform or working clothes. You don't need decent clothes to do housework.

It didn't matter to them whether we were decently dressed or not and they didn't appear to care what we looked like. They didn't take any pride in our appearance unless, of course, we had to appear in public on special occasions, when they magically produced the good clothes that they had hidden away so that the public wouldn't find out how they neglected us.

Some of the clothes the children wore were so old and shabby and had been passed down for so many years that any self-respecting rag and bone man would have turned up his nose at the sight of them. The nuns never bought the children anything new. Everything we wore was donated or recycled and nothing was ever wasted. There was a room called the sewing room where we had to darn and patch the clothes when they came back from the laundry, as they were so old and worn that they almost fell apart in the wash.

From time to time Mammy sent us new clothes. We would get to wear them for a few weeks, before the nuns appropriated them and they somehow found their way into the communal wardrobe or were put away for good. We greatly resented seeing other girls wearing our new clothes or even our shoes.

Usually, the children's clothes were provided from a massive built-in cupboard at one end of the dormitory. They were extremely unflattering, even though the concept of fashion had not been invented at that time. In an effort not to look too shabby and dowdy, the older girls, who were at a stage in their development when it was important to look and feel good, tried to adapt them as best they could by altering them. The clothes still looked awful as they had been passed down from many other people and were third, fourth or even fifth-hand; the day girls used to snigger when they saw us. I dreaded going to school and kept myself apart from the other girls.

The nuns didn't believe in girls looking nice or pretty and would often tell us, "It is a sin to be vain." They didn't care what they wore because nobody else did either. Who would want to look at them? It was an advantage for them to be as unattractive as possible so that no man would be interested in them and try to tempt them away from their religious path or show any sexual interest in them.

Ill-fitting second-hand shoes that were also passed down from child to child ruined our feet. I remember once getting new shoes from Mammy in the post. The shoes were made of tan-coloured leather and were the softest, most comfortable shoes I had ever worn. I owned them for about three weeks before they were then taken from me by the nuns and passed on to some other girl. I was heart-broken and cried my eyes out. We had reached an age when our appearance was becoming very important. Clothes and hairstyles were a major topic of conversation among the girls, along with the subject of boys.

My friend Pauline admired our class teacher Miss Ward's elegant look and tried to copy her hairstyle: "Don't you think Miss Ward's hair's gorgeous? I wonder if mine would look nice like that. Suzy, will you help me do the back the same way as her hair?" Pauline had lovely long dark hair. We spent ages trying to copy Miss Ward's style: a French pleat. Eventually we succeeded, and Pauline was thrilled with her new look. When she arrived in the refectory for her meal feeling really elegant, the nun in charge sneered at her in front of everyone: "What do you think you look like? Go and brush out that ridiculous hair, and don't come back here looking like a clown."

They tried to discourage us from taking an interest in the opposite sex, but couldn't stop human nature taking its course. We were adolescents who were becoming women and they couldn't control our hormones. There was nothing wrong with wanting to be normal teenage girls, but the nuns couldn't afford to lose control of the older girls. They had very primitive views on life and sexuality and seemed to think that anything pleasurable was a sin, especially anything to do with the body. All their femininity had been ironed out of them and they were like dried-up old husks.

Chapter Twenty-Eight

Most of the nuns were unattractive in looks and character, but none was as vile as Hoppy.

She was an unfortunate-looking person, having buckteeth, hairy moles and a hint of a beard. Her hair was styled in a Second World War fashion, brushed back from her face and curled at the bottom in a sausage shape from one ear round the back of her head to the other ear. This 'style' was achieved with the help of pipe cleaners. The hair was wound around them at night, and when they were pulled out in the morning, the sausage shape remained. The roll was then clipped into place to stop it from coming loose.

Hoppy was on the lower rungs of the hierarchy and she was given the jobs none of the other nuns wanted. In other circumstances we might have felt sorry for her, but her nature was so cruel and vile and she was so spiteful to the children that she forfeited any sympathy we might ordinarily have felt for her. We called her Hoppy because she had a deformed foot and wore one built-up shoe. You couldn't miss the sound of her coming to shatter our sleep in the mornings as she hopped along the corridor outside our dormitory, ringing a hand bell to wake us. We jumped out of bed immediately when we heard her bell clanging, to avoid having our bed covers rudely yanked from us and dumped on the floor.

After all the girls in the big dormitory had been woken (which wasn't difficult unless they were extraordinarily heavy sleepers) and were out of their beds, Hoppy clumped off through our dormitory and along the corridor to disturb the sleep of the little children and babies. On her way out of our room she turned and shouted, "Don't let me catch any of you still in bed when I get back or there'll be trouble."

When Hoppy had disappeared down the corridor, her uneven footsteps receding into the distance, we quickly got washed and dressed and then jumped back into our beds in our clothes and shoes to try to snatch a few minutes more rest before we reluctantly had to go to the chapel for the boring ritual of Mass. We jumped out again when we heard her heavy footsteps hopping back down the corridor.

About half an hour later she came back into our dormitory. "Are you lazy lot not ready yet?" she shouted. Then she made a big performance of checking the beds of the known bed-wetters to see if anybody had dared to wet theirs in the night, and appeared to take great delight in humiliating them in front of all of us if they had. She made a great performance of having them strip their beds while she shouted and screamed at them, calling them names and laughing her nasty little laugh. The girl who slept in the bed beside me used to wet her bed every night and cover up the evidence every morning. She had to sleep in a stinking wet bed, until one day she was found out from the smell and all hell broke loose.

Hoppy made a great show of pulling back the bedclothes, ostentatiously holding her nose between her fingers as she sneered, "What's this? You're disgusting; you're no better than a baby. Look, everyone, a 'wet-the-bed'." The unfortunate girl started crying. We turned away in embarrassment and felt sympathy for her humiliation, and revulsion and contempt for the loathsome Hoppy.

Sinead was unfortunate enough to be the target of Hoppy's anger for a time. Like most growing children, she was always hungry and was reduced to stealing apples from the orchard. After one such apple-scrumping expedition, when her pockets and knicker legs were full of illicit bounty, Sinead was on her way upstairs to hide them when the elastic of one knicker-leg broke. She turned and stood transfixed in horror as they tumbled down the stairs to land at the feet of Hoppy.

Hoppy looked up and saw her enemy, one of the children who openly defied her in front of the others and whose spirit she couldn't break. This was an opportunity to get back at her. She had caught Sinead red-handed and would make her pay dearly. Unfortunately for Hoppy, corporal punishment was out of the question. Then as Sinead turned to run up the stairs in an attempt to escape, her loose shoe somehow flew off and hit Hoppy in the face.

Hoppy was like a volcano erupting. Despite her lame foot, she ran up the stairs as if on fire. Catching up with Sinead at the entrance to the dormitory, she viciously grabbed her arm and had to exercise all her self-control to avoid hitting her. At that moment the mask slipped completely and if she had been allowed to physically punish Sinead, she would surely have killed her, so great was her anger. "You did that deliberately. You're coming with me to see Miss Brophy. She'll know how to deal with you," she snarled with fury.

Sinead desperately tried to escape Hoppy's clutches, which made her tighten her grip even more. She dragged the unfortunate Sinead down the stairs, still defiant and madly struggling in an effort to get away from her tight grip. Her shoe was still at the bottom and Hoppy scooped it up as they passed by without letting go of her grip on Sinead. They made a strange pair, both of them hopping along, one because she had a deformed foot and the other because one foot was shoeless. In other circumstances it would have been quite funny.

Unfortunately for Hoppy, Miss Brophy wasn't in her office: she was away from the convent for the day and so she had to punish Sinead herself. This took the form of extra chores on top of her already heavy workload, although Hoppy would have preferred physical punishment. It was against the rules, probably because an injured worker was no good to the management, so she had to be satisfied with that. She hissed at Sinead, "If I had my way, I'd beat you till you were black and blue."

How frustrating it must have been for her that she couldn't carry out her threat. The bruises from Hoppy's grip were visible on Sinead's arm for a few days after that.

Apart from waking the children in the morning, Hoppy's other responsibility was de-lousing the children's heads. She held a session every month when she checked all the girls' heads for nits, and de-loused those who were unfortunate enough to be infected.

At the start of each session, Hoppy hopped importantly into the washroom carrying her instruments of torture and with a look of happy anticipation on her face. She was going to enjoy this. This was one of the only times she appeared cheerful, apart from when she was humiliating some unfortunate child for bed-wetting. Setting up a chair in the middle of the washroom, she spread sheets of newspaper on the floor around the chair to catch any nits that might fall from an infected head. Her instruments of torture were a fine comb and a bottle of nit lotion, which she laid out on the counter that surrounded the hand basins.

Looking around, Hoppy said in a loud voice, "Who's first now? Come on now, don't be shy, get a move on, we haven't got all day." No one wanted to be first. The queue of reluctant children lined up, dreading what was about to happen. The younger ones would be pushed forward to the head of the queue. We old hands were wise enough to know not to be at the front, having attended many of these sessions and knowing just what to expect from Hoppy. After the first few victims had been assaulted, Hoppy ran out of steam and it wasn't quite so painful for the rest of the victims at the back of the line, as the assault on our scalps wasn't quite so fierce.

The first child sat squirming on the chair and a towel was wrapped tightly around her shoulders, pinning her arms to her side. Hoppy hissed, "Don't you dare fidget. Sit still or you'll get what's coming to you." When our turn came we remembered to keep our hands under the towel and tried to sit still during the ordeal because that made it quicker and we were soon free and on our way. We had long since learned to have combed the knots out of our hair by the time Hoppy attacked our heads, so that her nit comb wouldn't meet any resistance as it ploughed its way through our locks. If we involuntarily put our hands up to our heads when she scraped our scalp or tugged at a knot, she would hit us on the knuckles with the sharp edge of the steel comb, sometimes even drawing blood.

"Stop fidgeting. How do you expect me to do it properly if you keep moving?" she shouted angrily at any child who dared to move. This required no answer from the child, as the question was rhetorical. Hoppy wasn't concerned about what we thought or felt. Although we sometimes tried to hide from her to avoid her sessions, she always noticed if anybody was missing and came looking for us – nobody ever escaped her attentions; it was as though she had a mental list of names in her head. She was determined to get her full quota of satisfaction from this job and enforce her power over the children.

After she had viciously scraped the teeth of the steel comb through our hair, sometimes leaving bloody patches on the scalp, she cracked any unfortunate lice she might have found between her thumbnails. She seemed to take great satisfaction from murdering the lice; she considered them vermin, so therefore it wasn't really murder to her, although in the Catholic Church's teaching, they were all God's creatures and it was a sin to kill any of them. When she was satisfied that there were no nits left in our hair, she poured a liberal dollop of nit lotion into our wounds, which stung and burned for ages afterwards. It was irrelevant whether or not we had any nits: we still received a dose of her foul-smelling lotion.

Our two brothers visited us sometimes on Sunday afternoons, which was the official designated visiting time for families and relatives. The boys were scared of the nuns and sneaked in the side gate to avoid them. We met them without being seen and took them to our hiding place down the fields at the back of the poultry farm. There was an old shed there and we hid in it if the weather was bad and sat on the grass behind it in the summer, waiting while they hungrily ate the food we had stolen for them during the week.

One Sunday Callie noticed that their heads were infested with lice. They were scratching, so Callie examined them and noticed how badly they were infected. She thought for a moment: "You've got nits, that's why your heads are so itchy. I'll steal some of Hoppy's nit lotion to get rid of them. That'll soon stop them. Come back next Sunday. Be here at the same time when the nuns are not around and I'll do it then."

Later, when the nuns were in the chapel and the children were doing their homework in the classroom, we raided Hoppy's room to steal some nit lotion. It wasn't unusual for Callie to be in the vicinity of Hoppy's room at any particular time of the day, as she always had to do things for the little children on that floor. Usually there was nobody around at that time of the evening, but I kept watch all the same just in case Hoppy decided to come back early from her recreation. We were also wary of any of the sneaks seeing us because if they reported us to try to curry favour with the nuns, we would be in serious trouble. It would have been difficult, if not impossible, to try to explain what we were doing in Hoppy's room, which was strictly out of bounds to any of the children.

I checked to see whether anybody was in the dormitory or in the area around Hoppy's room. It was all clear. The door to her room was unlocked so Callie quickly entered and looked around for the nit lotion. I stood guard outside the door while she searched. It didn't take her long to find it in a cupboard beside the bed. Callie recognised the dark green bottle immediately, as she was familiar with it from the many nit-picking sessions we had attended.

The cupboard also contained the combs Hoppy used for her torture sessions, so it was obviously the right bottle. Without spilling any of the lotion, Callie carefully decanted it into a bottle she had brought with her for that purpose. She made sure that nothing in the cupboard was out of place or appeared to have been disturbed, left the room and closed the door firmly behind her.

But she was worried that she hadn't stolen enough: "I don't know if I've got enough for both of them but I can always come back again if there isn't enough." She then shuddered: "God, it's so creepy in there and smells horrible and musty just like her. Let's get out of here quickly before the old biddy comes back."

We bolted down the stairs and Callie hid the bottle in a secret hiding place, along with the food she had stolen for Anthony and Joseph ready for their Sunday afternoon visit. Strolling casually back to the classroom, we sat at our desks and did our homework as though it was an everyday occurrence to steal nit lotion from a nun's bedroom.

Chapter Twenty-Eight

It took two Sundays of treatment and a few more visits to Hoppy's room before the boys were free of lice. If Hoppy ever noticed that her supply of nit lotion was slowly diminishing, she could never have suspected that any of us was responsible – why would anybody want to steal nit lotion? That would have been a very weird thing to do. If she did notice, she probably thought it was just evaporating!

Chapter Twenty-Nine

Our days began by being woken by Hoppy at first light. She'd stand at the door to the dormitory and screech, "Wake up, wake up. Get up you lazy lot!" At a time when normal people were still asleep and dreaming happy dreams, we sleepily climbed out of our warm beds to get washed and dressed. At St Joseph's we made our beds in the same way that we had been taught at St Vincent's.

Still half asleep, we made our way to the chapel for Latin Mass. The priest droned on and on. If it wasn't for the fact that we had to stand up and then sit down again at the appropriate moments in the procedure, we would have fallen asleep. The fact that it was said in a language we didn't understand and sounded like mumbo jumbo made it even more difficult for us to be interested in the ceremony, as we didn't know what was happening nor did we particularly care.

The only thing that made it worthwhile for some of the older girls was seeing the altar boys. I wasn't yet at an age when the opposite sex held any interest for me and would have preferred to have still been in my bed fast asleep for a few more hours.

Chapter Twenty-Nine

After Mass, we took our seats in the refectory and had our breakfast of cold, grey, gluey, lumpy porridge and 'fried' bread. It was no surprise to us that the food here was just as bad as at St Vincent's, perhaps even worse considering that they had orchards and a poultry farm to supply the food. This menu, though, appeared to be the staple fare of orphanages everywhere. Most probably it was the cheapest food available to the nuns and could be bought cheaply in bulk. It consisted mostly of carbohydrates with a bit of protein and a few vegetables thrown in occasionally.

I don't suppose there were any vitamins left in the vegetables as they were generally overcooked and had been left lying around for ages before being served to us. Any meat that we received consisted mainly of fat and gristle, so there couldn't have been much nourishment in that either. The 'fried' bread wasn't actually fried, but was spread with dripping, layered in a big dish and cooked in the oven. Only the top layer was crispy. It was a treat to get one of those slices, so everybody competed for them. The lower layers were cold and thick with grease by the time they were served to us. It was most unappetising to be served this first thing in the morning.

The nun who was responsible for the kitchen delegated the job of cooking orphans' food to any of the girls who helped her while she cooked the nuns' food, taking great care over it. The girls were untrained and indifferent cooks and were always in a hurry. They resented having to work in the kitchen, so it wasn't surprising that they put as little effort as possible into the job. In all the years I spent in either of those institutions I don't ever remember having a decent meal.

At mealtimes, a lot of the food ended up on the floor under the tables as most of the children couldn't stomach it, even though they were always hungry. The toddlers, especially, hated it and they threw it under the table as it was forbidden to leave any. Even at that early age they were aware that they would be in trouble if the nuns discovered that they hadn't eaten their food, and they would be screamed and shouted at by whichever nun was on duty in the refectory. If we didn't get a crispy top slice of fried bread, we girls had devised ways to conceal the greasy bread that we couldn't face eating, for disposal later if we hadn't managed to somehow swallow it down. One of my jobs, which I particularly hated, was to clean the refectory after meals and scrape the greasy food off the floors under the little children's tables. To set the scene, our white enamelled teacups and plates were made of tin, and had worn patches from long use by the children over many years. We never had butter on our bread, only dripping.

The nutritional value of our food was most probably nil. The other meals that we received consisted mostly of mushy vegetable stew with any goodness cooked out of it. There was also a strange pie containing both tinned baked beans and peas. This made a frequent appearance, so it must have been very cheap to produce: a couple of big industrial-size tins of peas and beans and a few pounds of flour and some lard was probably sufficient to feed all the children for one meal.

On one occasion the stew was completely inedible as somebody in the kitchen had left a bar of carbolic soap in the pot. It tasted absolutely disgusting but was still served up. The nuns had no idea it tasted so bad as there was no way they would ever have eaten anything that was thrown onto our plates.

Often the carrots in the stew were rotten but they were still included. "Waste not, want not," was a particular saying the nuns were fond of, and when we objected to the horrible taste, we were told not to be ungrateful but to eat it or go hungry. The carrots arrived in big bags and the ones at the bottom would go bad, but nothing was ever wasted.

Although there was a poultry farm in the grounds, the only hen's egg I ever remember receiving was at Easter, when we were presented with one boiled egg each as a special treat.

Sometimes we were allowed to have the crusts from the nuns' sandwiches as treats; we looked forward to this as they had bits of egg and tomato clinging to them. I usually kept some back for my sisters when I brought them up from the kitchen. For dessert we also had rubbery pink blancmange and sago, which is harvested from the trunks of palm trees and has a similar consistency to tapioca. It always looked disgusting sitting there in the bowl and we quickly nicknamed that 'frog's eyes' too, as we didn't care much for that either! In fact there was nothing appetising about any of the food, ever.

When the autumn wind blew the apples from the trees, a few girls were taken for a walk along the coast road to Dalkey, not suspecting that, as usual with the nuns, there was an ulterior motive for this unusual break from work.

On the way back we stopped at local houses and the nun escorting us knocked on the doors. She asked permission from the owners for the orphans to pick up the windfall apples in their orchards. These were to be used to fill the apple tarts for the nuns' meals later. Although the convent had two big orchards, this wasn't enough for them. If they could get anything free, they would, and would use the 'poor orphans' as an excuse for their freeloading, although we never received any of the proceeds. It was extremely humiliating for us but as usual the nuns didn't consider our feelings. We didn't want to scrounge rotten apples from someone's garden, but we had no choice in the matter: we would have been hauled in for punishment if we had refused.

In the evenings, when the nuns were safely out of the way in the chapel saying their prayers, Callie and I raided the kitchens, orchards and storerooms to try to find something to eat, both for us and for our younger sisters. This was sometimes very productive. In a storeroom near the kitchen we sometimes discovered things like toothpaste or shampoo on the top shelf and appropriated them for our own personal use. It was nice to have toothpaste instead of salt for cleaning our teeth, and we hoarded it for when there was no nun around to wonder where we had acquired it.

Chapter Thirty

An elderly nun called DeeDee occupied a room on the first floor of the orphanage, just outside the refectory. This was a most unusual arrangement as she was the only occupant on the first floor at night.

At night, DeeDee was a long way from the other nuns in the convent and the children in the dormitories upstairs. We were puzzled about this mystery but never did find out why she had been banished to sleep there all alone. Maybe it was because she snored or walked in her sleep or perhaps she was there to guard the building. The other nuns who looked after the children slept either in the convent or on the top floors in cubicles in the dormitories with the children.

DeeDee could have been any age but looked like everybody's idea of a kind, old granny and was probably in her late 60s. There was always a slightly vague air about her and we assumed that she was a bit simple, as she appeared to be far away in another world for most of the time. When anybody spoke to her she snapped out of her daydream with a start. She had taken on, or had been assigned, the role of treasurer of the children's pocket money, that is for those children who were fortunate enough to receive any. As well as these activities, she also censored our mail and carried tales of any misbehaviour to Miss Brophy.

Although her room was just outside the refectory and she slept in the orphanage, she ate all her meals with the other nuns in their own dining room in the convent. On this same floor was a room where the clean clothes were placed on their return from the laundry. They were kept in cubbyholes, which were marked with our official numbers.

When it came to dealing with money, DeeDee showed a completely different side to her personality. She came to life then and was as cunning as a fox. She had obviously missed her true vocation in life. In another existence she would probably have been a little old lady in a corner shop doling out penny candies to children, whereas at St Joseph's she played at shops from her bedroom. She truly was a frustrated shopkeeper.

Her 'shop' consisted of a box of candies and some bars of chocolate that she brought out once a week so that we could go through the charade of spending our pocket money. We suspected that outsiders had donated these candies and chocolates as gifts for the children, but we never received them. They were not supposed to be for sale but somehow found their way into DeeDee's 'shop' and were sold to us, with the proceeds pocketed by the nuns.

This shop was where we also bought stamps for our weekly letters to Mammy in London. The nuns were so mean that they even charged us to keep in touch with our families. We had no alternative but to pay up because we couldn't just pop out to the shops if we needed anything. Even if there had been any near the orphanage, we wouldn't have been allowed to frequent them.

The only time any of the children managed to go into the town centre was when we were escorted there by one of the nuns. We were not allowed to deviate from the route determined by the nun escorting us, nor could we go into any of the shops along the way. Anyway, we were not supposed to have any money in our possession, other than that which DeeDee 'looked after' for us, and which we used for spending in her 'shop'.

DeeDee sold her wares at extortionate rates. She wasn't charitable enough to give free candies or chocolate to any of the children who didn't have money. If you didn't have cash you weren't welcome in her shop. There was no notice, as often seen in little corner shops, saying, "Don't ask for credit as a refusal often offends." But she should have used this motto, with the words 'especially orphans' added onto the end.

On Saturday mornings, after breakfast and when we had done the washing up and had cleaned the refectory from top to bottom, including scrubbing the tables and floors, DeeDee set up her stall in her bedroom. Saturday was the only day in the week when there was enough time for this activity. The rest of the week we were either at church services, meals, classes or working. But because there was no Mass on Saturdays in preparation for the big day on Sunday and the classrooms didn't have to be cleaned, it was more relaxed and DeeDee had time for her big performance. She relished it and probably looked forward to it all week. This was her big moment, which she appeared to have been anticipating all morning, as we had noticed from the aura of excitement that surrounded her.

There was a window at the front of her room that opened onto the corridor, and this became her stage. She would perform an elaborate charade of setting out boxes of candies on a table behind the window, with her cash register, which consisted of a tin box, on the side. Out of a drawer beside her bed she produced a cashbook in which she recorded each transaction. It had a stub of a pencil with an eraser on the end, so that she could rub out the total if she didn't like what she had charged and wanted to change it. The pencil was tied to the book with a piece of string just in case she lost it.

Occasionally, for a laugh, because it would inconvenience DeeDee when she discovered it was missing, one of the girls would steal her pencil while she was distracted. She would spend hours searching for her pencil, thinking she might possibly have lost it; whoever had stolen it would later leave it near her room for her to find.

After a long wait in the queue while she fussed around setting up her shop, the window eventually opened and DeeDee appeared glowing with pride: "Now, girls, line up nicely and wait your turn. No pushing and shoving please." She took so long over each sale that her customers became restless and would shuffle and sigh and complain: "For God's sake, hurry up. Are we going to be here all day?"

She popped her head out of the window: "Who said that? Don't blaspheme. You won't go to heaven if you take God's name in vain. If you're not patient you won't get anything at all." This was an empty threat, as everybody knew that DeeDee would never turn away a paying customer and a chance to make money.

Sometimes the chocolate would have a slight bloom on it because it had been there for such a long time. We suspected that Miss Brophy passed the candies on to DeeDee after eating the ones she and her friends liked. Miss Brophy had probably discarded the ones that were left as not being good enough for her refined palate and only fit for orphans. One of the jokers suggested, "Maybe DeeDee also has a good lick of it before she sells it to us." We all said in unison, "Ugh!" The joker continued, "Someone told me they saw her sucking the candies and those funny white bits on the chocolate are from her false teeth." We insisted, "We don't believe you. We'd know if she did. She wouldn't be able to put the paper back on properly because she's so clumsy. Whoever buys candies first, open one and check for signs of teeth marks. Angela, you always buy candies, so you go first."

But even Angela wasn't brave enough to risk buying DeeDee's candies after this conversation and instead bought bars of chocolate that were securely wrapped. Even though we were just joking around, we wouldn't have been at all surprised to have found DeeDee sucking on those candies and leaving the funny white bits on them.

Sometimes one of the girls, for a laugh, would shout out when she got round the corner, "Jesus Christ, hurry up woman," or, "Jesus, Mary and Joseph, what's she doing in there?" She then ran as fast as her legs could carry her, around the corner and down the stairs before DeeDee had a chance to see who had the impertinence to take God's name in vain. Her face would turn white from the shock, the colour draining away. She couldn't quite believe what she had just heard. She would then turn bright red and quiver with anger: "Who said that? Did anyone see who that girl was?"

Giggling, we pretended not to know who it was who had blasphemed. DeeDee was in a quandary about whether to come out of her shop to see who the culprit was, or to leave her goods at the open window and risk them being stolen. She had been caught out once before by that trick. When she returned to her shop some of her goods had disappeared, never to be seen again, and the girls denied all knowledge of the theft. The culprit had already eaten them, destroying the evidence. DeeDee decided that the sale of the candies was more important than any insult to God and continued serving the rest of her customers.

DeeDee also took on the role of censoring our mail, both incoming and outgoing. She examined every sentence and passed on to Miss Brophy anything she considered might be harmful to the image of the nuns or the Church. They must have feared that we might expose their cynical exploitation of the children to our families, if we had any, or perhaps it might somehow come to the attention of the authorities. Their moneymaking activities would be curtailed if the true extent of their exploitation of the children was uncovered. Miss Brophy would then send the letters back to us a few days later, with whole sentences or even paragraphs crossed out and nasty comments written in the margins.

Chapter Thirty

Occasionally a girl would be summoned to Miss Brophy's office and be accused of 'writing lies' about the orphanage or the nuns; she would be told to rewrite the letter to make it appear as innocuous as possible and shed a good light on the nuns. That usually had the desired effect of intimidating the girl. Callie once wrote to tell Mammy that one of us had had a minor accident. Miss Brophy sent for her and made her rewrite the letter while she stood over her, ensuring that she deleted every reference to the accident and dictating what she should write instead.

To pre-empt any complaints to our mother, Miss Brophy told her that we were lazy and ungrateful. We took this as a warning not to say anything, as we knew that it wouldn't achieve anything to tell Mammy the truth, as Turkey would take her revenge out on us later. If Mammy had tackled Miss Brophy, we would be punished for telling lies and our lives would be made a misery after Mammy had gone back to London. Besides, we didn't want to worry Mammy, as we knew how difficult things were. In London at that time it was difficult to find decent accommodation for a woman with children, and almost impossible with six children.

The nuns never praised us or said that we were doing well or that we had achieved anything or had some special talent. They only called us "lazy and ungrateful". I almost choked with indignation when I heard those lies spewing from Turkey's mouth.

On one occasion, when Mammy turned up unexpectedly to take us home for a few days, the nuns tried their hardest to prevent it. They used different ploys, such as saying that the house would be too cold and damp for us to stay in. Their apparent concern for our welfare wasn't convincing. It was out of character for them to be worried about our living conditions, as was evidenced by our quarters at the orphanage.

I suspect the real reason was that Christmas was coming and they needed our labour. Some children had recently left the orphanage and they were short of workers at such a busy time of the year, especially when there was extra work to be done because of all the extra visitors and entertaining that was required. There would be extra guests and social events when they would need lots of labour and our absence meant the other children would be burdened with the extra work.

When we arrived home, Mammy made big fires in the fireplaces in the dining and sitting rooms and brought down mattresses from the bedrooms to air. We all slept on the mattresses on the floor for the next few nights. It wasn't very comfortable, but we were so happy to be home we didn't care where we slept. I lay in the dark watching the firelight flickering on the ceiling, before happily drifting off to sleep, relieved to be away from the nuns for a short while.

We spent the short time we had at home meeting up with all our friends. We lived a normal life for a few days, enjoying our freedom from the restrictive regime at the orphanage. All too soon it was time to return to St Joseph's for us girls and to St Vincent's for the boys. Our hearts sank at the thought of parting from Mammy once more. It got harder each time and I would have given anything not to have to face the nuns ever again.

We arrived back in Dún Laoghaire in time for Mammy to catch the evening ferry back to England, after our usual emotional goodbye at the orphanage. We'd all be trying not to

Chapter Thirty

cry as Mammy told us, "Goodbye, I'll see you soon, it won't be long." It was still as difficult as ever to part. Callie, whose job it was to get the babies and toddlers ready for bed, stood at the window of the dormitory, watching until the ferry disappeared over the horizon, carrying her mother away from her once more. Then she turned her back on the window, dried her eyes and got on with her task of getting the little children ready for bed, comforting them and trying to get them off to sleep, before hand-washing their socks for the next day.

Chapter Thirty-One

Some of the other nuns ran their own little moneymaking schemes on the side. This usually meant extorting money from the orphans and the day girls, and even their parents, one way or another. Each nun had a different scheme. In some classes they collected for the babies in Africa. They didn't have a convent in Africa, so we can only assume that they passed the money on to Miss Brophy to forward to the babies in Africa. I'm sure she faithfully sent off a cheque to them every week, probably via the Vatican!

I was assigned to help in the kitchen. The nun in charge was called Miss Adams. The kitchen was her personal domain and she ruled over it with a rod of iron. She was a small, thin, nervous woman, with a bird-like face. Her brown hair was scraped back into a bun at the nape of her neck, over which she wore a hairnet that completely covered her head down to the middle of her forehead, with a knot tied in the middle. Nothing seemed to escape her beady little eyes, which seemed to swivel in all directions at once. Her face had a permanently harassed expression as she bustled around the kitchen dressed in a big apron. She was like a whirlwind as she hurried up and down the corridor leading to the convent and the nuns' dining room.

We came to recognise her footsteps, which had a sound all of their own, tapping on the wooden floor as she ran along the corridor, forever in a hurry. There was always a deadline to meet. She was full of anxiety, which she passed on to everyone who was forced to help her. She made us feel extremely harassed and jumpy when she was around: everything had to be perfect for the nuns' food and this just made her anxiety worse.

It was a pity she didn't pay the same attention to the orphans' food. This was left until after the nuns' meals had been made and little time or thought was given to its preparation. Her attitude was that we should be grateful for what we got and anything would do for us. Everything was thrown into a big pot and left to stew on the range with just an occasional stir with a big wooden spoon to stop it from sticking and burning.

The worst thing about working in the kitchen was the stress of being nagged and shouted at constantly by Miss Adams for every little thing. She'd yell, "Watch what you're doing! No, stir it properly! Watch the pot!" She was suspicious and didn't trust anybody, especially the orphans, who didn't volunteer to be there and given the choice would rather have been anywhere else.

We dreaded going to work in the hot, steamy, industrial-sized kitchen with its slippery red-tiled floors and big cooking ranges all along one white painted wall. There was a big wooden table in the middle of the room, which was laid with dishes and ingredients for the preparation of the endless meals. As soon as the washing up was finished from one meal, preparations began for the next. In the summer all the big windows were opened to try to let some fresh air in, but it didn't seem to make much difference: it was always steaming hot and uncomfortable in the kitchen.

All the ingredients for cooking, such as flour and sugar, were kept locked up in wooden boxes with padlocks on them. When a particular ingredient was needed, we had to go and ask Miss Adams to unlock the box and she measured it out exactly, before re-locking the padlock and rearranging the key in the bunch around her waist.

Did she perhaps imagine that if the boxes were left unlocked, one of us might decide to wander into the kitchen in the middle of the night and make a cake, maybe after a stroll through the orchard in the dark to collect some apples to make an apple tart? On reflection, though, it wasn't beyond the realms of possibility. We had now become so adept at manipulating the system to our advantage that it wouldn't have been beyond the scope of our imagination to think of doing something so surreal to assuage our constant hunger.

Despite her mistrust of other people, particularly the orphans, Miss Adams wasn't averse to making a bit of money on the side and had her own little racket going in the kitchen. At birthday times, girls who received money from their relatives could pay her to make a sponge cake with a bit of jam in the middle. This pathetic-looking cake was only big enough for the girl's immediate circle. All the other children had to watch with envy, salivating at the sight of the cake which assumed an unwarranted sumptuousness in their eyes, while the special birthday girl and her new best friends shared what appeared to be a fantastic-looking, mouth-watering concoction. In reality it was a simple little sponge cake with a tiny dollop of raspberry jam in the middle.

Those with no access to kind relatives with money never had a cake made for them. They just had to imagine how nice it would be to have one. When a girl's birthday was known to be approaching, she acquired lots of new friends. She would become the most popular girl in the orphanage until her cake had been eaten, then, like Cinderella, she turned back into an ordinary orphan when the cake was finished, but she didn't have to wait until the clock struck 12.

The fact that this was a dangerous place for children to work in didn't seem to concern the nuns. These conditions wouldn't have been tolerated in commercial premises, which are strictly controlled by the authorities, and where child labour is illegal. We were forced to carry heavy pans filled with boiling liquid and cook on the hotplates, even though some of us weren't very tall and couldn't see properly over the top. We also had to carry big dishes and utensils on the slippery floors and take heavy dishes out of hot ovens. The wonder was that none of us ever had a serious accident, apart from an occasional small burn or scald.

Unfortunately for Miss Adams, she couldn't be everywhere at once and didn't have eyes in the back of her head. There was a big industrial-sized walk-in fridge in the storeroom across the corridor from the kitchen. Just out of reach on the top shelf stood a big glass bowl full of juicy prunes in syrup. I developed an obsession with these prunes. Every time I was sent to get something from the fridge I looked at them with longing. With every day that passed, those prunes became increasingly tempting, and I was determined to have them. I racked my brains, trying to think of a way to get at them.

In the evenings, when the nuns were at prayers in the chapel and Miss Adams was safely out of the way for a while, the storeroom was left unlocked because other provisions were also stored there that might be needed, such as cocoa for their evening drink. But there was a padlock on the fridge door which Miss Adams locked before she left.

The storeroom was in a long corridor that led to the convent part of the building. At the other end was the laundry, which was also closed in the evenings. We hoped that Miss Adams might forget to lock the padlock, but it was a forlorn hope, as it was part of her routine to check everything: she had never forgotten to lock up in the evening.

I thought up various ways to try to get up to the top shelf, but most of my ideas, such as climbing up the lower shelves, I discarded as too dangerous. I probably wouldn't be able to get a good grip on the shelves with one hand and try to scoop the prunes out of the dish with the other. And what if the shelves were slippery? If I fell and made a noise somebody was bound to hear, maybe even Turkey, whose office was just along the corridor.

I eventually came up with a solution. Scouting around the storeroom, I spotted a big industrial-sized can of vegetables. I moved it near to the fridge and left it there to see if anybody noticed. After a few days I then moved it into the fridge, placing a few things in front of it to hide it from view. This made a

Chapter Thirty-One

perfect step and was tall enough for me to be able to stand and reach the shelf comfortably. Every time I was sent to get something from the fridge, I stood on the can and reached up for a prune. I was careful to take only one at a time so as not to arouse suspicion. Nobody ever noticed that there were less prunes in the dish and I was never caught.

It wasn't surprising that I had developed such a fixation for the prunes. We had frequent conversations about food. We were like prisoners who had been deprived of freedom too long and had become obsessed by the lack of decent food.

While I had my obsession with prunes, some of the older girls were also obsessed with boys or clothes. In the outside world this would have been recognised for what it was, normal teenage development. But here it took on a different meaning for the girls because it was outlawed by the nuns, who somehow thought it abnormal to be interested in things other than religion, especially the opposite sex.

Chapter Thirty-Two

The nuns were a strange collection of individuals. Most of them would have had difficulty surviving in the real world. It was obvious that the Church hadn't chosen them for their brains or personality and certainly not for their childcare skills. Most of the nuns who had day-to-day contact with us were extremely ignorant of the outside world and lived very different lives to people in the real world outside of their own narrow one. I am sure a psychologist would have had an interesting time assessing their suitability for looking after children, especially emotionally disturbed ones.

Some of the nuns stand out because they had their own peculiar characteristics or were particularly bad-tempered, but others were like ghosts who passed through our lives without ever speaking to us or even acknowledging our existence. We never knew their names or what they did in the convent. They weren't involved in the day-to-day running of the orphanage, the school or any of the businesses, as far as we knew.

We only had daily contact with the nuns who were directly involved in our lives, those who allocated the workload to us in the various houses or taught us in school alongside the secular teachers.. Most of them had nothing interesting or unusual about them to mark them out in my memory, but they all had one thing in common: they constantly criticised everything we did and always found fault.

They were drab, humourless people without personality or charm; these days they would be termed 'grey people' – grey hair, grey clothes, grey personalities. They appeared to live for no other purpose than to worship a god they couldn't be certain existed but had to take on faith, and hope that when they died they would go to a place called heaven.

Most of them were of an indeterminate age: they could have been anywhere between 30 and 100 but most were probably middle-aged. They all wore their hair scraped back in the same style buns. They wore suits over a blouse and, as a concession to the hot weather in the summer, they were allowed to take off the jacket. These suits were usually grey, black or navy, and made of tweed or gabardine. They also wore thick stockings and laced-up black shoes with a little stumpy heel, except for Hoppy.

Miss Brophy's suit is forever etched in my mind. It was made of rough grey tweed, and she wore it over a white blouse with a brooch pinned at the neck. This only served to accentuate the lump of loose skin that hung over the tight collar of the blouse. Her jacket was too small for her and only reached down to her waist. One of my most vivid memories is of the thick tweed jacket in front of my face, as she screeched with fury like a banshee.

Her face became red with anger as the fury spewed from her mouth. Her fat neck wobbled and I half expected her to explode in bits all over me. As I tried to back off, she leaned down further, screaming and almost spitting in my face. It was an unforgettable and thoroughly frightening experience for all the children, even those watching, hoping against hope that they weren't in the firing line, but knowing that their turn would inevitably arrive.

There was one exception to the other nuns: Miss Brannigan was in her mid-20s. She seemed totally out of place because she was so different from the others. She hadn't yet acquired the veneer of coldness and inhumanity like the rest of them. She was very thin and frail-looking, with an ethereal air about her. Her brown hair, fine features and elegant bone structure seemed out of place amongst the extremely plain or even ugly features of the other nuns.

Miss Brannigan was in charge of the babies and toddlers, but had no control over them. She would plead with them to behave but they took no notice of her, and she was frequently reduced to tears. Callie often took pity on her and helped her out by playing with the children, who adored her.

Miss Brannigan had lived all her life in institutions, as she was also an orphan. She suffered from ill health and spent long periods in bed. She died in her 20s, but we never knew what illness she had. As with all the nuns who died there, she was buried in a grave in the grounds.

One evening while the nuns were in the chapel saying their evening prayers, Callie was looking after the younger children in one of the classrooms. A little two-year-old girl called Sheila, who was climbing on the furniture, fell and hit her head on the edge of a broken desk. She was taken to the local hospital where she received stitches.

Later, when Callie was in hospital herself, this same child had an almost identical accident that resulted in her being blinded for life. Callie was very attached to little Sheila and is haunted by the thought of what happened to her, even though there was no way she could have prevented it. The nuns were more interested in saying their prayers and reserving their place in heaven than providing proper supervision or care for the children, so it was surprising that there weren't more serious accidents.

All of these nuns appeared to hate the children and we, in turn, despised them too, with their two-faced hypocrisy and sanctimonious ways, always preaching to the children but never practising what they preached. To the outside world they appeared to be caring people but we knew that our welfare didn't matter to them. They were not interested in us as people and we didn't know anything about them. The only thing they seemed to care about was making money. That appeared to be their driving force, not the love of God as they claimed, so no wonder we had no respect for them.

Their attitude towards us showed that they had no concept of the meaning of love. They couldn't appear to see the contradiction between their actions and what they preached to us. They really must have thought we were stupid to believe any of their lies.

There was one particular orphan, a girl called Anne, who had been in the care of the nuns for a long time, possibly since she was a baby. She was very disruptive and completely out of control most of the time. The nuns frequently put her forward for adoption to try to get rid of her as they couldn't handle her. They didn't appear to want her in the orphanage any longer, despite her behaviour probably being a result of their abuse and neglect. However hard they tried, she wouldn't do any work, was insolent to the nuns and fought with and bullied the other children. They decided that she had to go.

Anne was fostered with several unwitting families with the intention of eventual adoption after a settling-in period. She was sent to three families in one year but was returned to the orphanage each time, usually within a few weeks, because she was unable to settle and the families couldn't handle her. She was so disturbed, especially when there were other children in the prospective adoptive families, that it was impossible for her to live a normal family life. Everybody at the orphanage dreaded her eventually return. It was relatively peaceful during her absence, but we knew that she would try to bully us and cause trouble whenever she eventually returned, like a ball bouncing back and forth.

Cases of severely disturbed children weren't unusual in the orphanage, as at St Vincent's. They never received any help for their problems from the nuns but instead were punished for their personality defects and inability to interact normally in an abnormal environment.

Chapter Thirty-Three

We were very surprised and puzzled when one day the nuns started being nice to us and immediately suspected an ulterior motive on their part. It was most unusual, and we couldn't work out why they had changed their usual pattern of behaviour towards us. We knew, however, that it wasn't from the goodness of their hearts. "Maybe there's going to be an official inspection," we speculated. We didn't have long to wait, as the reason became apparent soon enough.

It appeared that the hierarchy was becoming concerned at the lack of new recruits to the order. The supply of fresh blood was dwindling, and more people were desperately needed to keep the business running. They decided to organise a recruitment drive among the orphans in an effort to enlist some new novices. The chaplain was appointed to interview applicants from among the girls who had 'volunteered' their services.

One or two of the girls, naive, unworldly, with no experience of the outside world or of real life, had been brainwashed into thinking they had what the nuns called a 'vocation' or a calling to the religious life. According to the nuns, they had been singled out, as only special people received this privileged calling from God.

As we were constantly told that we were no good and would never amount to anything, why would they want us as members of their order? They really must have thought we were stupid. Callie decided to pay the nuns back for insulting her intelligence. "They really must think we're dim. Here's what I'll do," she said. She volunteered as a joke and also to get out of work for a whole afternoon. An invitation was issued to each applicant to come to the parlour for afternoon tea and a chat with Miss Brannigan. As she was the only young nun in the order, they used her to try to persuade the girls that this was the life they wanted.

After serving tea and fairy cakes, she tried her best to convince them that it was a wonderful life and a great career choice. However, they all knew otherwise: they had seen what a miserable existence she led, surrounded by elderly, crabby nuns old enough to be her grandmother, looking after children she couldn't control and didn't appear to like very much. As an untrained and unwilling nursery maid was the best example they could come up with to promote the joys of religious life, nobody was convinced that it was a good career choice; also they didn't want to stay in that place a minute longer than was absolutely necessary.

The candidates were summoned one by one to the privacy of the confessional for an interview with the chaplain. When Callie's turn arrived, she grinned behind Miss Brannigan's back as she was escorted out of the room and down the corridor to

Chapter Thirty-Three

the chapel. Stopping at the entrance, the nun said, "Go straight into the confessional now. Father McCartney's waiting for you."

Callie entered the wooden box and sat down on the narrow seat on the opposite side to the priest behind the grille. She looked at him and smiled – she was going to enjoy this. Father McCartney got straight to the point: "Well, hello there, Callie. How are you today? Why do you want to be a nun? Have you got a vocation?" She played along with him: "What exactly do you mean by a 'vocation', father?" He replied, "A calling to the religious life." Callie tried not to giggle as she told him, "Not really but I'd like to go to Africa and look after babies." Father McCartney had to tell Callie, "But I'm afraid the order doesn't have a convent in Africa so you can't go there."

Callie continued her game: "Well maybe somebody else does." Father McCartney scrambled to convince Callie that she needed to stay there: "But we're not recruiting for anyone else, wouldn't you like to stay in Ireland and do good works here?" But Callie fired her final shot: "Well, if I can't go to Africa, then I'm not interested." But he wasn't going to let this one slip through the net if he could help it: "But just think, you could even go to college and train as a teacher! Now wouldn't that be grand?"

However hard he tried, there was no way that he could persuade Callie to join the order. She told him that she loved babies and was attracted by the glamour of foreign travel but if she couldn't go to Africa she wasn't interested. She then told him, "I don't want to be stuck in Dublin all my life. I want adventure!"

To save face, she was turned down as being unsuitable for the position; not serious enough was the verdict. After all, this was a business that needed to generate large sums of cash. Her romantic notions of helping people, and especially needy children, wouldn't bring money into the coffers. They needed a constant flow so that the upper echelons could continue to live in luxury and, besides, their empire had not yet expanded as far as Africa. All in all, she was the wrong person for the job.

When Callie came out of the chapel and back into the parlour, she smirked at the other girls sitting in a row waiting their turn. "Well, how did you get on Callie?" enquired Miss Brannigan. Callie told her, "The priest doesn't seem to be keen on the idea of me going to Africa and if I can't go there to be a missionary and look after babies, then I want to be an air stewardess instead!" All the girls giggled, and Miss Brannigan didn't know whether to laugh or tell Callie off for being irreverent.

The rest of the girls were ushered in to see the priest one by one and he spent the afternoon in a fruitless effort trying to recruit them. They said they wanted to be missionaries too. Eventually he realised that there was some sort of conspiracy going on and decided to give up the effort.

Then, when he had almost given up hope and was about to shut the confessional, one girl arrived who did actually want to be a nun. He must have thought he had died and gone to heaven! When she came out from the confessional with shining eyes and returned to the parlour, the other girls looked at her in astonishment.

One girl said, "You must be mad to want to join this lot. The very idea of staying here for the rest of my life gives me the creeps." Another added, "Me too. I can't wait until I'm 16 and can get as far away from here as I can." They thought she must have been not quite right in the head to want to give up normal life, and the opportunity in a few years' time to escape from the nuns and the orphanage forever.

However, this gullible young girl had always been considered a bit strange because she was so religious, and even more so now that she had actually chosen to spend the rest of her life living with the enemy. She was considered a 'goody-goody' who couldn't be trusted by the other children anymore; thereafter we avoided her like the plague in case she told on us to the nuns.

The children couldn't wait for the day they were old enough to escape from the nuns for good and longed for the time when they could leave that horrible place forever. We couldn't understand why this girl would want to live in such an awful place with those despicable creatures, becoming in time just as unhappy, frustrated and bitter as them. It was beyond our comprehension how the nuns could think that anybody would want to follow in their footsteps and be like them. But this girl proved to be the exception to the rule.

The recruitment drive was deemed to be extremely successful, and the poor soul was accepted into the order as a novice. She was whisked away for training at Carysfort College and entry into the sisterhood before she had a chance to change her mind and realise that she didn't have a 'vocation' after all.

Chapter Thirty-Four

Even though we lived in the same institution as our siblings, we lived quite separate from each other. Most of the time we didn't see that much of each other because we were at school or working in one of the numerous buildings. Sometimes we were lucky if we saw each other at meals or when we eventually staggered to bed, worn out from the day's work.

There were days when we didn't see our sisters at all if our work extended beyond our bedtime or we had an extra early start in the morning, for instance when we had to cater to outsiders attending religious retreats. The guests stayed in the retreat house across the playground and there was a lot of work involved in looking after them.

The people taking part in the retreat expected their breakfast to be ready for them on their return from Mass, and the girls had to prepare it. Their beds had to be made and the retreat house had to be cleaned from top to bottom every day, and of course an evening meal had to be provided. I don't know whether they had a midday meal because

Chapter Thirty-Four

we were at lessons, but it wouldn't surprise me if some of the girls had been kept off school to make lunch for them.

If it hadn't been for Callie we wouldn't have been as close to each other as we were. She made sure that we kept our identity as a family. Callie also worked in the two retirement homes, which were located elsewhere in the grounds, serving meals to bedridden old ladies and generally looking after them in the evenings when the nuns were at prayers and recreation or even nursing them in some cases.

After a time she discovered new ways to manipulate the system to her advantage. When the nuns were safely out of the way and the old ladies were asleep, she had total control of the whole place. She was left in charge of the old ladies in one of the two retirement homes for the evening. Their bedrooms were upstairs, while she was stationed downstairs in the office/parlour to answer the telephone and the door in the event of unexpected visitors. This meant that the telephone was left unguarded: an open invitation to Callie.

Settling herself at the desk with a tray of tea and a plate of fairy cakes, she spent the evening chatting to her friends on the phone. There was never any danger of the nuns finding out about her use of the phone from the bill, because itemised bills didn't exist at that time. They never caught her because she had plenty of warning of their return from the chapel or recreation, as they had to ring the front doorbell to be let in.

Sinead was still a rebel and was always in trouble. She was punished regularly by the nuns but no matter how much they tried, like Sister Magdalena at St Vincent's, they couldn't break her spirit and she defied them to the bitter end, right up until the moment she left the orphanage for good, without any regret on either side. They were as equally relieved to see the back of her as she was to leave them.

Imelda was still very quiet and withdrawn. She craved affection but that wasn't forthcoming from the nuns. They were incapable of providing any love or affection to the children, even the tiniest babies or toddlers. Imelda had developed a nervous habit of biting her fingers until they bled. Once, to try to get the attention she craved, she stole a nun's keys and hid them, hoping that when she found them later she would be praised her crazy scheme wasn't discovered. But sadly her behaviour wasn't unusual among the children, starved as they were of attention and affection.

I was physically run down from the constant hard work, lack of proper food and disturbed sleep. This manifested itself physically in boils on various parts of my body, styes on my eyes and whittles on my fingers. All of these ailments were very painful and went untreated by the nuns, except once when Hoppy lanced a boil with a darning needle, which she sterilised by holding the tip in a match flame for a few seconds. Thick pus oozed out when she lanced it, but when it healed, another erupted on a different part of my body and the whole process was repeated.

I had never before or since suffered from boils or styes, except many years later when I went on a vegetarian diet and developed the same sort of boils that I had experienced in the orphanage. They were obviously due to a lack of something, probably protein, in my diet.

All of us suffered from the poor diet at St Joseph's, which hadn't improved with our transfer from St Vincent's, and consisted mostly of carbohydrates with some vegetables with all the nutrients boiled out of them, and the occasional piece of very poor-quality gristly meat. The food wasn't enough for growing children, never mind those engaged in hard manual work. It was of the poorest quality, and we were all underweight and malnourished.

Apart from the physical neglect and the lack of proper nourishment, no regular dental treatment or medical care was provided for the children. When Callie was in severe pain with a toothache, it was only after three days, when her face began to swell so badly that her eye was almost closed, that she was taken to visit a local dentist. Her tooth had to be extracted because of a bad abscess.

Of course, the nuns made no allowances for her condition, and she was still expected to do her allocated work as well as attending school. The only concession they made was to allow her to go to bed early some nights even though her homework wasn't done: the nuns didn't consider homework to be important in the grand scheme of things, because they had no expectations for Callie's future and didn't expect her to go on to higher education.

All of the children suffered problems from the lack of dental treatment, probably as a result of the lack of calcium-rich food in our diet. They never received regular medical checks, except when there was an accident or a sudden illness requiring emergency treatment.

Callie had developed a persistent hacking cough a short while earlier. When she was at Mass in the chapel, Miss Coote, sitting behind her, would thump her in the back each time she coughed. The nuns never thought to seek any medical treatment for it; it was just a nuisance when it disturbed proceedings in the chapel. She had also started sleepwalking, to the amusement of the other girls and the annoyance of the nuns.

One of Callie's first jobs every morning was to arrange the priest's tray and leave it on the parlour table in readiness for his breakfast after Mass. The tray was laid with a white linen cloth and a little vase of flowers. It always contained a tempting glass of chilled orange juice that had been lovingly poured out by the nun in the kitchen into a sparkling, polished glass.

Sometimes the priest didn't drink his juice, and one morning Callie was so tempted by the sight of it sitting there, unwanted on the tray, that she surreptitiously drank it behind his back while clearing the table. He was so engrossed in reading the morning paper that he didn't appear to notice that she had drunk his juice. This gave Callie an idea.

She loved and coveted orange juice but until then had not found a way to drink it without being caught by the nuns. One morning, knowing that most of the time the priest didn't drink it, she couldn't resist gulping almost all of it down before he arrived for his breakfast. She was then so desperate to replenish the glass that she filled it up with water. That wasn't a good idea because it didn't look like orange juice anymore.

Then she had a brilliant idea: while the nun was busy in the kitchen cooking the bacon and eggs, she crept into the walk-in fridge and found a raw egg, which she beat up with the fork on the priest's tray and then put in the glass to cover up her crime. The priest never appeared to notice that his juice had been tampered with, so Callie became bolder and started drinking the juice and replacing it with a beaten egg every day, mixing it into the little drop of juice at the bottom of the glass so that it didn't smell too much of egg.

Thereafter, on her way back to the kitchen with the breakfast tray, she found a place to dispose of the new drink before the nuns became aware something fishy was going on. One day she was disappointed to discover that the orange juice had been changed to grapefruit juice, which wasn't to her liking, as it tasted too sharp.

Chapter Thirty-Five

It appeared from the nuns' way of thinking that secondary education was a complete waste of time for orphans. We shouldn't have any expectations in life and should only expect to work as servants and skivvies. In that case why would we need higher education?

Callie had now turned 15 and the nuns had their own ideas for her future. She was to become a domestic servant, working in the business full time for what amounted to little more than pocket money. Mammy's wishes didn't count as far as they were concerned, and it didn't even occur to Miss Brophy to consult her.

The nuns decided that they needed someone to work in the retirement home and simply chose Callie. Mammy was astonished when Callie tearfully told her the news by phone one evening when the nuns were in the chapel. Choking back tears, she told Mammy, "Miss Brophy is insisting I work in the retirement home. She says I can't go to college, I have to stay here and work for them." Mammy immediately contacted Miss Brophy to discuss the matter.

Chapter Thirty-Five

Fortunately for Callie, Mammy insisted that she be sent to Dún Laoghaire College to take a course in shorthand, typing and bookkeeping. After much resistance from Miss Brophy, she eventually relented and allowed Callie and four other girls to be released daily from the orphanage to attend college. The other girls were astonished and couldn't understand the reason why they were permitted to attend college but were thrilled all the same. It was unheard of in the history of the orphanage.

Perhaps Miss Brophy realised there might be some benefit to be gained in having them learn shorthand and typing. It might bring some benefit to her business; otherwise she would never have released the girls. Apparently she had told one of the girls that when she had finished her course in shorthand and typing, she would obtain a job for her in the local solicitor's office and she could continue to live at the orphanage. This was another moneymaking scheme for the nuns that would help swell the coffers, and this is why Miss Brophy's opposition melted away.

The five girls loved going to college and the freedom of being away from the nuns for a major part of each day. They could pretend they were normal, and the orphanage and nuns didn't exist. They soon made friends and enjoyed being the same as everybody else for a little while, although they stood out from the other pupils by their clothing and 'less than carefree' attitude. All the other girls were dressed in good quality clothes, while the orphans had to make do with hand-me-downs that had been owned by many other children before them.

Although they didn't tell anybody that they were from the orphanage, it must have been obvious, because no self-respecting mother would have allowed their child to leave the house in such awful clothes. The girls were never able to invite their new friends back to their house for tea or to meet their family; it was their guilty secret that they lived with the nuns up the road, and they didn't want to become objects of pity.

As far as the opposite sex was concerned, the only contact – it could hardly be called contact – was when we saw the altar boys and the priest at Mass and confession. The nuns considered it a sin to think about boys. In their eyes the opposite sex was an alien species that would probably make us pregnant just by looking at us. If they had known of the existence of the yashmak and chador, worn by women in Middle Eastern countries, we would probably have been forced to wear it.

Yet in the company of men, especially priests, the older girls behaved like giggling schoolgirls. They twittered and simpered like repressed Victorian women. As with teenage girls the world over, a lot of their conversations were about boys: "Have you seen the new altar boy? He's gorgeous." Another girl would chime in: "Of course we have, don't we spend most of our lives in the chapel? How could we miss him?" They were desperate to know if the altar boy had noticed them: "Do you think he likes any of us?" "I think I saw him looking at you this morning, Frances," said Mary. Frances blushed and giggled. "I wish he had," she said, as we all laughed. We endlessly discussed the merits of the newest recruit, who was just an ordinary boy but was elevated to the heights of a movie star in the eyes of the love-starved girls.

It was evident that something was not quite normal about the nuns in their repressed attitude to sexuality. Their primitive views of life outside their own little enclosed world, where it was a sin for healthy teenage girls to be interested in boys, were extremely Victorian and there was no such thing as sex education for the girls. Their teaching over and over again was: "It's a sin to kiss a boy and any girl who does so will immediately become pregnant and burn forever in the flames of hell."

It was also a sin for teenage girls to harbour any fantasies about boys, which they should confess to the priest at the weekly confessional. Despite this and their attempts to prevent the girls from mixing with the opposite sex, human nature always found a way.

During daily Mass, different altar boys attended the priest in serving the sacraments. They were objects of desire, those poor gangling, spotty youths, and some of the girls wrote them little love notes. Unfortunately, these letters somehow found their way into the hands of Turkey. She was apoplectic with rage and determined to teach the offenders a lesson. Although the letters were unsigned, she somehow found out who had written them. The girls were sent to the priest next day to confess their sins, but he just laughingly told them not to be silly and to go away.

On another occasion, the nuns held a dance for the parish helpers and invited the altar boys to attend. Some of the older teenage girls, who were aged about 16, went for a walk with them. This terrible crime was discovered by some busybody and reported to Miss Brophy. The girls were summoned to her office first thing the next day. They were made to wait outside her office, aware that they had committed some awful crime but not completely sure what it could be.

They were herded, one by one, into the room where a furious and intimidating Turkey sat behind her big desk. The girls standing quaking in their boots outside could hear her shouting and screaming at the offender standing before her. They desperately tried to prepare for their coming ordeal by trying to guess what they might have done wrong and think of something that might mitigate their crime.

When their turn arrived and they were called into her room, she accused them: "You are sex-mad and are going to hell. You are no better than tramps and prostitutes just like your mothers." Ironically, she was the one with a mind like a sewer as she could imagine all the awful things she accused their mothers of. Although they had only been for a walk down the road and were entirely innocent of any wrongdoing, they were sent to see the priest next morning to confess their 'sin', the sin of being normal teenage girls. Father McCartney once again laughed when he heard their made-up confessions and told each and every one of them not to be so silly and to go away.

This wasn't good enough for Turkey. She wanted revenge and summoned all of them to her office once more. From that day on, none of the girls were to be allowed anywhere near the vicinity of the front of the chapel and the altar boys. They were forced to sit in the back pews and were watched to make sure they didn't make any eye contact with the opposite sex. The girls who had the job of cleaning the chapel were transferred to other work far away from any sight of the altar boys; only those deemed 'holy' enough were allowed this privilege.

Callie's punishment was to clean the refectory from top to bottom. She did such a good job and the nuns were so impressed with her work that she was promoted to permanent cleaner, which taught her a valuable lesson: Never let them know what you're capable of as they will only exploit you.

Still, even Turkey's disapproval couldn't prevent the girls from lusting after the altar boys and their conversations soon returned to normal. One of the older girls fell in love with a local teenage Teddy Boy and sneaked out in the afternoons to meet him. She also met him sometimes in the evenings when the nuns were at prayers. After a while she became pregnant by him. One day she and her sister disappeared from the orphanage, never to be seen or spoken of again.

It wasn't surprising that occasionally one of the older teenage girls became pregnant. They yearned for the love and affection which was not forthcoming from the nuns. None of the girls knew anything about the facts of life. How were we supposed to find out about the birds and the bees in that environment? Sure, we gossiped with each other, but the nuns never sat us down and explained how things happened.

The girls were not supposed to have normal teenage fantasies. Callie, on one of her visits home, discovered the music of Elvis Presley and bought a little book about him.

On her return to the orphanage she hid it in her locker. Later she found it torn up into little pieces under her pillow. It was considered by the nuns to be a 'sin' to possess such a thing.

Surprisingly, she wasn't sent to confession for this: the book's destruction was obviously considered warning enough. Miss Boylan had earlier been seen rooting through the lockers and we took it for granted that this was her doing. Any of the other girls would just have taken it for themselves, hidden it and then taken great joy in sneaking a look at Elvis and his 'pelvis'!

On another occasion we were taken to the cinema at Easter to see a religious film in which we had no interest. But it was a great opportunity to get out of work and away from the orphanage for a while. When we arrived at the cinema we discovered that it had finished the previous week, and an Elvis Presley film was on instead. We teenage girls were very excited when we saw this and begged to be allowed to see it, saying, "Please Miss Boylan, please," but she refused, probably because she had no power to make such an independent decision.

Full of disappointment at the outcome and frustrated at the stupidity of the nuns, we were quickly marched back to the orphanage. We hated them and their stupid rules more than ever and longed for the time when we could be free of them and live normal lives like other girls our age.

If we ever had to go out in public, either down into the town or for a walk with the nuns, we tried to avoid being seen with them, especially in the town centre. It was acutely embarrassing for teenage girls to be seen in the company of women old enough to be our grannies, so we would lag as far behind them

Chapter Thirty-Five

as we possibly could. There was also a stigma attached to being an orphan, as though it was our fault and we were somehow responsible for losing a parent or parents.

Chapter Thirty-Six

One day a mass X-ray van came to the college and stationed itself outside the front door looking for patients. Callie decided to avail herself of the opportunity, along with some of her classmates, as an excuse in order to 'go on the ockie', meaning to play truant. About three weeks later, Miss Coote was waiting for her when she returned to the convent at lunchtime. She was instructed to get her wash bag and hairbrush and come to the front door of the convent when she was ready. Callie was curious about the reason for this strange command. Miss Coote told her, "When you're ready, Patrick will be waiting for you with the car outside the front door. Get everything packed in your bag and meet him there. Hurry up."

Before Callie has a chance to ask her anything, Miss Coote disappeared. There was no explanation and Callie was given no time to tell anybody or even to say goodbye to us.

Patrick the chauffeur was waiting in his car at the front of the convent. He instructed her to sit in the back seat and kept the windows open, even though it was a cold day and the wind whistled through the car. Callie assumed that it was because he smoked, and Miss Brophy wouldn't have approved of the smell of stale cigarettes in the car. Callie turned round to look at the door of the convent, expecting at any minute to see a nun coming out to join her. Without warning the car jolted forward. A nervous Callie asked, "Isn't anybody coming with us?" Patrick told her, "No. There's just you and me."

Naturally Callie was curious about the reason she was alone in the car with him. "Where are we going?" she asked. It was only then she found out where they were headed, as Patrick replied, "We're going to the hospital in the Phoenix Park." She was puzzled: "Why, is somebody sick?" She became worried when Patrick added, "It's the TB hospital." Callie demanded to know, "But why are we going there?" He then dropped the bombshell. "Didn't the nuns tell you? You've got TB."

And that was how Callie discovered she had tuberculosis. She was stunned, so shocked for a moment she was at a loss for words. She finally managed to get out, "Are the nuns going to meet me there?" But Patrick had no idea. He had just been given his orders to drive Callie to the hospital, he hadn't been given any more information: "I just don't know. They didn't tell me anything else. Maybe there will be somebody there to meet you."

When they arrived at the hospital, Patrick didn't even take the time to park; he just stopped the car outside the front door for a minute and said, "Take your bag and go in there," pointing to the hospital entrance. Callie got out and closed the door. He drove away, leaving her standing on the pavement not knowing what to do, feeling completely abandoned and confused.

Inside, a woman at the reception, noticing her confusion, called her over. "What's your name?" she asked. She told her. The receptionist was friendly, something Callie wasn't used to. "Ah, yes, we've been expecting you. The orphanage phoned us to say you were coming. Sit down for a moment Callie.", she said. She picked up some papers and made a phone call. A little while later a nurse arrived to collect Callie. She smiled and said, "Hello Callie. I'm Nurse O'Brien and I've come to take you to the ward. Follow me."

Callie followed her along endless corridors until they arrived at a door leading to a ward. Inside were rows of beds against one wall, with open doors on the other side leading out to a garden. They entered the ward and passed a row of beds filled with inquisitive occupants, who stopped chatting as Callie passed by. Some smiled at her and said, "Hello." The nurse stopped at an empty bed in the corner. Pulling the curtains around the bed, she instructed Callie: "Undress and get into the bed. I'll be back in a minute when you're finished."

Callie got undressed, put her clothes in the bedside locker and changed into a hospital gown that was lying on the bed. The sheets had been tucked so tightly under the mattress that it was like a straightjacket. As usual, the pillows and mattress were rock hard. She got into bed and sat there waiting for the nurse, curious to find out what would happen next.

Nurse O'Brien came back with a covered jug of water and a glass for Callie, which she put on the bedside locker. She told her, "I have to take your blood pressure and temperature now." She put a thermometer in Callie's mouth. "This will take a few minutes. Then we'll do your blood pressure," she said. Callie, with her mouth full, could only nod.

The nurse then brought out the blood pressure equipment. This was a new experience for Callie. She placed the cuff around her upper arm and then pumped it up using the attached bulb. Placing her stethoscope on Callie's arm, she listened for a little while. When she was satisfied with the reading she deflated the cuff and took it off. Nurse O'Brien wrote the result on Callie's chart and put the equipment back in its box. "That's you done for now. The doctor will be around to see you later. Let me know if you need anything."

After all the admittance procedures had been completed, Nurse O'Brien pulled the curtains back and Callie was able to see her new neighbours again. She was curious about them, and they were just as curious about her, and they immediately started chatting.

"Hello, love," said the woman in the next bed. "What's your name? I'm Mary." "I'm Callie." Mary was full of questions: "You're a bit young to be in here. How old are you?" Callie said she was 15. Mary smiled as she added, "15? You're just a baby, so you are."

Another woman asked, "Where's your mammy? Didn't she come with you?" After hearing Callie's explanation, the other patients eagerly joined in the conversation. Callie regaled them with tales of the nuns and the orphanage. Later, when the doctor came to examine her, he told Callie that she would need many months of complete bed rest and drug therapy to cure her. She would also need building-up, as she appeared to be malnourished, he said.

He prescribed a bottle of Guinness every day for her. This was because it contained a lot of iron, necessary to help build her strength up.

After her admittance to the sanatorium, Callie never saw or heard from the nuns again. They never called to see her, never wrote to her or even acknowledged her existence. This was probably because of the impact it would have had on their businesses had it become public knowledge that there was TB in the orphanage.

As well as the effect on the nuns' other businesses, the day girls would probably have been withdrawn from the school and the building closed down. Making money was more important than the health of the orphans; why else would they so callously dump Callie at the sanatorium and have nothing more to do with her?

The nuns didn't even think it necessary to tell us, her sisters, that Callie had been admitted to hospital. It was only later that we realised that she was no longer in the orphanage. We kept asking, "Where's Callie? Where's our sister?" It was only after several hours and endless questions that we found out she had been taken away.

So we only found out the facts that evening when we discovered that Callie's bed had disappeared from the dormitory. For a while we stood looking in puzzlement at the empty space, unable to grasp the implications. What had happened to Callie? Where was she?

I was shocked and frantic with worry, as I knew that she hadn't been feeling well for some time and was worried that something awful had happened to her. When I found Miss

Chapter Thirty-Six

Coote, I asked, "Where's Callie? Her bed's gone. What's happened to her?" She coldly replied, "She's been taken to the hospital, she's not well." I asked frantically, "Has she had an accident? Why didn't you tell us?"

Miss Coote then revealed what was wrong with Callie but her voice and tone were so disinterested she could've been telling me something as boring as it was raining outside for all she cared: "No, she hasn't had an accident, she's got TB." I was stunned – I had heard people talk about it and knew it was serious.

I asked, "What hospital? Where? Can we go and see her?" But letting us go and visit Callie would've involved some kind of caring, and that wasn't about to happen any time soon. Miss Coote almost sneered as she informed me, "No, you can't see her. Not now. Your mother's been told that your sister's in hospital. She'll be coming over from London to see her soon. You'll be able to visit her then."

She was more concerned – and annoyed – that Callie's TB was going to disrupt the daily routine. Bristling with annoyance she told me, "The whole school's going to have to be inoculated against TB now because she's brought those germs here." She then coldly turned her back on me, signalling the end of the discussion, and walked rapidly away. I should not have been surprised at her lack of humanity. Even so, her insensitivity took my breath away. She had no thought for Callie but was only concerned at the inconvenience it would cause them.

I was sick with worry but she didn't care how I felt. We had to deal with the trauma and continue as though nothing had happened. As it later transpired, unbeknownst to us, one of the nuns from the convent was already infected with TB and was in the same sanatorium where Callie had been taken. She had been a patient there even before Callie had been diagnosed and was probably the one who had spread it around. The hypocrites knew this but were trying to offload the blame onto Callie.

Who knows how many other cases of TB had been hidden by them in the past? Sometimes other girls left in a hurry, and were never heard of again. The older girls always assumed that they were pregnant, but could they have had TB too? Only the nuns know what really happened to them.

Callie could have contracted the disease anywhere but most probably she caught it in the orphanage. TB thrives in places where people are poor, ill-nourished and live crowded together. Those most at risk of developing the disease are people with weakened immune systems and without access to proper health care. Apparently TB is spread through the air when an infected person coughs or sneezes. People nearby may breathe in these bacteria and also become infected. They can settle in the lungs and begin to grow. From there, they can move through the blood to other parts of the body, such as the kidney, spine and brain. People with TB are most likely to spread it to those they spend time with every day. This includes family members, friends, schoolmates and co-workers. TB, which was often known as consumption, had many famous victims in earlier times.

Dozens of well-known people have contracted the disease over the years and some of them sadly died. These include: Vivien Leigh, Anton Chekhov, Frédéric Chopin, Igor Stravinsky, Franz Kafka, Nelson Mandela, Robert Burns, John Keats, Robert Louis

Stevenson, George Orwell, the Brontë sisters, Dylan Thomas, Tom Jones and D.H. Lawrence. After World War Two, a new antibiotic called Streptomycin provided the first cure for TB and paved the way for other drug treatments. Before antibiotics, the death rate was around 50 per cent, but after the war, it was brought down to around 2 per cent in Western industrialised countries; it was still spoken of with dread, however.

I was very upset and shocked at the news and went to the other dormitory to find Imelda and Sinead to tell them what had happened. All three of us were in tears. Sinead asked me, "Oh, God. Is she going to die like Daddy?" I desperately tried to reassure my younger sisters: "No. They'll make her better in the hospital." I didn't know that but had to do my best to reassure them that Callie wasn't going to die. I wasn't too sure myself.

Hoppy appeared at the door: "What are you doing here? You, get back to your own dormitory and stop making that awful racket. The rest of you go to sleep. You're keeping everyone awake with all the noise you're making."

I returned to my own dormitory and sat down on my bed. The other girls crowded around me. They were eager to know what had happened to Callie. There had been lots of speculation since they had discovered the empty space where her bed had stood. They had tried to find out what had happened but there was no nun around to ask and nobody else had any details.

"Did you find out anything?" asked her friend Jo, who worked with her in the retirement home. I told them she was in hospital. The questions came thick and fast: "In hospital? Has she had an accident?" Again I tried to reassure everyone, even though I didn't really know how Callie was or how sick she might be: "No. They think she's got TB but they said not to say anything." One of the girls took the Lord's name in vain as she said, "God, that sounds serious." Another girl added, "Shush, you'll upset her and what if the nuns hear you, you'll be in trouble." Somebody else asked, "Will she be okay Suzy?" I had no idea but tried to keep upbeat: "I hope so."

The girls were appalled and shocked when I told them the news, but not in the least bit surprised at the lack of sympathy from the nuns. My friend Niamh, a kind girl, tried her best to comfort me, saying, "Try not to worry. I'm sure she'll be okay. At least she's out of this place and in hospital where she'll receive proper treatment. They'll take good care of her, better than they would here."

The nuns had removed Callie's bed from the dormitory while we were at school, along with all her belongings, and burned them in case they might infect the rest of the children: a bit late in the circumstances. As TB was a communicable disease, the health authorities should have been informed that it had been discovered in the orphanage. That would probably have meant the end of their business. The children would be taken away from them; the nuns would have no more free labour and might actually have to pay people to do their work. That would certainly eat into the profits and certainly couldn't be allowed to happen.

With hindsight, some things began to make sense. We remembered that for some time Callie had been feeling extremely tired, even to the extent of dragging herself out of bed in the mornings. This was most unlike her as she was normally full of energy. She also had a hacking cough. A persistent cough is the main symptom of tuberculosis, along with night sweats, chills, weight loss, fever and fatigue.

The nuns must have informed Mammy immediately of Callie's illness, because she soon arrived from London to visit her in hospital and then to see us in St Joseph's. She comforted us and obtained permission from Miss Brophy for us to visit Callie in the sanatorium. Unfortunately she was only able to stay for a very short time, as she had to go back to her job in London, from which she had taken a few days' unpaid leave.

I don't know whether the nuns ever informed the health authorities, but all the premises remained open and no health check was carried out on the other children. Shortly afterwards, all the children in the day school, as well as the orphans, were lined up and inoculated against TB by a nurse who visited the school for that purpose.

Chapter Thirty-Seven

Some weeks later Miss Brophy gave me permission for a Sunday visit to Callie in the hospital, but my younger sisters were not allowed to come with me, as the nuns couldn't spare three workers. I was expected to find my own way there even though I was only 12 years old. Miss Coote grudgingly gave me my bus fare, allocated from money Mammy had sent for that purpose.

She counted it out into my hands very carefully and then double-checked to make sure that she hadn't given me too much, telling me, "Don't forget to bring back your bus ticket and any change." She never asked how Callie was or sent any good wishes for her health. All she was concerned with was the change from the money she had given me.

I was glad to get away from the petty atmosphere of the orphanage for a while. I relished my short freedom and happily set off down into the town centre to try to find my way to the hospital. I didn't know how to get to Chapelizod, which turned out to be to the west of Dublin. I was in Dún Laoghaire, which was in the south-east. I decided to ask a bus driver who was standing beside his bus smoking a cigarette.

Chapter Thirty-Seven

He looked down kindly at me and smiled before giving me directions: "Chapelizod. Now that's a long way off, so it is. You'll have to go into the city centre and change buses there. You see that bus stop just along there, catch a bus from that stop and tell the driver where you want to go."

I waited at the stop he indicated until a bus pulled up, then climbed on and asked the driver, "Is this bus going to Chapelizod?" Again, the bus driver spoke to me more kindly that I was used to: "No, you'll have to change in the city centre. I'll let you know when we get there. Aren't you a bit young to be travelling by yourself? Where are your mammy and daddy?" I bluntly told him, "My daddy's dead and my mammy's in London." He asked me where I lived, and I decided to tell the truth: "St Joseph's orphanage."

The bus driver looked concerned: "Do the nuns know where you are?" But he seemed to relax a bit when I told him, "Yes. I'm going to visit my sister at the hospital in Chapelizod. She's sick." He shook his head and gave me my ticket, then put his head out of his cab to look behind him. He spied a woman sitting by herself and shouted to her, "Hey Mrs B, do us a favour, look after this young girl for us and see that she gets off at the right stop."

I sat down beside the woman who had been listening to my conversation with the driver. She stood up and let me in to the window seat so I could see out while she sat in the aisle seat. She shifted around on the seat to make sure I had enough room. She turned to me and said, "Are you comfortable there pet? I'm Mrs Brennen, what's your name?" I told her: She was like a friendly old granny. "Have you got enough room there?" she asked. She shifted her ample behind on the seat and smiled kindly at me: "Don't you worry your pretty little head about a thing, I'll look after you."

It turned out Mrs Brennen was a grandmother, plump and cuddly with soft brown curly hair and a kind face. She wore a flowery print dress and a hand-knitted red cardigan. Chatting away as the bus pulled away from the stop, she told me that every Sunday she travelled to the other side of Dublin for her weekly visit to see her daughter, her son-in-law and her grandchildren, a boy and a girl: "About the same age as you," she revealed. Her grandson was called Sean and her granddaughter was Anne. She chattered away as we drove along. This was the bus with the same driver that she caught every week, "as regular as clockwork". Her daughter would have a lovely dinner ready for her and she had bought candies for the grandchildren.

I relaxed and settled into my seat. Opening a white paper bag, Mrs Brennen offered me a candy from a selection of boiled fruit drops. I debated whether to have an orange or a strawberry one and eventually decided on the strawberry, which I slowly sucked for ages, savouring the lovely taste until it eventually melted on my tongue.

Mrs Brennen knitted a multi-coloured garment as she chatted away. The bus lurched but she manoeuvred deftly to avoid stabbing both of us with her knitting needles. She knew lots of the other passengers and said hello to everybody who boarded the bus, some of whom turned out to be other Sunday regulars. They spent a lot of the journey gossiping about various people they knew. Some of them sat on the seat in front of us and turned round to chat to Mrs Brennen.

They gossiped away: "I haven't seen Mary for a while now. I'm a bit worried about her. Do you think everything's all right?" and: "I heard that she was having problems with that husband of hers." When they didn't want me to know what they were talking about, they spelled it out: "Have you heard? Mary Kennedy is p-r-e-g-n-a-n-t again. How many is that now? Five or six, I can't remember." They also spoke about people they knew that had passed away and they all made the sign of the cross when they spoke of the dead.

All of them were curious about me and enquired whether I was her granddaughter. Mrs Brennen said no, but that I was from the orphanage in Dún Laoghaire and that I was finding my way to the hospital in Chapelizod all by myself. They were shocked but intrigued: "Is that right now? You don't say." They were concerned that I wasn't accompanied by a nun: "Sure, and wouldn't you think the nuns would send someone with her. She's only a little thing. God bless us and save us. They should be ashamed of themselves. Allowing a young girl to wander around the city by herself. Anything could happen to the poor mite. It's a disgrace."

They all nodded their heads in agreement. One of them offered me an apple, which I accepted with thanks. "Here, buy yourself some candies, my dear," said a kindly old lady, pushing some money into my hand. Others followed her example and gave me small amounts of money, a penny here and tuppence there. All in all, it amounted to a fair bit. The great thing about it was that the nuns wouldn't know that I had it and I could hide it in a secret place when I got back to the orphanage.

"Are you all right there?" they asked. "Yes thank you," I assured them and basked in their kindness. It was the first kindness that had been shown to me in over three years. It felt like I was basking in bright sunlight. It felt so good, and I still remember that initial feeling of wonderment that these strangers could be so kind towards me when the nuns I spent every day with were the complete opposite. Even though I was still only a child, it restored my faith in humanity

Our route took us around the coast road on the south side of Dublin Bay. As the bus rattled along I turned to look out of the window and admired the beautiful scenery and the sparkling blue sea. The white foam-tipped waves rolled in to lap at the shore and then pulled back out again. White seagulls flew overhead and the sun shone on the water. It was a beautiful day and I was happy to be away from the nuns and the orphanage. I would have stayed on the bus all day if I could and never have gone back there.

In between chatting with her friends, Mrs Brennen turned, beamed at me and offered me more candies: "Are you all right there, would you like another candy?" It was so good to be with this friendly, motherly woman and I relaxed and enjoyed the journey. I found comfort in Mrs Brennen's kindness. It had been a long time since an adult had been so nice to me, apart from my mother.

As the bus wound its way through the southern suburbs of Dublin Bay, we passed families returning home from church after late Sunday morning Mass. They strolled along without a care in the world. I imagined that, after a leisurely lunch, they would probably have a relaxing family day, before the routine of work and school began all over again on Monday.

They reminded me of how happy our life had been before Daddy died and how our family had been abruptly torn apart. I envied them and felt very sad. Although I wished that everything could be normal again, I knew that was never going to be possible now. I sighed a deep, melancholy sigh.

Mrs Brennen turned to me with a look of concern: "What's the matter?" I told her, "I was just remembering when I lived at home." She opened her bag: "It won't be long before you see your sister, darling. Here, have another candy. How about a nice green one this time?" She started gathering her bags. "We're nearly there now. Make sure you check around the seat in case you've left anything behind. Don't worry about finding your bus to Chapelizod, we'll ask the bus inspector where to get it."

I had been very worried about finding my way around Dublin, so it was a relief to have her help in finding my way to Chapelizod; I was happy to leave that task in Mrs Brennen's hands. It would have been difficult for me to try to find my way around the busy city centre all by myself as I wouldn't have known whom to approach to ask for directions.

Although it was Sunday, the city centre streets were crowded with people rushing around getting on and off buses. It was a confusing place for a 12-year-old child from the suburbs who wasn't used to travelling alone on public transport. I was lucky to have found Mrs Brennen to guide me. I shudder to think now what peril I could have been in if I had asked the wrong person for directions.

When the bus arrived in the centre of Dublin, Mrs Brennen took charge. She gathered up all her possessions and checked around and under the seat again to make doubly sure that she had not missed anything. We got off the bus and found an inspector to ask directions for the next part of my journey. He directed us to the bus stop at the end of O'Connell Bridge, on Aston Quay near the famous Halfpenny Bridge. When she found my stop we waited until the bus drew up. Mrs Brennen held my hand as we climbed on. She told the driver, "This child is going to Chapelizod. Be sure to let her out at the right stop for the St Mary's Chest Hospital."

The bus driver told her, "I'll do that, missus." He then smiled at me: "It's in the Phoenix Park and the bus stops right outside it at the Chapelizod Gate. Don't worry. I'll see that she gets there okay. Come on, girl, hop on and sit at the front. I'll tell you when to get off." Mrs Brennen gave me a handful of candies out of her bag and waited until I was settled in my seat before she got off. She waved to me through the window as the bus drew away before setting off on the rest of her journey to see her own family.

The second journey didn't take as long as the one from Dún Laoghaire, but I felt a bit anxious because I didn't have the comforting presence of Mrs Brennen beside me and was afraid I might miss my stop. However, the driver poked his head out of his cab when we reached it. "This is your stop. Can you see the big gates across the road? That's the Phoenix Park and

Chapter Thirty-Seven

the hospital is just inside the park. Just walk up to that big white building you can see at the top of the avenue."

I thanked the driver and he waited while I crossed the road. When I was safely across, he waved goodbye to me, revved up his bus and chugged off into the distance.

I was lucky to have met such kind and decent people to help me on my journey. It obviously didn't occur to the nuns that it was extremely dangerous to let a 12-year-old child wander around Dublin by herself, asking strangers for directions. Most probably they just didn't care. On the other hand, what would they do if one of their workforce went missing? They were taking a big chance.

Chapter Thirty-Eight

I stood for a moment looking at my surroundings. There was a big iron gate leading into the park and I could see a long tree-lined drive leading up to a huge white building standing on the top of a hill. People were walking up on the left-hand road towards it, so I followed them.

The road divided into two a short way up. At the fork a sign pointed to the left, which indicated the way to the hospital. The fork to the right led to a place called Furry Glen, an area of the park with scenic walks that was also home to a lake with wildlife. The name caught my imagination, and I would have liked to explore it as it reminded me of St Anne's Estate behind our house in Clontarf, but I didn't have the time. I had to find Callie.

Just inside the entrance to the hospital there was a wooden reception desk manned by a woman. She asked, "Who are you here to see?" and then looked up Callie's name on a list and directed me to her ward. She told me it was in the "TB unit in the chalets". I wasn't sure what a chalet was, or even TB for that matter. Apparently, the hospital had been a military school before the war and the chalets were converted from army huts when TB had become a big problem in Dublin and there were not enough hospital beds to cater for all the patients who needed them.

Seeing my look of confusion, the woman said, "Just follow the signs that say 'TB unit' and you'll soon find it." After becoming lost a few times in the maze of corridors and having to stop frequently and ask passers-by for directions, I eventually came to the TB unit and found Callie's ward. The long room was completely empty of beds and people. This was very strange. One side of the ward had French windows that were open to the garden and I could hear the sounds of conversation drifting through them.

I headed in that direction and discovered a verandah, beyond which was a lovely garden with a large lawn and flowers. All the patients were lined up on the verandah in their beds. They had been moved there so that they could breathe the fresh air. This was part of the treatment for TB patients then, along with the drugs prescribed by the doctors.

The visitors were sitting on chairs or draped on the patients' beds. Others sat on blankets on the grass and their children played in the garden. It was all very relaxed and friendly. I stood for a moment and tried to spot Callie. Her bed was in the middle of the row, and she was propped up on plump pillows. Anthony and Joseph were sitting on the end of the bed eating a bunch of grapes. They hadn't changed at all since I had last seen them.

Callie saw me and excitedly waved me over. I hadn't seen any of them for ages and felt quite shy. I soon relaxed when we got chatting and it felt like we had never been apart. This was the first time I had seen Callie since she had been spirited away from the orphanage, never to be spoken of again by the nuns. It was also quite a while since the boys had made their sneaked Sunday visits to us at St Joseph's to get food and their heads de-loused. I discovered that they came to see Callie on Wednesdays and Sundays as these were the official visiting times and it wasn't too far for them to travel from their orphanage. They weren't as scared of the nurses as they were of the nuns. Unlike the nuns, the medical staff were normal human beings and actually liked people. Besides, the Christian Brothers didn't care where the boys were or what they did so they could come and go at will.

"Where are Imelda and Sinead? Why didn't they come with you?" Callie asked, disappointedly. I told her, "The nuns wouldn't let them. They said I couldn't look after them properly and they could come next time." Callie was mad: "God, how I hate those lying old hags. I know that's not the reason at all. They needed them to work."

I tried to calm her down by telling her I'd try to bring them next time. That seemed to settle her and she focused on me instead: "How did you manage to get away from them?" I really had no idea but said, "It must have been because Mammy insisted. They told me I was to come to see you and gave me money for my bus fare."

Anthony made room on the bed and offered me some grapes. "Where did you get those from?" I asked him. He grinned: "They're Callie's. She's got lots of money. There's a shop in the hospital and she can buy what she likes. There's plenty more where they came from." I offered each of them a candy from the supply Mrs Brennen had given me. We unwrapped them and sat there chewing contentedly. I had brought some of my comics for Callie to read and she put them in her locker for later. She sat up on her plumped-up pillows at the top of the bed like a queen with her audience spread out before her.

"What's it like here? Do they do horrible things to you?" I asked. We were so fascinated by the gruesome things they might have done to her that we couldn't wait to hear about her experiences. "God, no. I love it here," she said. "We have X-rays and blood tests where they put a needle in my arm to take blood. But they don't do anything too horrible to me. I look away when they take the blood and it's not too bad." I shuddered at the thought of needles being stuck in her arms. Looking around the ward, she continued, "The other patients are so nice and friendly and really look after me. I've made lots of friends and I know all the nurses and doctors' names." That didn't surprise me one bit.

What she said next made us all screw up our faces in disgust: "They give us a bottle of Guinness every day to try and build us up." We knew it tasted horrible because we had sampled some of the supply Daddy got free from Guinness, and it tasted revolting. It was enough to put anyone off drink for life. Seeing the look on our faces, she hastened to reassure us: "I don't drink mine. I give it to the other patients in exchange for lemonade. They save the Guinness up for a party at the end of the week."

I wanted to know if Callie had seen or heard from Mammy. She revealed that she'd been in contact with her every week, via mail if she couldn't visit in person: "She writes every week and sends me money to spend in the hospital shop. They sell candies and comics and things." I felt slightly envious of Callie and wished we could have nice food and lots of fun too, but then we weren't sick, just sick and tired of the orphanage and the nuns.

She took out a big bottle of lemonade: "Here, have some of this." Our eyes lit up at the sight of it. I took a swig from it and in turn handed it to Joseph and he took a great big gulp. It dribbled down his chin and he wiped it with his sleeve and passed the bottle to Anthony. Callie told me, "I don't miss the orphanage and those horrible old witches at all but of course I miss all of you and my friends and the babies." She looked sad at the mention of the babies: "How are they?"

I didn't have the heart to tell her about one of the toddlers who had suffered as a consequence of Callie's sudden removal to hospital. She had come to look upon Callie as a mother because she had looked after her all the time and had even potty-trained her. The child was distraught at her sudden disappearance, but the nuns hadn't offered her any comfort. Instead, it was left to the other children to care for her. She stood in her cot crying and calling "Mamma," until she became exhausted and fell asleep. This scene was repeated daily for a while until eventually she came to accept the fact that Callie wasn't coming back.

Joseph, as usual, entertained us with his dry humour and we laughed along with him. We reminisced about our trips to the zoo and the seaside and St Anne's, our friends and life as we used to know it. Before we knew it the bell rang to signal the end of visiting time. We reluctantly said goodbye to Callie.

Chapter Thirty-Eight

I promised her, "I'll come back soon and next time I'll try and bring Sinead and Imelda with me." We then left the hospital for the walk down the avenue to the bus stop. Running around in the parkland and hiding behind the big trees, playing hide-and-seek, we made our way out to catch the bus. The boys suggested exploring the right-hand road, but it was getting late and I had a long return journey ahead of me. Besides, I was tired as I had been up since dawn without much to eat.

I told the boys, "I haven't got enough time now. It's going to take me ages to get back to Dún Laoghaire." It was okay for them: their orphanage was almost in the city centre and it wouldn't take them long to get back there. Anthony said, "We're in the Phoenix Park. Do you remember when we went to the zoo with Mammy and Daddy and rode in a seat on the elephant's back? The zoo's in this park."

We all caught the same bus for the return journey back to the city centre and rode on the upper deck. Because it was a Sunday afternoon we were the sole occupants and played around like all kids do. I parted company with my brothers when we reached the city centre. It didn't take me long to find the bus stop for the second stage of my return journey to Dún Laoghaire, as it was just across the road from where it had stopped when we arrived in the city centre. The next bus ride was uneventful and I eventually reached the orphanage after a long and tiring day.

It was getting late and I was worn out from all my travelling. I hadn't eaten since the morning, except for the candies and apple on the bus, Callie's grapes and a few biscuits I had eaten in the hospital. My stomach was rumbling and I hoped I hadn't missed dinner; otherwise I would have had to wait until the next morning for something to eat. Luckily I was just in time.

The other girls crowded around to ask how Callie was. This was the first time anybody had been to see her since her abrupt departure from the orphanage. I told them all about the hospital and how much she was enjoying her stay there. The nuns never asked me how she was. They didn't want to know and couldn't have cared less. It was one less problem for them.

Afterwards I had to go down to the nuns' kitchen and do my usual shift there. The fact that I had been away for most of the day had been noted and I was made to do my normal work, probably to put me in my place just in case I thought that I might be entitled to special treatment. Later, after rosary and benediction in the chapel, I was also given the job of getting the little children ready for bed, even though I was so tired that I was just about ready to fall into my own bed and sleep until morning.

Before I got into my bed I crept into the other dormitory to see Sinead and Imelda. They were eager to know how Callie was. They bombarded me with questions: "How was Callie? Was she better? Did she miss us?" I told them all the news and how Anthony and Joseph had been at the hospital. They were upset because they had not been allowed to go and cried at the unjustness of it.

The next day the other girls also questioned me at length about what had happened to Callie, why she had just disappeared without a word. When they had asked the nuns where she was, they were told that she had been taken into hospital and they refused to discuss the matter further. They didn't say how long Callie would be there or whether she would return to the orphanage, and none of her friends were ever allowed to visit her. That was the last time they ever saw her. She had been like a sister to some of them and it was terribly traumatic for them too. The nuns never mentioned her name again. As far as they were concerned, she could have been dead for all the interest they took in her existence. They didn't care either whether we were emotionally affected by the trauma: our feelings didn't matter to them at all.

It was not unusual sometimes for other girls to disappear from the orphanage, never to be heard of again. We would be warned by the nuns not to talk about that particular girl, but of course the girls couldn't resist discussing the scandal in hushed whispers when the nuns weren't around. Their beds were never burned, though, so obviously they couldn't have had TB. The fact that Callie's bed had been burned caused much more interest and speculation than would normally have been the case. Even though the nuns wanted to hush it up, the girls speculated on the cause of her disappearance until they learned the true facts from me. Even then it didn't come as a surprise to them that the nuns could be so scheming and hypocritical, nor that they would go to such lengths to hush it up, because nothing they ever did surprised or shocked us.

One Sunday, some weeks later, I was sent for by Miss Coote to be informed that I would be going to the hospital in the car with the chauffeur and one of the nuns. She was visiting one of the nuns from their order who also had TB and was in a private ward at St Vincent's Hospital. The chauffeur was waiting at the front of the convent with the engine running.

Miss Coote gave me some battered windfall apples from the orchard to take to Callie. Some had suspicious holes in them that might have contained worms. I sat in the front seat with the chauffeur and the nun sat in the back. When we arrived at the hospital she got out of the car, turned to me said, "I'm going to see Miss Brickley in her ward. You go and see your sister and I'll meet you back here at the end of visiting time."

Sinead and Imelda had not been asked to accompany us in the car to visit to their sister in the hospital. I later discovered the reason for their exclusion from this charitable act, when Mammy told me, "The nuns had sent me a bill for the petrol used for the journey and the apples they gave you for Callie." They hadn't cared whether Sinead or Imelda saw Callie; the whole point of taking me in the car was to be able to charge Mammy for the expense. They didn't miss a trick when it came to making money. They never took me in the car to the hospital again but soon I was allowed to visit Callie most Sundays. I was relieved as I loved travelling with my friend Mrs Brennen, Joe the bus driver and all the Sunday regulars, and looked forward to seeing them. I missed them when I wasn't allowed to make the journey.

Callie was surprised one day when the orphanage chaplain paid her a visit. He told her that he had had TB and had also been a patient in the hospital. He was the only visitor she ever had from the orphanage, but he hadn't come especially to see her but had only popped in to see her on his way out from visiting the nun in the private ward. To add insult to injury, he offered to say prayers for her recovery. That was the only time she ever saw him.

Chapter Thirty-Eight

Every Sunday afternoon when I went to visit Callie I waited for the same bus so that I could sit beside Mrs Brennen. She always looked out for me and I enjoyed her company. After that first time when I hadn't brought anything with me to eat, I took some money from my little hoard that I had secreted away and bought some biscuits to keep the hunger at bay on the journey.

One week, just as I was about to set off, they said that I couldn't go, as I was needed to look after the younger children. I had told Callie that I would come to the hospital that day and there was no way of letting her know that I wouldn't be able to come. That didn't matter to the nuns: the fact that I was upset was neither here nor there.

Callie, who was never the type of person who lay in bed doing nothing, had become restless after a period of enforced bed rest and begged the doctors to allow her out of bed. Eventually she was given permission to get up and started doing errands for the other bed-ridden patients, things they couldn't do for themselves, such as going to the shop and posting their letters. Callie became the unofficial ward clerk, helping the nurses by taking around 'certs' – sickness certificates for the patients to claim sick pay from their jobs.

There was a girl who came to the ward to cut patients' hair and Callie learned the rudiments of hairdressing from her. She assisted her, holding scissors and combs. Later, when the hairdresser left the hospital, Callie took over her role and looked after all the patients' hair in her ward.

Callie spent nearly a year in the sanatorium before she was discharged as cured. When she left the hospital she went home to our house in Clontarf and never again set foot in St Joseph's, nor did she ever see any of the nuns or the other children again. It is possible that if she had called to visit St Joseph's to see her friends, she would have been turned away in case she infected anybody, even though she was now completely cured.

Chapter Thirty-Nine

One of the lessons I most looked forward to at school was the weekly cookery class. This lesson was held in the kitchen of the Retreat House that stood beside the school. The day girls had to bring their own ingredients from home, while the kitchen nun Miss Adams gave us anything that we needed from her supplies that she kept locked up.

For my first lesson we were going to make a cake and I looked forward to it with great excitement. How stupid of me.

I took great care making my cake. I followed the instructions and mixed everything carefully. It was a labour of love for me. When it was assembled it looked delicious and I was very proud. I couldn't wait to show it to the others.

As soon as the cookery lesson was finished – the last class of the day – I carefully carried my creation back to the orphanage. Old Adams appropriated it before I could even show it to my sisters and friends. I never even had the pleasure of tasting it. The nuns had it for their tea and I cried with anger. I shouldn't have been surprised: the next time I vowed that I would put so much salt in it that they would choke on it.

I had fantasies of punishing the nuns by poisoning my cake, especially if fat, greedy old Turkey and her visitors, including her horrible creepy brother with the ginger hair, who was often seen loitering around the convent, were scoffing my cake for their afternoon tea.

They took away any enthusiasm I had for cooking, and it was to be many years before I re-discovered my talent and enjoyment for cake making.

Later on I was able to get my own back on the nuns. While at St Joseph's, Callie had been given the job of going down to the local teashop, which sold tea, sandwiches, cakes and lemonade to the tourists and local shoppers. Callie instituted a tradition that was to be carried on even after her departure, of eating most of the fancy cakes on the way back up the hill.

After Callie had been spirited away to hospital, Miss Coote told me that I would have to take over the job of going down to the town to collect the cakes every evening before the shop closed. I pretended it was the last thing I wanted to do: "Do I really have to go? It's such a long walk." Miss Coote said, "Yes, I can't spare anyone else." I tried to wriggle out of going, claiming I had too much work on: "But I haven't got the time, I've so much to do." But she wasn't going to give in to my complaints: "Don't give me any of your cheek; just do as you're told. Get on your way without any of your backchat."

I turned away so she couldn't see the smile of satisfaction on my face and realise that she had been hoodwinked. I couldn't let her know that I coveted the job with all my heart and would have done almost anything to get it. If she had even suspected that I was interested, that would have been the end of my chances of going, so I had to pretend that I didn't want to do it.

I left as quickly as I could, before she had a chance to change her mind. Not wanting to take the risk of being seen by any of the other nuns on my way out and being sent to do some other job, I left by a side door where I was unlikely to be waylaid by any of them at that time of the day.

So, it was with great delight and anticipation that I made my way down to the teashop in the town centre. My imagination conjured up visions of the luscious cakes waiting for me: éclairs covered in chocolate and bursting with thick cream, mouth-watering fresh fruit strawberry tarts, cream slices with layers of pastry sandwiched together with cream and jam and topped with icing. There were also fondant fancies and myriad other mouth-watering cakes that Callie had described to me.

Arriving at the shop, I stopped before entering to look through the window. If there had been any customers sitting at the tables, I would have been embarrassed if they had seen me receiving charity. The sign on the door said 'open' but there were no people in the shop. As I pushed the door, a bell jangled to alert the staff that they had a visitor.

A pretty assistant, dressed in a white frilly apron over a black dress and wearing a white cap, came out from the back room and peered at me over the counter: "Hello there. What can I do for you?" I shyly told her, "I'm from St Joseph's and I've been sent to collect some cakes from you." She wanted to know where Callie was, so I had to tell her, "She's in hospital. The doctor said she's got an infection and they're keeping her in for a while. The nuns sent me instead. I'm her sister Suzy."

I was wise enough by now not to mention that Callie had TB. The assistant's reaction might have been one of horror and I might not have been allowed in the shop ever again if they had known that Callie had the disease. I really would have been in trouble with Turkey then, if her free supply of cakes was stopped because I had told the truth. The girl was too polite to delve any further: "I'm pleased to meet you, Suzy. My name's Deirdre. Tell Callie I was asking for her when you see her and I hope she gets better soon." I smiled and told her, "I will. Thanks Deirdre."

She began filling white cardboard boxes with fancy cakes and fruit scones. When she had finished, there were three boxfuls. "I'll put these in a bag for you so you can carry them easier," said Deirdre. She came out from behind the counter and handed me the fancy bag with the name of the shop printed on the front. I could hardly contain my excitement: "Thanks, Deirdre. I'll see you again tomorrow." She held the door open and I smiled my thanks and walked out, straight round the corner and out of her sight.

I was exhilarated at the thought of what was in the bag and couldn't wait to have a look. There was a little park nearby beside the Marine Hotel and I went in and found a secluded bench. There were a few people strolling through the park but they didn't take any notice of me. There was nothing unusual in the sight of a child eating a cake – unless it was a child who lived with the nuns in St Joseph's – now that would indeed have been a miracle.

It occurred to me that it was getting a bit late, so I hastily ate an éclair and rearranged the remaining cakes in the box. I made

Chapter Thirty-Nine

my way back up the hill to the orphanage, making sure to wipe my mouth clean of the telltale signs of my crime before handing the boxes to Miss Boylan. She took them without a word of thanks and never noticed that anything was missing. Why should she? She didn't know how many cakes had been in the boxes to begin with and couldn't query the amount with the people in the shop. I felt safe in the knowledge that she wouldn't know, as Callie had told me that the amount varied daily, according to the quantity that remained unsold at closing time. The nuns never knew how many or what type of cake to expect.

When the weather was very hot, I sometimes sat on a bench in a little garden on the seafront overlooking the pier where there was a cool breeze. I ate the cakes and looked out to sea, admiring the view and watching the ferries sail in and out of the harbour. If time was short, I had to eat them while I walked back up the hill to the orphanage. This wasn't very satisfactory as I ran the risk of being spotted, perhaps by one of the nuns out on an errand, so I was careful to make sure that nobody was approaching in either direction before I took a furtive bite.

The fact that the nuns never discovered that I was eating their cakes gave me a secret thrill and I didn't feel at all guilty. Why should I? I'm sure the shop thought they were handing over the cakes for the 'poor children' in the orphanage and had no idea that they were ending up on the nuns' dining table every night instead.

Chapter Forty

Turkey was a tyrant. People from outside the orphanage who didn't know her said how "good" she was and "what a saint" for looking after those poor orphans. If they only knew the truth: that she had come from the same mould as Sister Magdalena. But whereas Sister Magdalena's motivation had been sadism, Miss Brophy's main aim in life appeared to be to make money, lots of money, and for this she needed able-bodied workers. But in order to maximise profits, the least money that was spent on the children the better. Only the barest minimum was spent in order to keep our bodies and souls together.

Another of her moneymaking schemes was to hold a charity fair at the school with the profits going to the school fund. All of the girls were ordered to make goods to sell, and Turkey came to inspect our efforts. We lined up in a row in the corridor outside the schoolrooms while we waited for her arrival. At the terrifying sound of Turkey pounding up the stairs, with her entourage following timidly behind her, we all quaked inwardly, while at the same time trying to shrink into ourselves in an unsuccessful effort to become invisible.

Chapter Forty

Claire Murphy was first in the firing line. "What have we got here?" asked Turkey. "A scarf I knitted, Miss," said an agitated Claire. "Why has it got these knots in it?" Claire was flustered. "I don't know." "It's not good enough. It's only fit for the bin." Turkey turned away. I was next in line. As she moved nearer to me I felt sick to my stomach. My feet were stuck to the floor in terror and although I tried, I couldn't move back when she leaned down to shout at me. Her fat neck with the loose skin wobbled and swung backwards and forwards. Her breath was in my face as her pent-up rage washed over me in waves. I cringed and tried to move my head away. I proffered my item and she said, "This is good," and attempted a smile. Everybody's mouths opened in astonishment. I was so stunned I couldn't remember anything else after that. When she finished her inspection, she stalked out of the room and down the stairs, followed by her lieutenants.

Shortly after that I was assigned to work at the poultry farm. One of the older girls. Margaret O'Brien, sniggered, "You're going to see the Lezzy on the poultry farm." I was confused: "What's a Lezzy?" Someone laughed, "She doesn't know what a Lezzy is, someone tell her." Margaret informed me, "Someone who likes girls." She smirked and looked at her friends and they all laughed again. In my naivety I was relieved that someone in this place might actually like us and really looked forward to going to the farm. It didn't seem like hard work just to feed a few hens and collect eggs.

The next day was a sunny Saturday and after breakfast was finished and the washing-up done, the crowd of girls rushed for the door, I was stopped by Miss Coote. Some of the others looked back at me and giggled. She scanned the list in her hand: "You, you're to help Miss Barrow on the farm."

I couldn't wait to get away. As I idled along in the sunshine I relished the thought of being free from the nuns for a little while and not to have to work in the kitchen on this hot, humid day.

There was nobody in sight so I took my time and strolled slowly along the winding path through the orchard. The gooseberry bushes low down on the ground were laden with luscious purple fruits that looked soft and juicy. I bent down and squeezed one. It burst open and the juice oozed out onto my fingers. I licked them clean of the sweet liquid and made a mental note to harvest some on my way back. I said to myself, "Wouldn't it be nice not to have to go back to the orphanage ever again? I wish I could stay here forever."

In the middle of the orchard stood an old tram that was used for our weekly sewing lessons conducted by Miss Robinson. The whole scene was very picturesque and peaceful. It was a nice change. Normally on a Saturday afternoon I would be slaving away in the kitchen or looking after the young children in the concrete yard. I was feeling very smug at that point: "Bet the others would be jealous if they could see me now, especially that stupid Margaret O'Brien."

The gate to the poultry farm was locked and I had to climb up on the rungs and bend over the top to open the latch on the other side. It swung open as I stood on it and I could see what they called 'the farm'. I really don't know what I had been expecting, but this was disappointing. It was just a collection of wooden sheds with corrugated roofs and a concrete path running down the middle. The turkeys lived in the right-hand hut behind high wire fences. They rushed up and down the runs trying to peck me through the wire. Squawking hens rushed around pecking madly at the grain scattered on the ground.

At the entrance to one of the sheds a woman stood staring at me. I had never seen her before but assumed that this must be Miss Barrow. She was an ugly-looking creature with a weather-beaten face and scraggy ginger hair tied back in a bun. She was dressed in a shirt and skirt with an apron made from sacking, and wore a pair of battered old Wellington boots.

She didn't seem surprised to see me so she must have been expecting me. "What's your name?" she squawked at me, sounding like one of the chickens. I told her, "Suzy. I've been sent out to help you." She beckoned me over: "Come over here and let me have a look at you."

I did as I was told. She smelled musty and I held my breath to avoid inhaling her odour. She turned me around and looked me over: "You're a skinny little thing. There's not much meat on you. How old are you?" After I told her I was 12, she gave me some instructions: "I just hope you're able for the work. Okay. Let's not waste time. There's a lot to be done. Take this pail and follow me to the pens. When we've fed and watered the hens I'll show you how to collect the eggs."

She gave me two very heavy pails full of food for the hens and I followed her to the hen house, staggering under the weight. My arms were almost pulled out of their sockets, while she carried her two pails with ease. "You must always make sure the gate is closed behind you so that the hens can't escape," she explained.

As we entered the big shed, light filtered through cracks in the roof, and dust and feathers floated in the air. The smell from the droppings was overpowering and the noise from the hundreds of hens was thunderous. Some of them scattered out of our way flapping and squawking but others rushed to get at the food. I felt scared that they would bite me so I edged along the walls and tried to keep away from the chickens, but they knew I had food in the pails and crowded around me.

"Come on. Get a move on. They won't hurt you," she shouted. I could see she was annoyed but I was more scared of the hens than her. We emptied the pails into the food troughs and the hens rushed between our legs pecking and trying to get at the food. After the food troughs were replenished, she showed me how to refill them with buckets of clean water from a tap just outside the shed.

She then demonstrated how to collect the eggs from the nesting boxes, putting some straw in the bottom of the pail and gently putting the eggs in and then layering them with more straw, then putting more eggs on top and then more straw so that they wouldn't break. We repeated this operation in all the other pens. The last pens to be done were the turkeys. These were big ugly creatures and even scarier than the hens. Gathering my courage, I quickly opened the gate, ran into the pens and dumped the food in the troughs and got out again as quickly as I could, making sure to fasten the gate securely so none could escape.

After we had completed the job of feeding and watering the poultry, she showed me how to wash and grade the eggs and put them in cardboard trays when they were ready. She seemed happy with my work. At the end of the day she told me, "You can go back to the orphanage now for your supper." When I got back to the refectory the other girls asked me how I was getting on with 'Chick'.

"Chick. Oh, do you mean the chickens?" I was confused. The girls told me, "Chick is the Lezzy. She's called Chick as in chicken." I thought she was fine: "She seems okay." They all laughed. I thought it was a funny nickname. As it turned out, the joke was on me. Chick had been softening me up and was ready to pounce.

Next Saturday I ambled through the orchard to the poultry farm. When she saw me standing at the door, Chick said, "Don't just stand there, come in and sit down." I entered the shed where she was washing and grading the eggs. She pointed to a chair. I sat down on the ancient, rickety old chair with its torn leather seat. She was so creepy and the way she was staring at me was making me feel very uneasy.

As I made a move, I knocked an egg off the table. She shouted, "You stupid girl, look what you've done." She lunged at me and grabbed hold of my arm. As her ugly old face came near me I twisted away and in the struggle knocked an entire tray of eggs off the table onto the ground. She let go and we both looked in horror at the smashed eggs.

She yelled at me, "Look what you've done now, you stupid girl. You're in big trouble." In terror, I shouted, "I'm going to tell on you. I'm going to tell Miss Boylan," and ran to the door. I was in a state of sheer panic, scared that she might follow me and try to grab me again. She was desperate for me not to go running and telling tales: "Come back. Don't be silly. Here, have an egg." She held one up to try to entice me back.

But I fled out of the farm as fast as my legs would carry me and ran straight back through the gate into the orchard and all the way to the orphanage without looking back, terrified that she might catch up with me. As I ran back up the path through the orchard and out into the playground, I bumped into Miss Boylan. She grabbed me by the arm to stop me getting past her.

She demanded, "Where do you think you're going, you should be helping at the poultry farm!" I was near tears as I told her, "I'm never going there again." She demanded, "Why not?" I managed to get the words out: "Because she attacked me." Weirdly she didn't insist that I went back to the farm, telling me instead, "Don't be silly. Go and help in the kitchen instead."

I was really puzzled by her reaction but relieved that I didn't appear to be in trouble for leaving the poultry farm without permission. This was totally unexpected and extremely puzzling. When I told the other girls what had happened, they said, "We wondered how long it would take. Chick does it to everybody. That's why she's called the Lezzy."

I still didn't know what a Lezzy was and it wasn't until many years later that I finally discovered what the girls were talking about. At the time I was just glad to be back in the orphanage and away from Chick. Nobody ever mentioned me going to the poultry farm ever again, neither Miss Boylan nor Miss Brophy.

For a long time afterwards I had nightmares and woke up in a sweat after a wild-eyed, scary-looking Chick had chased me through my dreams.

Chapter Forty-One

I had reached the age of 14 years and it was time for my secondary schooling. The day girls in my class were moving up to the next stage of secondary education, but not me. The nuns didn't want me to continue with my education, as they needed my labour in the kitchen, looking after the younger children and cleaning the classrooms, etc. They thought I'd had enough education. After all, why would orphans need higher education? In the eyes of the nuns we were only destined for menial jobs that befitted our perceived low status.

Mammy wanted me to learn shorthand and typing at Dún Laoghaire Commercial College in preparation for my future, the same college that Callie had attended when doing her commercial course. She insisted I enroll in the college, but the nuns didn't approve of Mammy's plans for me and made it as difficult as they possibly could for me to attend, including keeping me off school frequently on the flimsiest of excuses, so that I was too far behind the other students to catch up. They also made it almost impossible for me to do any homework, as I had no time left after I had finished my various jobs in the convent.

One day my schoolbooks inadvertently got locked in the dormitory – the nuns had taken to locking it during the day so that nobody could lie on the beds after Callie had started a trend when she was suffering from TB – and out of petty spite they refused to open it so that I could retrieve them.

Worn down by overwork and bad food, constantly tired, hungry and depressed, I could no longer endure the stress of living with the nuns or their petty spitefulness. They were like vampires or leeches, sucking out all my energy. If I didn't leave now I would become more and more ill and probably end up in hospital like Callie. Sinead and Imelda were so upset when I told them I was going to leave. I warned them not to say anything in case it got back to the nuns, and they assured me that they wouldn't. It broke my heart to leave them behind but I was literally at breaking point. I don't think I would've survived another day in there.

So on a rainy morning in late November I left the orphanage for good. Instead of going to college I headed for the bus stop with just the clothes I stood up in and my bus fare in my hand. My only desire was to get as far away as possible from the nuns. The relief I felt was enormous and a big weight was lifted from my shoulders. I was determined that I was never going back and that nobody or nothing in this world could make me.

I took the now familiar bus from Dún Laoghaire into Dublin city centre and then changed to another one on Eden Quay for the rest of the journey home to Clontarf. Callie had by then been discharged from the sanatorium and was living at our family home. She wasn't at all surprised to see me and didn't send me back to the orphanage. The nuns never tried to find me and, as far as I am aware, didn't send anybody to look for me. Nobody ever came to our house in Clontarf to check if I was there, although they must have assumed that was where I would go.

Miss Brophy must have contacted my mother in London to give her the news and to try to explain why I had run away from her care. Later Mammy phoned the neighbour across the road and spoke to Callie about the situation. She told Callie, "I'll be home in a few weeks and we'll sort things out then. I'll send you and Suzy some extra money in the meantime for food."

Although she must have been shocked at my unexpected departure from the orphanage, there was never any reproach from Mammy. We had never told her about our ill treatment at the hands of the nuns and she didn't know the true extent of our unhappiness. No doubt the nuns made up some kind of story to cover up their ill treatment of us, in an effort to try to convince Mammy that I was at fault, but she obviously didn't believe them. I never saw the nuns again.

The knowledge of my unhappiness seems to have hastened the removal of my brothers and sisters from the institutions a very short time later. What a shock it must have been for the nuns to lose three workers all at once. We must have accounted for a good 10 per cent of the workforce, not counting the little children who were too young to work. The burden would have to be passed on to the other children, who were already badly overworked, but that wouldn't matter to the nuns. Their only concern would be about the inconvenience I had caused them and the adverse impact on their profits.

During that time, Mammy sent us money every week in the mail to buy food. Because it was close to Christmas, the volume of letters and Christmas cards were often delayed in the post. When it was time for the postman to make his round, I stood at the gate in the snow anxiously watching for him, waiting for the letter from London that I hoped he carried with him. Finally, I saw him turn the corner into our road. I watched expectantly as he went in and out of each gate until he reached ours. With a big smile he held out the bundle of letters: "Are you waiting for these?" I was so relieved. "Yes, thanks," I smiled gratefully.

I rushed inside to check that the expected letter from Mammy was in the bundle. It was, and contained the money she sent us every week. It had arrived just in time as we were now completely out of food. For the past 24 hours we had existed on a pack of dry cream crackers and tap water, but I would have preferred to starve to death than to have to spend another day with the nuns. There was no hardship in having to do without food now and then because we were free from them and would never have to be in their company again.

I hurried to the shops at St Gabriel's, passing the convent where we had spent a few weeks 'holiday' in our first summer at St Vincent's, and set off home with a bag filled with fresh food. On my way back I devoured lumps of fresh bread. Nothing had ever tasted so good. When I arrived home we had a meal of fresh boiled eggs and soft white bread and butter. It tasted like a banquet compared to what we had eaten for the past few years. Later Callie and I had another feast until the bread was all gone.

Chapter Forty-One

In the few weeks leading up to Christmas before Mammy arrived back in Dublin, Callie and I lived at home very contentedly. The relief at being away from the nuns was enormous and while I felt guilty at leaving Sinead and Imelda behind, we revelled in the freedom to do things that most girls our age took for granted. We were glad to be among normal people again and did the simple things that had been denied to us for so long, like going to the department stores in town and trying on pretty clothes. I had my hair cut in a fashionable style and we listened to pop music on the radio.

Callie got herself a part-time evening job in a shop on Eden Quay beside the River Liffey and she proudly brought home her pay packet every week. I was very impressed. While Callie was working I stayed inside the house and hid just in case the nuns were after me. I was very cautious and didn't open the door to anybody.

After a while without incident, it occurred to me that maybe they were not going to send anybody to look for me. I relaxed a bit, but was still a bit wary and looked for strangers whenever I went out of the house. Sometimes I went out the back way and down the lane to my friend's house to see her after school.

The stores were once again decorated for Christmas and full of families shopping for presents. I felt extremely sad because it reminded me of when we had made our visit to see Santa Claus just before Daddy died: it had been a day I would never forget as long as I lived.

Our neighbours looked out for us, including a particularly kind one, a widow without any children of her own, who looked after me when Callie was at work in the evenings. She made me banana sandwiches and I listened to Radio Luxembourg, which was probably the only radio station at that time to broadcast pop music. Unlike the nuns, she didn't expect payment but did it out of the kindness of her heart.

It was one of the happiest times of my life since Daddy had died, but I felt desperately sorry for the unfortunate children we had left behind. I never saw any of my friends again and don't know what happened to them during the 50 years that have passed since then.

My sisters and brothers soon arrived home for Christmas, which was a very special one for me. I was so happy that we were reunited at last. Our best Christmas present of all was when Mammy surprised us with the news that we were all moving to live in London very soon. We all looked forward to the adventure to come and were very excited.

After our experiences of the past few years, we were wise beyond our years and now viewed life in a different way to that of our childhood friends. We had made a detour from our once safe suburban lives and had seen a world they would never know or even imagine existed. Our whole outlook on life had been changed by our experience. They were just skimming the surface of life, but we had dug deeper and seen many things that would remain forever beyond their knowledge or comprehension. Unlike them, we were no longer innocent and never would be again, nor would our lives take the same safe path as theirs. Everything that we had been taught or believed had been turned upside down and we had become disillusioned and cynical.

Chapter Forty-One

Shortly afterwards, almost four years to the day after we had entered St Vincent's orphanage, we left the land of our birth without any regret, or even a backward glance. It was a place forever tainted in our memories by the abuse and exploitation we had endured at the hands of the representatives of the Catholic Church.

We had no desire to ever see them or to set foot in a church again as long as we lived, although it would take time to rid ourselves of the Catholic guilt and fear of everlasting damnation that every member of that Church is burdened with because of their indoctrination from a young age.

There was only one thing of value that we carried with us to our new life: our beloved daddy would be forever in our hearts and memories.

Although we didn't know it then, we had been irrevocably damaged by our experiences and carried deep within us the scars of the emotional, psychological and physical abuse inflicted upon us, along with the callous neglect of the previous four years. The problems associated with that abuse would take time to manifest, and it would only be many years later that we came to realise the impact of the damage as it took its toll on our lives over the following decades.

We departed from the seaport of Dún Laoghaire on an early summer's day in 1962, headed for the bright lights of Swinging Sixties London. Free from the suffocating confinement of the orphanage, we were glad to be able to put the nightmare of those traumatic years behind us and eager to embrace the new and exciting life that awaited us.

Standing on the deck of the ferry taking us across the Irish Sea to England, with the waves rushing below and Dún Laoghaire receding into the distance, Callie was already making plans for her new life and couldn't wait to get started.

The boys were running around exploring the ship but I was just content to be free of the nuns and to be able to relax at last.

Epilogue

By Melissa Walsh – Suzanne's daughter

My mum was a survivor.

She was brave, courageous, with a wonderful outlook on life despite all she and her siblings had been through. None of them escaped unscathed from their time in the orphanages – least of all my mum – but she was my hero.

She spent her later teens in South London after my nan brought them over. She loved to travel and experience new places and cultures. She also loved reading and cooking and used to make me the best fruit cake I've ever had!

Later on in life, she spent time traveling to Los Angeles, where I live and work as a celebrity make-up artist. She was so proud of me for following my dreams – but I was just as proud of her and her always positive attitude, generosity and talent for writing.

My mum battled many health issues in her life – all stemming from the malnutrition and abuse in the orphanages. She had Crohn's Disease and suffered five heart attacks before making it through open heart surgery. But sadly she passed away in October 2018 from cancer.

I miss her every day: she was my world. Although it's bitter-sweet that's she's not here to see it, she had been working on this book for several years and it was one of her last wishes that it be published so people could finally know what happened behind those convent doors.

I'm so happy to be able to honour her last wish and I hope her story shows that despite no matter what life throws at you, it's your faith in yourself that will always win.

To the most wonderful Mum in the world. I love you. You did it!

Acknowledgements

Melissa and Nicola would like to thank the great, hardworking team at Mardle Books. It was a pleasure and a joy to work with Jo, Mel and Kaz.

Melissa would also like to thank:
Her aunts Carol, Marguerite and Damhnait for their unwavering support and love always.

And to Nicola for her hard work and dedication in getting the book published!

Also by Mardle Books

The Missing Pieces of Mum
By Sally Herbert

Born out of wedlock in Dublin in 1937, Phyllis grew up in a brutal, church-run orphanage. She thought by fulfilling her dream to become a nurse in England, her life might change for the better. But her loveless childhood predisposed a loveless marriage. Her feelings of being worthless, instilled by the orphanage, perpetuated a series of poor choices and things spiralled out of control for her – and, shockingly, for her daughter, Sally.

As her mother's health deteriorated, Sally began looking for answers to why it seemed inevitable that their lives would go so spectacularly wrong. She asked questions about the true identity of her mother: "Who was she? Why was she abandoned? I needed to find answers before it was too late." After a mission that lasted nearly a decade, searching archives and contacting countless organisations and anyone who would listen, Sally finally uncovered the truth and opened the door to a world so many of us take for granted.